ADVANTAGE AND DISADVANTAGE:
A Profile of American Youth

ADVANTAGE AND DISADVANTAGE:
A Profile of American Youth

R. Darrell Bock
University of Chicago

Elsie G.J. Moore
Arizona State University

1986

LAWRENCE ERLBAUM ASSOCIATES, PUBLISHERS
Hillsdale, New Jersey   London

Lawrence Erlbaum Associates, Inc., Publishers
365 Broadway
Hillsdale, New Jersey 07642

Library of Congress Cataloging-in Publication Data

Bock, R. Darrell.
    Advantage and disadvantage.

    Bibliography: p.
    Include index.
    1. Youth—United States. I. Moore, Elsie G. J.
II. Title.
HQ796.B58   1986   305.2′35′0973   86–4601
ISBN 0–89859–686–6

Printed in the United States of America
10 9 8 7 6 5 4 3 2 1

Contents

Preface

In this monograph, we offer the reader a critical view of a large body of factual information describing the cognitive skills and potentials of young people in the United States in the 1980s. The initial source of these data was a nation-wide survey conducted for the Departments of Labor and Defense by the National Opinion Research Center (NORC) of the University of Chicago. This survey has the distinction of being the largest study of cognitive and vocational test performance ever attempted in a complete cross-section of this country. The young people were located, not through school systems, but by sampling of households drawn from urban and rural areas, cities and suburbs, and affluent as well as impoverished neighborhoods.

Not surprisingly, the survey revealed wide differences in the vocational potential and preparation of these young people as they begin their transition to independent living. These were differences that would inevitably put them in positions of advantage and disadvantage as they attempted to continue their education, find jobs, or begin careers.

Past experience suggests that caution must be exercised in interpreting data of the kind obtained in this survey. There are obvious implications of inequality, but it is far from obvious why it exists or what action might be taken to lessen it. The facts call out for a theory that will identify the sources of these disparities and provide a rational basis for a public response. But no generally accepted theory exists—only proposals, speculations, opinions, and little empirical support for any of them. The best that can be done at present is to analyze the profile data in a way that brings its implications into sharp focus, then to judge various theories in the social science literature by how well they account for these facts. Our purpose is to put the results of this analysis and our assessment of the relevant literature at the disposal of a broad audience. With this goal in mind, we have tried to make the greater part of this material accessible to the general reader. But to provide also for the needs of the specialist, we have included technical appendices that document the sampling, measurement, and statistical methods used in the study.

This book is the product of our joint efforts. Most of the material in Chapter 2 and Appendix B concerning the vocational tests, and the statistical discussion in Appendix C, were prepared by the first author, R. Darrell Bock. The second author, Elsie G. J. Moore, was primarily responsible for Chapters 3, 4, and 5, in which the effects of the various background factors on the test scores are examined. An exception is Section 5.4, devoted to sex differences in spatial visualizing ability, a topic of special interest to both authors and to which both of us contributed. Section 3.6 was also a result of our joint discussions. Appendix A, dealing with sampling issues, was prepared by the first author with the assistance of Harold McWilliams of NORC. The final assembly of the material and the writing of the first and last chapters were tasks of the first author.

Although we alone are responsible for our conclusions, we had the help of many others in all phases of this work. We acknowledge in particular the support and encouragement of A. J. Martin, former Director for Accession Policy, Office of the Secretary of Defense; W. S. Sellman, Director for Accession Policy, Office of the Secretary of Defense; Zahava D. Doering, Defense Manpower Data Center; Brian K. Waters, Human Resources Research Organization; and Michael E. Borus, Principal Investigator, National Longitudinal Survey of Youth Labor Force Behavior, Center for Human Resource Research, Ohio State University.

Staff of NORC directly responsible for sampling and data collection were Martin Frankel, Celia Homans, Mary Cay Burich, Shirley Knight, and Harold McWilliams. Harold McWilliams, Suzanne Erfurth, Susan Campbell and Steven Ingels were responsible for the final editing. Computer data processing was carried out by Robert Gibbons and Robert Mislevy. Michele Zimowski, Mary Jo Petersen, and Ernest Froemel assisted in the review of the literature. Word processing was accomplished by Jean Hirsch, Anne Buckborough, Mary Okazaki, Chris Lonn, Irene Edwards, Mia Moore, Cassandra Britton, Karla Maze-Darby, Arturo Landeros, and Linda Budd. Linda Budd also prepared the graphs and figures. Peggy Nolin prepared the index and assisted in proofreading.

R. Darrell Bock, *University of Chicago*

Elsie G. J. Moore, *Arizona State University*

1 Profile of American Youth

In the spring and summer of 1980, the National Opinion Research Center of the University of Chicago (NORC) administered a set of cognitive and vocational tests to a nationwide sample of nearly 12,000 young people 15 to 23 years of age. The immediate purpose of this survey, called the "Profile of American Youth," was to obtain normative distributions for the tests that comprise the Armed Services Vocational Aptitude Battery (ASVAB). The test norms used by the Armed Services at that time were extrapolations from World War II data and no longer accurately described the population of potential recruits. The data from the NORC study would make it possible for military personnel psychologists to calculate up-to-date percentile ranks for the test scores in the contemporary youth population and its various subpopulations.

The sample for the Profile study was the youth panel of the Bureau of Labor's National Longitudinal Study (NLS) of labor force participation, selected in 1979. Using this same panel for the Profile study made available the extensive background information that had been obtained in personal interviews in the NLS. The responses to these interviews, combined with the ASVAB test scores, comprise the data we examine and discuss in this book.

It was clear from the beginning of the Profile study that the results of a nationwide administration of cognitive and vocational tests would be of interest well beyond the technical objectives of test standardization. The respondents were examined at a time when they were in transition from childhood dependence to independent living. Many of them were making the first meaningful choice of a direction in which to find a livelihood. In our analysis of the Profile data, we are asking, "What are their prospects for suc-

1

cess or failure in their first steps toward financial independence and a productive life?" Relatively, at least, the Profile data allow us to assess their prospects by comparing the average test performance of respondents who are members of various subpopulations in the United States and have certain personal characteristics identified in the NLS interviews.

Although not the first attempt to survey the vocational potential of American young people, the Profile study is the most extensive and detailed. No similar study has encompassed all regions of the country and all segments of society. The Profile study is the first to reach a complete cross-section of this age group by means of a sample of persons in households rather than a sample of students in school. It is the first to employ both cognitive and vocational tests for this purpose. In so doing, it presents a detailed picture of job and career potentials of American young people of the 1980s. In the chapters that follow, we use this detailed information to test a number of contemporary theories about the origins of individual and group differences in vocational prospects. Out of this confrontation of theory and data we have tried to find reasons for the positions of advantage and disadvantage in which young people find themselves as they begin their life careers.

1.1. ASSESSING VOCATIONAL POTENTIAL

The assessment of vocational potential in this study is, of course, indirect; it depends on the power of the test battery to predict how the examinees will fare when they attempt to enter college, enlist in the Armed Services, find a job, or otherwise make their way in the world. Because these tests include the scales of the ASVAB that are used to select recruits, there is little question about their power to predict qualification for the Armed Services. Provided they meet age, physical, and moral requirements, persons who score high on the ASVAB tests have a very good chance of being accepted by the Armed Services. The power of the ASVAB to predict scores on college entrance tests, such as the Scholastic Aptitude Test (SAT), is also not in doubt. The SAT measures only general verbal and quantitative skills, and these are well represented in the ASVAB. Only the capacity of the battery to predict actual success on the job, which is difficult to demonstrate for any test, is open to question. Predictive validity of such tests must be demonstrated empirically. The validity studies of the efficacy of the ASVAB that have thus far been attempted are reviewed in Appendix B. They show that these tests, the latest of a long series of personnel selection and classification tests going back to World War II, perform reasonably well both as predictors of success in military training courses and as performance ratings reported by supervisors of civilian workers. Thus, we can have some confidence that, in examining the average ASVAB scores of various groups of respondents, we are in effect comparing their vocational potentials. As more data from the National Longitudinal Study become available for the participants in the Profile study, it will be possible to verify further the predictive validity of the ASVAB tests for success in a wide variety of jobs and careers.

1.2. ANALYZING THE DATA

The data of the Profile study are subject to a certain amount of uninformative variation, some from the sampling of persons for the NLS panel, and some from the less-than-perfect reliability of the ASVAB tests. Quantitative methods are therefore required to reveal the statistical regularity in the relationships among the variables. Many investigators would analyze this type of data by first combining the test scores into a single index of attainment. They would then attempt to assign variation in that index to sources in various explanatory variables. Multiple regression methods that show percent of additional variation accounted for as the explanatory variables are added to the statistical model are often used for this purpose. Examples can be found in the work of Duncan, Featherman, and Duncan (1972), Jencks et al (1979), and Solomon and Taubman (1973).

Our approach is different: although we use quantitative statistical methods, we attempt to retain much more qualitative detail. We use multivariate analysis of variance to examine average levels of performance in detailed subclasses of respondents—retaining throughout the identity of the individual ASVAB tests. Where the statistical significance of the effects warrant, we are then able to study interactions among background characteristics of the respondents that are often obscured when multiple regression methods are used. Retaining the tests as distinct dependent variables also enables us to discuss the results in psychological and cognitive terms that are not of interest to sociologists. In this way, we can connect to a wider literature, drawn from the fields of psychology, education, and human development, in which these more specific qualitative distinctions are discussed. Although our approach does not give as neat a summary of the quantitative variation, we believe that the greater detail obtained by examining relationships among subclass means of the original test variables gives a better understanding of its sources.

1.3. LARGER IMPLICATIONS OF THE PROFILE STUDY

To appreciate the implications of the Profile data, we must see these young people, born in the 1960s, in the social and economic context of their times. On the brighter side, they belonged to a generation enjoying wider opportunities and greater freedom of choice than any before it. Although the children of troubled times, they entered the adult world with the nation at peace, the economy healthy, and freedom of movement virtually unrestricted. The majority of them were favorably situated for their first attempts at independent living. Census figures indicate that about 4 million of them turned 18 in 1980. Of these, nearly 70% continued with some form of full- or part-time education, often with a job on the side. This is an extraordinarily favorable proportion relative to other countries and to previous generations in the United States. With some college or a college degree behind them, their prospects for employment will, on the whole, be good. Similarly, another 10% who join the Armed Services can expect quite satisfactory careers in the military or in jobs learned while in the services. At the present writing, with an economic upturn under way, these prospects are even more favorable.

On the darker side, one that we shall see reflected in the Profile data, some sections of society were still experiencing an unremitting intergenerational poverty when the majority of Americans were enjoying the rewards of a prosperous economy. Although the 8-year cohort in the Profile study was the first to benefit from the legislative programs of the 1960s and 1970s aimed at extending educational opportunities, it was far from clear that these efforts had not ameliorated the effects of years of segregation and social isolation. Most young people in these excluded groups were still not acquiring the credentials and skills required in an increasingly technological society. Education was not proving to be quite the great "equalizer" that it was supposed to be. Black, Chicano, Puerto Rican, and other subordinated minorities were not sharing in the uplift that universal public education offered, in principle, to all.

Still, young people find it hard to realize that their actions arise out of a social and historical context. To most of the Profile study respondents, the times must have seemed permissive, and the choice of a direction in life largely their own. They were not required by law to attend school any longer, and, unlike the youth of many countries, they had no military training obligations. Whatever their parents' desires and expectations, they were not likely to be forced against their will to go to college, to stay on the farm, to enter the family business, or to marry the boy next door. In the midst of this apparent freedom, their perspectives would have been too limited to allow them to see the restrictions that the confines of their personal space had imposed on their choices.

We, however, see them from the outside and have a statistical basis in their test scores and background characteristics for judging their chances of success. From this vantage point, we recognize again the problems arising from the unequal incidence of social and economic advantage and disadvantages in the United States of the 1980s. Although we have no ready-made solutions to these problems, we see in our analysis of the Profile data some indication of the direction in which progress might be made. Some of these issues are considered in Chapter 3 on sociocultural group differences; others are discussed in the summary in Chapter 6. Fundamentally, the problems to be solved are as old as the nation: how to maintain unity in the midst of diversity; how to create a vital and open national society and economy while retaining the independence and uniqueness of the local community.

2 Outline of the Profile Study

This chapter describes the main features of the Profile study, including how the sample was drawn and the respondents located, the nature of the tests and how they were administered, the selection of background data, and the statistical analysis. The account here is intended for the general reader. Technical details are relegated to Appendices A, B, and C.

2.1. THE SAMPLE

Most studies of the cognitive abilities of young people are based on the test performance of students in high schools and colleges. It is relatively easy to test respondents in these settings, and national and even international data are available for a wide variety of achievement measures. Obtaining test results from a nationally representative sample of youth and young adults is a vastly more difficult undertaking. Because there is no institutional route to obtaining such persons, they have to be located by interviewing them or their parents in their homes. Once identified, the respondents must be persuaded to spend several hours in arduous testing sessions.

As a matter of economy, and having available a greater variety of data, the sample for the Profile study was initially drawn from the current National Longitudinal Survey of Youth Labor Force Behavior (NLS). Subjects in the sample represent a cohort of persons born between January 1, 1957 and December 31, 1964. The NLS study design called for annual personal interviews beginning in 1979 and continuing for 6 years. Among other things, the interviews covered the participants' educational and vocational experiences,

6

their income, their state of health, and demographic characteristics. By the time the ASVAB was administered in 1980, the respondents had completed two annual NLS interviews. All of this information was available in the analysis of the respondents' scores on the ASVAB.

The NLS/Profile sample consisted of three independent probability samples: (a) a cross-section sample designed to represent the noninstitutional civilian segment of American young people aged 14 to 21 as of January 1, 1979, in their proper population proportions; (b) a supplemental oversample of civilian Hispanic, Black, and economically disadvantaged non-Hispanic, non-Black (poor White) youth in the same age range; and (c) a military sample designed to represent youth aged 17 to 21 as of January 1, 1979, who were serving in the military as of September 30, 1978. The data from all three of these samples are examined in the present study.

For the civilian sample, a total of 6,812 persons were identified and selected for interview. Of these, 6,111, or 89.7%, cooperated in completing the interviews, and 5,766, or 94.4% of the latter took the ASVAB tests. For the supplementary sample of Blacks, Hispanics, and the economically disadvantaged, 5,969 were selected for interview; 5,295, or 88.7%, completed the interview; and 4,990, or 94.2% of the latter took the tests. For the military sample, 1,280, or 71.5% of those selected completed the interview, and 1,158, or 90.5% of those took the tests. As an inducement to take the tests, all respondents who completed them were paid $50. In total, 11,914 persons took the ASVAB tests.

2.2. BACKGROUND INFORMATION

Although the personal interviews elicited data on a wide range of demographic and other background characteristics, the present study is concerned with only those characteristics that previous research suggested would be most associated with score variation on the 10 ASVAB tests. These characteristics are: age, sex, education level, sociocultural group, economic status, region of residence at age 14, and mother's education. The classes within each of these factors are as follows:

1) Age: 15 to 17, 18 to 19, 20 to 22.
2) Sex: male, female.
3) Education level (highest grade completed): 0 to 8, 9 to 11, 12, 13 plus.
4) Sociocultural group: White, Black, Hispanic.
5) Economic status: poor (at or below the official poverty level), non-poor.
6) Region of residence at age 14: Northeast, Southeast, Midwest, West.

7) Mother's education (highest grade completed): 0 to 8, 9 to 11, 12, 13 to 15, 16 plus.

To give some idea of the kinds of persons on which these classifications are based, we present tables showing frequency counts of the number of respondents in the categories of each background factor. These frequency counts are unweighted and cannot be used to estimate the distribution of these characteristics in the population. They reveal, however, the qualitative variety of the responses and the minor extent of missing or unusable information. In addition, we describe the definition and construction of each background factor. Weighted figures are shown in Tables 2.8 through 2.18.

Age.   Table 2.1 shows the distribution of the 11,914 respondents by year of birth. Since the test battery was administered during the summer of 1980, about half of the respondents in each cohort were older than the January 1980 age indicated in Table 2.1.

Sex.   Of the 11,914 respondents tested, 5,969 were male, and 5,945 were female.

Education Level.   Information on highest grade completed was obtained in both the 1979 and 1980 interviews. Subjects interviewed in 1980 are classified according to their response to the question, "What is the highest grade or year of regular school that you have completed or received credit

TABLE 2.1
Profile Cases by Year of Birth

Year of Birth	1980 Age[a]	Number of Cases
1957	22	1,545
1958	21	1,542
1959	20	1,597
1960	19	1,534
1961	18	1,447
1962	17	1,538
1963	16	1,488
1964	15	1,223
TOTAL		11,914

[a] Age as of January 1, 1980.

for?" Those respondents not interviewed in 1980 are classified according to their 1979 response to the same question. The distribution of respondents by highest grade completed is shown in Table 2.2.

Sociocultural Group. From the many possible ways to disaggregate the United States population, we have chosen a scheme that classifies the population in three broad sociocultural groups: White and other, Black, and Hispanic. These same broad groupings are widely used in social science research and in government reports such as the Current Population Reports published by the U.S. Bureau of the Census.

Table 2.3 shows the distribution of Profile respondents across the three sociocultural groups. The sociocultural group categories are based on classes in the sampling design determined from the screening interview conducted with an adult member of the respondent's household. After the screening fieldwork was completed, individuals were assigned to one of the three sociocultural groups based on three types of information obtained during the screening interview: (a) race (White, Black, or other) as observed by the interviewer; (b) origin or descent as indicated in response to the question,

TABLE 2.2
Profile Cases by Highest Grade Completed

Highest Grade Completed	Number of Cases
0	2
1	7
2	2
3	15
4	15
5	16
6	72
7	170
8	700
9	1,783
10	1,864
11	1,756
12	3,606
13	829
14	539
15	317
16	208
17	3
No information	10
TOTAL	11,914

TABLE 2.3
Profile Cases by Sociocultural Group

Sociocultural Group	Number of Cases
White	7,043
Black	3,028
Hispanic	1,843
TOTAL	11,914

"What is [interviewee's] origin or descent?"; (c) whether Spanish was spoken in the home as a child. On the basis of this information, NORC's sampling department assigned individuals in the eligible age range in the screened households to one of three sociocultural groups. Individuals were assigned to the Hispanic group if their origin or descent had been recorded as Mexican–American, Chicano, Mexican, Mexicano, Cuban, Cubano, Puerto Rican, Puertorriqueno, Boricua, Latino, other Latin American, Hispano, or of Spanish descent. In addition, individuals whose descent was other than those listed above were assigned to the Hispanic group if they met all of the following criteria: (a) they were not of Filipino or Portuguese descent; (b) Spanish was spoken in the home as a child; and (c) the family's surname appeared on the U.S. Census Bureau's list of Spanish surnames.

Individuals were classified as Black if the interviewer had coded their race as Black, and their origin or descent was not Hispanic. In addition, individuals who identified their own origin or descent as Black, Negro, or Afro-American were classified as Black regardless of the race recorded by the interviewer. Thus, self-identification took precedence over the interviewer's classification. All individuals not classified as Hispanic or Black were classified as members of the White sociocultural group.

The three sociocultural groups, in fact, contain considerable ethnic diversity. Thus, in Table 2.4 we show the unweighted frequency counts of the responses to a question in the 1979 Year 1 NLS interview, "What is your origin or descent?" These counts, based on the self-identifications of the Year 1 respondents themselves, give some indication of the heterogeneity of the three broad groupings.

Our intention in using this classification of sociocultural group is not to distinguish races in an evolutionary sense but, rather, to identify the origins of the respondents in the broad subcultures that exist in the United States at the present time. Our decision to use these three broad groupings was based on the fact that most young people in the United States are nurtured in one or another of these three broad cultures; few belong simultaneously to more than one, even when their parents are the products of different cultures. The definition of the culture is elusive, but its collective influence through family, peers, and community is unmistakable. It heavily determines manners and dress; spoken language; preferences in reading, music, entertainment, and sports; personal values; and, most important for our purposes, educational and vocational aspirations. Among other things, it is the effects of these influences that we expect to see in the test scores of our respondents when we examine them by sociocultural group in Chapter 3.

TABLE 2.4
Profile Cases Self-Reported Origin or Descent
Classified by Sociocultural Group

Origin or Descent	Number of Cases
White	
Chinese	24
English	1,424
Filipino	41
French	274
German	1,268
Greek	27
Hawaiian	19
Native American	577
Asian-Indian	18
Irish	873
Italian	451
Japanese, Korean, Vietnamese	22
Polish	211
Portuguese	92
Russian	40
Scottish	116
Welsh	34
Other	725
Black	2,893
Hispanic:	
Cuban	96
Mexican, Mexican-American, Chicano	1,104
Puerto Rican	287
Other Latino	110
Other Spanish	86
Unclassifiable	
American	703
None	128
Refused, Don't Know, or Missing	271
TOTAL	11,914

Economic Status.   Economic status, as measured by the income available to a family, exerts a pervasive and powerful influence on vocational prospects in most societies, including the United States. Economic status cuts across and acts within each of the broad sociocultural groups defined earlier. Therefore, in the analysis that follows, it is often used in combination with the sociocultural group factor to differentiate between the higher and lower income segments of the three sociocultural groups.

Subjects are classified on the economic status dimension as either poor or nonpoor based on definitions formulated by the Office of Management and Budget (OMB). These definitions of poverty take into account family size and urban or rural residence, as well as total family income. For nonfarm families living in the continental United States, poverty is defined as a net 1979 family income less than or equal to $3,770, plus $1,230 times one less than the number of persons in the family unit. For farm families the formula is $3,220, plus $1,040 times one less than the number of persons in the family unit. For a nonfarm family of four, this translates into a net family income of $7,460 or less per year. By many standards, this is a stringent definition of poverty, and, as we see in Section 2.5, only a small percent of the population falls within it.

Table 2.5 shows the distribution of Profile respondents by economic status based on their 1979 family income or, if they were not interviewed in 1980, based on their 1978 family income (using 1978 poverty definitions). Unfortunately, this definition of poverty-line households does not distinguish between young people living with their parents and those living independently and thus classified as heads of household. The latter include, of course, students who are supporting themselves while in college or graduate school or in other types of occupational training. Such persons are not genuinely poor; within a few years their earnings will be above, often far above, the poverty level.

TABLE 2.5
Profile Cases by Economic Status (Unweighted)

Economic Status	Number of Cases
Poor	2,779
Nonpoor	8,813
No information	322
TOTAL	11,914

Note: Economic status is based on OMB criteria using 1979 and 1980 NLS interview data on family size and net family income.

Residence at Age 14. For purposes of the present analysis, respondents are classified according to the region of the country in which they were living at age 14. Residence at age 14, rather than residence at the time of testing or interview, is used because it is assumed to be a better indicator of where participants spent their formative years. It is possible, of course, that some respondents spent only a few years or even months in the region where they were living at age 14. Internal evidence (presented in Chapter 6) indicates, however, that residence at age 14 is an informative classification.

The assignment of respondents to regions is based on their response to a question in the 1979 interview that asked where they were living on their 14th birthday. Subjects were classified first by state or territory of residence. The 50 states were then grouped into Northeast, Southeast, Midwest, and West regions according to the definition used by the National Assessment of Educational Progress. The few respondents residing in outlying territories of the United States were assigned to one of the four regions as described in the note to Table 2.6. The number of respondents in each region is shown in Table 2.6.

Mother's Education. In order to have more information about family background than is conveyed by the subpopulation classification, we have

TABLE 2.6
Profile Cases by Region of Residence at Age 14

Region	Number of Cases
Northeast	2,595
Southeast	3,018
Midwest	3,019
West	2,934
Elsewhere	265
No information	83
TOTAL	11,914

NOTE: Northeast region includes the following states and territories: CT, DE, DC, ME, MD, MA, NH, NJ, NY, PA, RI, VT, and Canal Zone, Puerto Rico, and Virgin Islands.

Southeast region includes the following states: AL, AR, FL, GA, KY, LA, MS, NC, SC, TN, VA, and WV.

Midwest region includes the following states: IL, IN, IA, KS, MI, MN, MO, NE, ND, OH, SD, and WI.

West region includes the following states and territories: AK, AZ, CA, CO, HI, ID, MT, NV, NM, OK, OR, TX, UT, WA, WY and Pacific Trust Territory and Other Pacific Islands.

also included the respondent's report of mother's highest grade completed. Mother's education is more satisfactory for this purpose than father's because: (a) as we point out in Chapter 5, there is reason to believe that the mother is more influential in determining the linguistic skills and educational aspirations of her children than is the father; (b) in the case of broken homes, the mother is more likely to have custody of the children; (c) the respondent is more likely to know the mother's than the father's education. Classification by mother's education is based on the 1979 interview question, "What was the highest grade or year of regular school that your mother completed?" The breakdown of responses to this question is shown in Table 2.7. For purposes of our analysis, we have collapsed Mother's Highest Grade Completed into 0 to 8, 9 to 11, 12, 13 to 15, and 16 or more years.

2.3. POPULATION COMPOSITION

We can regard the NLS sample as a sort of minicensus of the United States populations between the ages of 15 and 22 in the spring of 1980. As such, the proportions of respondents in certain subclasses of the seven-way

TABLE 2.7
Profile Cases by Mother's Highest Grade Completed

Mother's Highest Grade Completed	Number of Cases
0	117
1	22
2	87
3	184
4	162
5	199
6	415
7	265
8	798
9	690
10	987
11	1,083
12	4,602
13	361
14	536
15	178
16	630
17 plus	97
No information	354
TOTAL	11,914

classification, suitably weighted to account for allocation sampling, should approximate those of the Current Population Survey (CPS) around that time. In particular, figures are available in the CPS that enable us to check the distribution of cases in the important sociocultural groups by age by highest grade classification.

The weights for reconstituting a probability sample were calculated to match the proportions of Whites, Blacks, and Hispanics, male and female, in the relevant age cohort as given in the CPS. This weighting takes into account any differential loss from these groups in the sample at screening and interviewing. (Details are given in Frankel & McWilliams, 1981).

The data presented in the tables in this section are based on the weighted 1979 NLS interview sample and not on the slightly less complete sample of respondents who actually took the tests in 1980.

Sociocultural Group by Economic Status and Region at Age 14. We see in Table 2.8 that, notwithstanding the internal migration following World War II, the number of Blacks relative to non-Blacks is still substantially greater in the Southeast than elsewhere in the country. And, by the same token, Blacks are relatively more numerous in the Northeast than in the Midwest or West. (Refer to Table 2.6 for the states included in these regions.)

We see also that the influx of Cubans into Florida, though locally concentrated, has not produced any appreciably greater proportion of Hispanics in the Southeast than in the Midwest. A somewhat larger proportion of Hispanics is found in the Northeast, but their relative numbers continue to be much greater in the Western States.

TABLE 2.8
Percent[a] of NLS Year 1 Sample in Each Sociocultural Group and
Economic Status, by Region of Residence at Age 14

Sociocultural Economic Group	Region of Residence at Age 14				
	Northeast	Southeast	Midwest	West	All Regions
Poor White	7.6	8.6	8.4	6.7	7.9
Nonpoor White	73.5	63.3	81.6	68.0	72.4
Poor Black	4.5	12.1	2.8	3.1	5.5
Nonpoor Black	8.8	14.1	5.5	5.8	8.4
Poor Hispanic	2.3	0.3	0.3	4.9	1.7
Nonpoor Hispanic	3.3	1.6	1.3	11.6	4.1
TOTAL	100.0	100.0	99.9	100.1	100.0
Percent in Region	23.8	23.8	30.9	21.5	100.0

[a] Weighted.

The proportions of people classified as being in poverty varies among the regional and sociocultural groups. We can calculate from Table 2.8 that among Whites 9.8% are in poverty; among Blacks, 39.6%; and among Hispanics, 29.3%.

Highest Grade Completed by Region. Table 2.9 shows that education level (as highest grade completed) in this sample is not as variable among these regions as one might suppose. The Northeast continues to send the greater proportion of its young people to college, especially when compared to the Southeast. The Southeast also has relatively more respondents with less than 9 years of education the percentage in that group being nearly twice the percentage in the 0 through 8 group in the Northeast and Midwest. Other than these differences, regional variation in highest grade completed is not especially striking. For example, the proportions of respondents with 12 or more years of schooling varies only a little more than 10%. In terms of numbers of pupils completing high school, all regions are doing about equally well.

Highest Grade Completed by Age. It is important to understand that the overall proportions of respondents from the Profile sample at the various education levels cannot be interpreted in Table 2.9 because of the respondents who are too young to have completed high school, or to have entered college. More useful figures are shown in Table 2.10 where the educational levels for respondents in the age ranges are shown. As mentioned above, the actual basis for the age classification is date of birth: Reading left to right,

TABLE 2.9
Percent[a] of NLS Year 1 Sample Completing Each Grade
Category by Region of Residence at Age 14

Highest Grade Completed	Region of Residence at Age 14				
	Northeast	Southeast	Midwest	West	All Regions[b]
0-8	5.2	8.6	4.8	7.0	6.3
9-11	41.3	48.1	45.1	46.9	45.3
12	30.4	27.9	33.1	27.9	30.1
13 plus	23.1	15.3	17.0	18.2	18.3
TOTAL	100.0	99.9	100.0	100.0	100.0
Percent in Region	23.8	23.8	30.8	21.6	100.0

[a] Weighted.

[b] This marginal distribution differs slightly from those in Tables 2.10 and 2.17 because complete classification data were not available for some cases in the sample.

TABLE 2.10
Percent[a] of NLS Year 1 Sample Completing Each
Grade Category, by Age Group

Highest Grade Completed	Age Group			All Ages[b]
	15-17	18-19	20-22	
0–8	12.8	3.0	3.2	6.6
9–11	86.2	31.6	14.7	45.0
12	1.0	50.5	43.7	29.9
13 plus	0.0	14.9	38.4	18.5
TOTAL	100.0	100.0	100.0	100.0
Percent in Age Group	36.4	25.2	38.3	99.9

[a] Weighted.

[b] This marginal distribution differs slightly from those in Tables 2.9 and 2.17 because complete classification data were not available for some cases in the sample.

the age categories represent subjects born in 1962 and later, in 1960–61, and in 1959 and earlier, corresponding roughly to the ages 15 through 17, 18 and 19, and 20 through 22. Table 2.10 shows clearly that those members of the sample aged 15 through 17 who have completed 8 or fewer grades are behind merely by virtue of their age and will eventually move at least to grade 9 and possibly beyond. This is apparent in the very small numbers o respondents in the lowest educational level among those 18 years of age and older. Highest grade completed among the 18- and 19-year-olds and the 20- through 22-year-olds can also be obtained from the Current Population Reports for 1979 and 1980.

That the figures shown in Table 2.11 agree within a few percentage points with the figures in Table 2.10 is an indication that the NLS probability sample closely mirrors the population it is intended to represent.

Highest Grade Completed by Sociocultural Group and Economic Status. Comparable to the regional variation in highest grade completed is the variation between the sociocultural groups shown in Table 2.12. In terms of the proportions in each group with high school education or better, the percentages range from 52.0 in the nonpoor Whites to 24.2 in the poor Hispanics. In terms of the proportion with some college education, however, the special nature of the economic status classification mentioned above comes into play. The sample contains a number of White college students who are living independently and are considered heads of households. Their income as students is low enough for them to be classified as poor by the

TABLE 2.11
Percent of Noninstitutional United States Population
Completing Each Grade Category by Age Group[a]

Highest Grade Completed	Age Groups 18–19	Age Groups 20–22
0–8	3.5	3.4
9–11	34.7	12.7
12	49.3	45.3
13 plus	12.5	38.6
TOTAL	100.0	100.0

[a] Figures based on the March 1979 Current Population Survey. See U.S. Bureau of the Census, Educational Attainment in the United States: March 1979 and 1978, Current Population Reports, Series P–20, No. 356, Table 2, p. 20, August 1980.

criteria used here, even though this may be a temporary poverty. The result is, however, that the nonpoor Whites and poor Whites show about the same percentage of respondents completing one or more years of college.

The genuinely poor Whites are, of course, much more represented among those not completing more than 8 years of school. This group constitutes 15.5% of the poor Whites. Among the nonpoor Whites, 4.2% fall in this lowest educational level, and most of these are behind for their age and will eventually reach at least the ninth grade.

TABLE 2.12
Percent[a] of NLS Year 1 Sample Completing Each Grade Category
By Sociocultural Group and Economic Status

Highest Grade Completed	White Poor	White Non-Poor	Black Poor	Black Non-Poor	Hispanic Poor	Hispanic Non-Poor	All Groups Poor	All Groups Non-Poor
0–8	15.5	4.2	12.9	6.2	25.4	12.0	15.8	4.8
9–11	42.7	43.8	58.6	45.6	50.5	49.0	49.4	44.3
12	22.6	32.1	19.3	30.4	15.2	23.6	20.5	31.5
13 plus	19.3	19.9	9.2	17.8	9.0	15.4	14.4	19.4
TOTAL	100.0	100.0	100.0	100.0	100.0	100.0	100.1	100.0
Percent in Group[b]	7.9	72.0	5.5	8.3	1.9	4.4	15.3	84.7

[a] Weighted.

[b] This marginal distribution differs slightly from that in Table 2.16 because complete classification data were not available for some cases in the sample.

In all, the distribution of educational levels for the nonpoor Blacks is somewhat higher than that for the nonpoor Hispanics and not very different from that of the nonpoor Whites. The poor Blacks, and to an even greater extent the poor Hispanics, have the least favorable distribution of education. These are quantitative comparisons that do not necessarily reflect quality of education. We come back to this point when we discuss sociocultural group differences in responses to the vocational tests in Chapter 3.

Highest Grade Completed by Sociocultural Group by Age.   The sociocultural differences in highest grade completed are shown in a more detailed cross-classification by age group in Table 2.13. Comparing Table 2.13 with Table 2.14, which contains corresponding percentages calculated from the Current Population Survey, we see a possible tendency to undersample low-education respondents from the Hispanic population aged 20 to 22. The lowest education group is underrepresented by 5.3%, and the highest over-represented by 10.3%. In spite of this problem in sampling the low-education-level Hispanics, we do not expect our analysis to be much affected. As mentioned in Chapter 1, the group comparisons, based on the interaction plots in Chapter 7, assume arbitrary numbers of respondents in the subclasses and are not influenced by differences between the sample and population proportions. They would be affected only if there were differential misrepresentation of high- and low-ability respondents within education levels, and any such effects are likely to be small.

Highest Grade Completed by Sex.   There is an interesting trend over educational levels in Table 2.15. Relatively more males are held back or drop out without completing more than 8 years of education, and relatively fewer males go on to 1 or more years of college. This effect is especially prominent among Blacks, where 17.6% of females reported 1 or more years of college, as opposed to 10.9% of Black males. Some reasons for the greater educational attainment of Black women are discussed in Chapter 7. In the other sociocultural groups, the sex effect on the distribution of highest grade completed is in a similar direction as in Blacks, but much weaker.

Mother's Education by Sociocultural Group and Economic Status.   The other important two-way associations in the population classification involve mother's education. As might be expected, the variations in mother's education with respect to region and sociocultural group are similar to those of her children, except stronger because they reflect origins of the parents and the state of education a generation earlier. Differences among sociocultural groups shown in Table 2.16 are especially dramatic, the most striking figure being 68.7% of poor Hispanic mothers reported to have no more than 8 years of education.

TABLE 2.13
Percent[a] of NLS Year 1 Sample Completing Each Grade
Category by Sociocultural Group and Age Group

Highest Grade Completed	White			Black			Hispanic		
	15–17	18–19	20–22	15–17	18–19	20–22	15–17	18–19	20–22
0–8	10.8	2.5	2.4	18.9	2.8	3.3	22.9	9.9	13.1
9–11	88.2	28.5	12.3	79.7	42.3	25.5	75.8	47.7	23.0
12	1.0	53.1	45.0	1.5	43.1	30.6	1.2	34.4	32.7
13 plus	0.0	15.9	40.2	0.0	11.8	30.6	0.1	8.0	31.3
TOTAL	100.0	100.0	99.9	100.1	100.0	100.1	100.0	100.1	100.0

[a] Weighted.

TABLE 2.14
Percent of Noninstitutional United States Population Completing Each Grade Category by Sociocultural Group and Age Group[a]

Highest Grade Competed	White		Black		Hispanic	
	18-19	20-22	18-19	20-22	18-19	20-22
0–8	3.3	3.4	4.9	3.9	10.5	18.4
9–11	32.7	11.5	48.7	21.9	42.5	20.1
12	51.4	45.4	35.5	45.4	38.5	40.2
13 plus	12.7	39.8	10.8	28.7	8.5	21.0
TOTAL	100.1	100.1	99.9	99.9	100.0	99.7

[a] Figures based on the March 1979 Current Population Survey, See U.S. Bureau of the Census, Educational Attainment in the United States: March 1979 and 1978, Current Population Reports, Series P-20, No. 356, Table 2, p. 20, August 1980.

TABLE 2.15
**Percent[a] of NLS Year 1 Sample Completing Each Grade
Category by Sociocultural Group and Sex**

Highest Grade Completed	White		Black		Hispanics		All Groups	
	Male	Female	Male	Female	Male	Female	Male	Female
0–8	6.3	4.6	11.2	6.9	17.2	14.9	7.6	5.6
9–11	44.6	42.8	51.6	48.9	50.0	48.9	45.9	44.1
12	30.5	31.9	26.3	26.6	20.6	21.4	29.3	30.5
13 plus	18.5	20.7	10.9	17.6	12.2	14.7	17.1	19.9
TOTAL	99.9	100.0	100.0	100.0	100.0	99.9	99.9	100.1
Percent in each	40.7	39.2	7.0	6.9	3.2	3.1	50.9	49.2

[a] Weighted.

TABLE 2.16

Percent[a] of NLS Year 1 Sample Whose Mothers Completed Each Grade Category, by Sociocultural Group and Economic Status

Mother's Highest Grade Completed	White		Black		Hispanic		All Groups	
	Poor	Nonpoor	Poor	Nonpoor	Poor	Nonpoor	Poor	Nonpoor
0–8	20.2	7.3	23.1	11.4	68.7	44.5	27.2	9.6
9–11	24.0	16.7	42.6	32.1	16.1	19.5	29.6	18.3
12	40.3	51.9	28.0	37.3	11.1	25.2	32.3	49.1
13–15	8.7	12.5	4.4	11.5	2.6	6.0	6.4	12.1
16 plus	6.8	11.6	2.0	7.8	1.4	4.9	4.4	10.9
TOTAL	100.0	100.0	100.0	100.0	100.0	100.0	99.9	100.0
Percent in Group[b]	7.8	72.5	5.3	8.2	1.9	4.3	15.0	85.0

[a] Weighted.

[b] This marginal distribution differs slightly from that in Table 2.12 because complete classification data were not available for some cases in the sample.

This figure probably reflects the agrarian and working-class origins of many of the poor Hispanic mothers, especially those from Puerto Rico and Mexico, where at the time (circa 1960) it would not be unusual for such girls to have only a grade-school education. We have more to say about these kinds of migrational effects in Chapter 5.

The data in Table 2.16 also show more clearly than elsewhere the connection between the classification of households by income level and characteristics of parents of the Profile respondents. The nonpoor Whites have a much more favorable distribution of mother's education than do poor Whites, whose distribution across levels of mother's education resembles that of the nonpoor Blacks.

Mother's Education by Offspring's Education. Not surprisingly, a mother's education has a strong association with that of her children. Table 2.17 shows the distribution of highest grade completed among the NLS sample in each of the mother's education groups. Having a mother with some college education greatly increases the probability that the respondent will have some college education. Inasmuch as only about 50% of the sample had reached college age when this information was obtained, the effect of mother's education on the probability of her children attending college is even stronger than Table 2.17 indicates. We see in Chapter 6 that mother's education is also strongly associated with the performance of her offspring.

TABLE 2.17
Percent[a] of NLS Year 1 Sample Completing Each
Grade Category, by Grades Completed by Mother

Case's Highest Grade Completed	Mother's Highest Grade Completed					All Grades[b]
	0-8	9-11	12	13-15	16 plus	
0-8	17.7	9.7	3.9	2.8	1.8	6.4
9-11	47.5	53.4	43.0	39.0	40.0	44.9
12	27.1	28.9	34.7	23.1	20.8	29.9
13 plus	7.8	8.1	18.4	35.0	37.4	18.8
TOTAL	100.0	100.1	100.0	99.9	100.0	100.0
Percent in each Mother's Grade Category	12.2	20.1	46.5	11.2	10.0	100.0

[a] Weighted.

[b] This marginal distribution differs slightly from those in Tables 2.9 and 2.10 because complete classification data were not available for some cases in the sample.

2.4. THE TESTS

Understanding the results of the Profile study requires some familiarity with the tests that make up the ASVAB. Like all such psychological measures, these tests can be described from a number of points of view—history of development, scientific rationale, construction and use, content, psychometric characteristics, and correlations with other measures. The best way to begin is to examine sample items to obtain a first-hand impression of the content. Unfortunately, because the version of the ASVAB administered in this study is still in active use, its items cannot be publicly disclosed. In this section we have therefore simulated as realistically as possible some of the items in each of the tests. For 8 of the 10 tests, we have also displayed the simulated items for a scale indicating their relative difficulties for the respondents in the weighted sample. For the remaining two tests, which are speeded and cannot be scaled in this way (see Appendix B), we show the practice items that actually appear in the test booklet. These displays, and other information presented in this chapter, give some idea of the actual skills and knowledge measured by the tests. Sample items taken from earlier versions of the ASVAB can be found in Maier and Fuchs (1973).

History of the ASVAB

The Armed Services Vocational Aptitude Battery consists of 10 tests resembling in many respects those in the well-known General Aptitude Test Battery (GATB) or the Differential Aptitude Tests (DAT). The ASVAB is the latest of a long line of selection and classification instruments developed by the Armed Services beginning with the famous Army Alpha and Beta tests of World War I. By World War II, the Army Alpha and Beta had evolved into the Army General Classification Test (AGCT), which was made up of three subtests—verbal reasoning, numerical ability, and spatial reasoning. Recruits in the World War II mobilization were screened with this test to ensure a minimum of reading and general learning ability.

As the need for detailed job classification became more evident following World War II, special ability tests including shop mechanics, automotive, radio, and electrical knowledge were added to the Army and Navy classification batteries. The Army, Navy, and Marine Corps used these batteries to assign recruits to the numerous military occupational specialities and training schools. The Services carried out many studies of the validity of the tests in predicting final course grades and instructor ratings in these schools. Correlations between the predictor tests and these criteria were consistently high enough to justify continued use of the tests. (Similar studies of the ASVAB are discussed in Appendix B.)

Prompted by the Selective Service Act of 1948, Army psychologists developed, on the model of the AGCT, a selection test called the Armed Forces Qualification Test (AFQT). When introduced operationally in 1950, the AFQT consisted of the arithmetic reasoning, vocabulary, and spatial relations scales from the AGCT; the Navy's tool usage test was added later to supply more practical content. The AFQT remained the initial selection instrument for all the Services through the Korean and Vietnam conflicts and up to 1973. In that ‚ear, the Services discontinued use of a common AFQT, and from 1973 through 1975 each Service estimated AFQT scores from its own classification test battery.

During the time when each Service had its own classification battery, the Air Force began using shortened versions of its tests in a voluntary testing program for high school students. High school seniors were given the opportunity to take the test to find out whether they would qualify for the Air Force and, also, to learn something of their prospects for success in various vocations. This testing program was sufficiently popular to be broadened into a joint effort of the Services. The high school students were tested on a form of the ASVAB similar to that used in the Profile study.

In a further move to unify and reduce the cost of testing (by eliminating the administration of separate selection and classification tests to the same recruits), the Defense Department adopted a single battery, the present ASVAB, and implemented its use for service-wide selection and classification of recruits. Although some compromise in differential efficiency had to be accepted to accomplish this goal, satisfactory ASVAB Forms 6 and 7 were developed and put into operational use for selection and classification in 1976. Development of Forms 8, 9, and 10 was initiated at the same time. Further details are available in a report entitled "History of the ASVAB," prepared by the ASVAB Working Group for the Principal Deputy Assistant Secretary of Defense (Manpower, Reserve Affairs, and Logistics), March, 1980.

The tests used in the Profile study are those from the current operational ASVAB, Form 8A, which was introduced in October, 1980. It is entirely a paper-and-pencil instrument and contains 10 independently timed and scored subtests as follows, (in order of administration):

	Subtest	Code	No. of Items	Time (Min.)
1)	General Science	GS	25	11
2)	Arithmetic Reasoning	AR	30	36
3)	Word Knowledge	WK	35	11
4)	Paragraph Comprehension	PC	15	13
5)	Numerical Operations	NO	50	3
6)	Coding Speed	CS	84	7

Subtest	Code	No. of Items	Time (Min.)
7) Auto and Shop Information	AS	25	11
8) Mathematics Knowledge	MK	25	24
9) Mechanical Comprehension	MC	25	19
10) Electronics Information	EI	20	9

Numerous studies on various forms of the ASVAB have investigated their reliability, predictive validity, and comparability with standard batteries such as the GATB and DAT. A review of these studies, prefaced by a brief introduction to psychological measurement is presented in Appendix B.

Description of ASVAB Form 8

With the exception of Numerical Operations and Coding Speed, the ASVAB tests are "power" tests—that is, tests with time limits sufficiently generous to allow most examinees to attempt all items. Differences in test scores result primarily from numbers of right and wrong responses due to differences in the difficulty of the items and not from differences in the number of items attempted. Generally speaking, the items become progressively harder from the beginning to the end within each power test. Figure 2.1-a, b, c, and d conveys something of the range of item content and difficulty within each of these tests. Easy, medium, and hard items are shown in their respective locations on the measurement scale for each test. The units on these scales have been set so that the mean is 500 and the standard deviation 100 in the total sample correctly weighted to reflect the population composition. Each item is represented at the point on the scale where the probability is 50% that persons with that score will correctly answer the item. (These points are called the item-50% thresholds.) Because the content of the ASVAB Form 8A must be kept secure so that it can be used operationally and for standardizing other forms, we show only simulated items in Figure 2.1a. They are similar to items at these thresholds, but words and other details have been altered to disguise the item and the location of the correct response. They nevertheless provide an indication of the progression of the item difficulty along the scale.

The speeded tests, Numerical Operations and Coding Speed, are well represented by the practice items from ASVAB Form 8A shown in Figure 2.2. All items in these sets are about equal in difficulty and cannot be scaled in the manner of power-test items.

In the construction of vocational aptitude batteries, the goal has been to find a relatively small number of tests, administered in not more than 3 or 4 hours, that have useful predictive validity for a range of occupations and jobs. Because test constructors are under great pressure to keep the battery short and simple, they are interested in finding tests that relate to very gen-

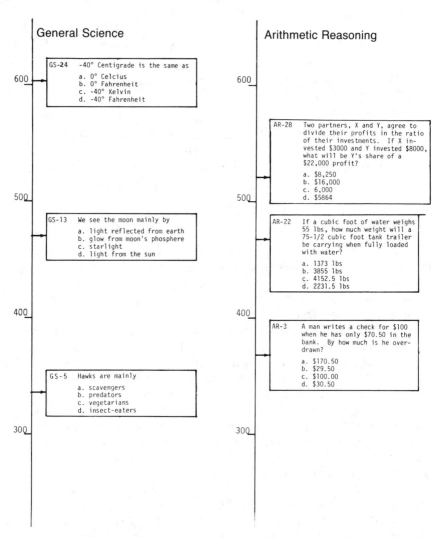

FIG. 2.1a.   General Science and Arithmetic Reasoning: Selected item difficulties (higher scale numbers indicate greater difficulty)

eral dimensions of skill required in varying amounts in many or most occupations. At the same time, they may need to assess very particular areas of information that are required for specific jobs.

The approach to finding general dimensions of vocationally relevant skills that should be represented in such tests has been greatly influenced by the thinking of L. L. Thurstone (1887–1955) who, with Truman Kelley (1884–1961), introduced multiple factor analysis for this purpose. With the help of factor analysis, dimensions or clusters of related tests can be identified in

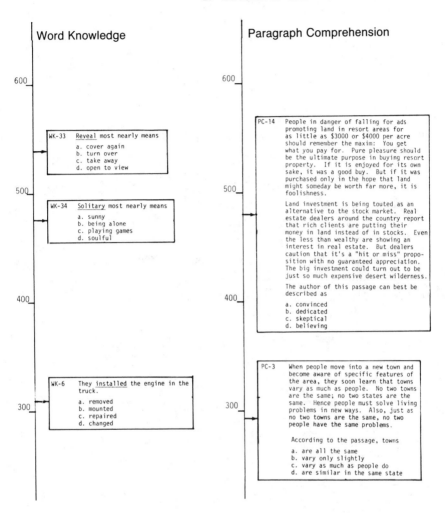

FIG. 2.1b. Word Knowledge and Paragraph Comprehension: Selected item difficulties (higher scale numbers indicate greater difficulty)

greater or lesser detail. The dimensions or clusters correspond to distinct abilities in which the respondents vary, and which can be reliably measured by two or more tests. Many such systems for classifying factorially identified abilities exist (Cattell, 1967; Guilford & Hoepfner, 1971; Thurstone & Thurstone, 1941). Differing in particulars, these systems still identify much the same skills at higher levels, although sometimes with different terminology. Most factors analysts would agree at least on the importance of the three major sources of variation in mental-test scores discussed in Bock (1973)— namely, verbal ability, spatial ability, and fluent production. They appear in

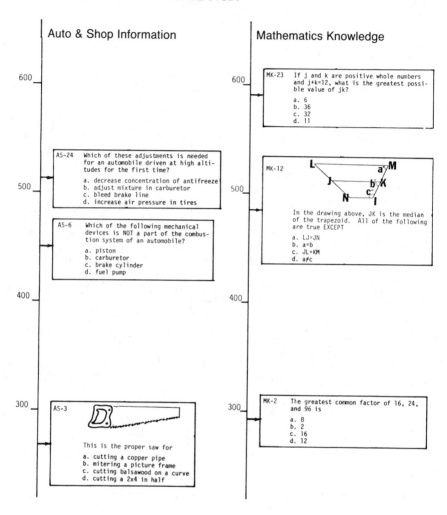

FIG. 2.1c. Auto & Shop Information and Mathematics Knowledge: Selected item difficulties (high scale numbers indicate greater difficulty)

the factor analysis of many cognitive test batteries, and there is evidence from research on twins that they have a genetic component (Bock, 1973).

At an intermediate level, most factor analysts would also concur in identifying the skills related to the intellectual tools of our culture—namely, reading, arithmetic ability, spelling, and other language usage. Variation in these more basic abilities is probably due to differences in educational and cultural background. At a still more detailed level, factors relating to specific content may appear, depending on the particular tests used and on the populations to which they are administered. Variations specific to these factors reflect a

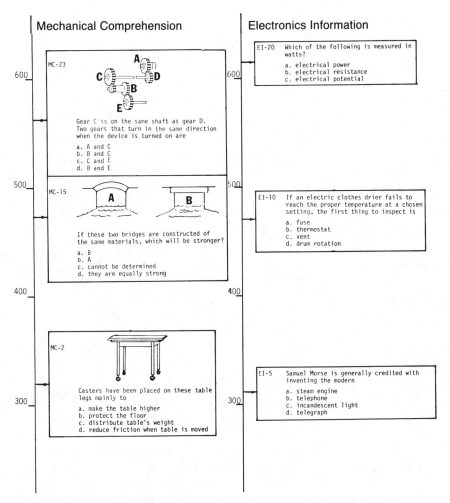

FIG. 2.1d. Mechanical Comprehension and Electronics Information: Selected item difficulties (higher scale numbers indicate greater difficulty)

wide variety of experiential differences. From the content of the ASVAB, we can see that the tests are aimed simultaneously at these several sources of variation.

The test of **General Science**, although certainly relevant for predicting success of further education in scientific field, appears in the ASVAB both as a test of the extent of exposure of respondents to technical topics, and as a measure of the efficiency, capacity, and accuracy of the long-term memory and recall of information. Because the military occupational specialties are becoming increasingly technical, recruits who have an interest in science and have learned basic scientific facts and concepts are at an advantage in many

Numerical Operations

Now look at the sample problem below

3×3

A 6
B 0
C 9
D 1

The answer is 9, so the C answer is correct.

Coding Speed

Look at the practice Key and the five sample questions below.

KEY

| green .... | 2715 | man .... | 3451 | salt .... | 4586 |
| hat .... | 1413 | room .... | 2864 | tree .... | 5972 |

SAMPLE QUESTIONS			ANSWERS		
	A	B	C	D	E
room	1413	2715	2864	3451	4586
green	2715	2864	3451	4586	5972
tree	1413	2715	3451	4586	5972
hat	1413	2715	3451	4586	5972
salt	1413	2864	3451	4586	5972

FIG. 2.2. Sample problems: Numerical Operations and Coding Speed

of the training courses and military specialities. The General Science test was constructed from what were originally separate tests of physical science and biology, and the distinction is still evident among the items. Bock and Mislevy (1981) have shown that there are differences between men and women in their response to these types of items: Men do slightly better on the physical science items, and women slightly better on the biological science items. The accuracy of the tests for classifying men and women would be improved, albeit at the cost of greater complexity of reporting, by scoring the physical science and biological science items separately.

The **Arithmetic Reasoning** test requires the ability to implement the arithmetic operations of addition, subtraction, multiplication, and division of integers and fractions. Mental arithmetic is not required; the respondents are given scratch paper and told that they may use it in the calculations. The test does not simply measure the ability to perform these formal operations. Rather, the items require the respondent to recognize the correct operation to apply in the various situations set by the problem.

The items shown in Figure 2.1-a are typical: Most are rate, pro rata, and ratio problems. Eleven of the items deal with money, and another 11 with physical dimensions; 5 have some connection with homemaking (e.g., extending recipes); only 1 contains a military reference; 2 are unclassifiable. The four multiple choice alternatives of each item are always numbers with the units of measurement indicated. Wrong alternatives represent obvious types of conceptual or computational errors that the examinee might make.

Although men tend to score higher on the Arithmetic Reasoning test than women, Bock and Mislevy (1981) found no evidence of differential sex bias among these items. The items that seem directed more toward women are not actually any easier for them relative to the items with physical and mechanical content. The only apparent trend is that as the items become more difficult the proportions of correct responses of the male respondents increase relative to that of females. Either the female respondents make errors on the more difficult items, or they do not complete, or do not attempt to answer, the more difficult items that appear later in the test.

Word Knowledge is a straightforward vocabulary test. The items, like those in Figure 2.1-b, consist of a sentence in which one word is set in boldface type and underscored. The respondent is to choose from four alternatives the word or phrase that "means the same, or most nearly the same" as the underlined word. Twenty-two of the 35 items take the form "so-and-so most nearly means"; the remaining items give some minimal indication of the context in which the word is used. In Bock and Mislevy's (1981) analysis of the sex and sociocultural group effects on item difficulty, the item thresholds showed a significant sex difference for at least one of the words— a sporting term that appeared to be relatively easier for males than for females. The sociocultural group interactions with Word Knowledge item difficulties were confined to contrasts between Whites and Hispanics, with certain words being relatively easier for each of these groups. As we discuss in Chapter 3, the word knowledge of persons who speak both English and Spanish is affected by the fact that a somewhat infrequent and unusual word in English may have a Romance language cognate that is a relatively common word in Spanish. In fact, many of the items in Word Knowledge take the form of a stem word of Latin origin and alternatives that include a more common Anglo-Saxon equivalent. Since the bilingual Hispanic speakers are likely to know both types of words, these items are relatively easier for them. The exception is, of course, the occasional false cognates where the English meaning has become quite unrelated to the Spanish word. These words may be relatively easier for the English speakers. Most of the English-Hispanic effects on the difficulty threshold for the Word Knowledge items can be explained in these terms.

Paragraph Comprehension is a conventional reading test in which the examinee is presented a brief passage and asked one or more questions about it. In the field of reading instruction, it is now considered important to distinguish between literal reading ability and reading comprehension. An item measuring literal reading should ask only about the facts and relationships actually mentioned in the paragraph. In reading comprehension items, the examinee may be required to generalize the theme of the paragraph or infer relationships implied by it. This latter kind of reading ability obviously places a greater premium on the experiential background of the respondent. A good test of whether or not an item is a measure of literal reading is the extent to which it can be answered without reading the paragraph. If it can be so answered, it is drawing on general information and reasoning ability in addition to reading ability. In this respect, the items in the ASVAB lean rather heavily on general knowledge. A well-informed person has a good chance of answering many of the items correctly without reading the paragraph. This means that the better educated among the Profile respondents, having both the benefit of reading the passages and already knowing many of the facts contained in them, should have found this test very easy. That this is the case is evident in the distribution of scores shown in Section 2.5.

The **Numerical Operations** test measures the speed with which the respondent can perform the simplest arithmetic operations on whole numbers, in most cases with single digits, and mark the correct alternative on the answer sheet. The time limit is so stringent that very few respondents, even in the most educated groups, are able to respond to all 50 items in the time allowed. A practice item from this test is shown in Figure 2.2.

Coding Speed is similar in many ways to Numerical Operations but requires no arithmetic knowledge and draws more heavily on short-term memory. Typical examples of the Coding Speed items are those shown in Figure 2.2. Subjects are given a key that associates a common word with a four-digit number; they are then required to mark the number corresponding to the word in a series of 28 random presentations of the words. The key then changes and another 28 presentations of the words follow; then the key changes a third time, and 28 more presentations follow. The short time limit for the test leaves little probability of anyone's completing all 84 items.

Tests similar to Coding Speed, sometimes called "Clerical Speed," appear in many vocational aptitude batteries. They are believed to predict the speed and exactness with which clerks or secretaries can process information from one list to another, but the ability required by the test seems more general. Because the scores on this type of test correlate fairly strongly with general verbal ability, a test of this type called "Digit-symbol" appears in the Wechsler Adult Intelligence Scale. Why this test should correlate with general intelligence is not well understood, but studies by Hunt (1976) and others indicate that persons who preform well in general information and verbal tests seem able to process the semantic information in symbols more rapidly than those who do less well. Such persons spend more of their time working with written symbols and language and overlearn more thoroughly the basic processes of identifying symbols and retaining words and numbers in short-term memory. They can therefore perform the task of comparing symbols and transferring information between the test booklet and the answer form more quickly than persons with less facility in processing this type of material. Another factor that must enter into performance on this test is the motivation of the examinee. Both the Numerical Operations and the Coding Speed tests are fatiguing, not to say boring, and put a premium on the concentration and persistence of the respondent. Those persons who can marshal these resources in a trivial task set by the Coding Speed tests must have qualities that will serve them well in many work situations. It is perhaps not too surprising that tests of this type have reasonably good predictive validity for a wide range of clerical occupations.

The remaining tests in the battery appraise knowledge more specifically required in particular vocations.

Auto and Shop Information, with items similar to those in Figure 2.1-c, deals with the everyday facts that one encounters in automobile repair and in metal and wood shops. Of the 25 items on the test, 14 require knowledge of automobiles, 8 of metal shop practice and tools, and 4 of woodshop tools and practice. This knowledge could readily be acquired in high school shop classes, on the job, or by reading magazines such as *Popular Science* or *Popular Mechanics*. It is not at all the kind of knowledge that would be covered in a liberal arts undergraduate education.

Bock and Mislevy (1981) find considerable sex differences in the difficulties of some of these items. Male respondents tend to find all of these items much easier than do female respondents, especially items about parts of automobiles. Female respondents do slightly better on items that can be answered on the basis of general principles rather than on specific facts of auto and shop work.

The **Mathematics Knowledge** test is the most educationally demanding of the 10 tests. Unlike the Arithmetic Reasoning test, it does not require the solution of "word problems." All 25 of the items are similar to those shown in Figure 2.1-c in requiring knowledge of mathematical terms and concepts and the ability to perform formal algebraic operations. The content of these items would be known only to persons who had some exposure to high school algebra and geometry, or who had studied text books on these subjects.

The **Mechanical Comprehension** test appraises knowledge of the properties of materials and structures and how mechanical devises operate. This knowledge could come from direct experience with machines, simple and complex; from formal study of mechanics; and from reading on technical subjects. Many of the items require the examinee to interpret pictures of mechanisms in the style of mechanical drawings. Exposure to mechanical drawing and drafting would assist a person in responding to these items. A number of these drawings depict the movement of parts that the examinee could visualize in order to solve the problems. Equally important, however, is a familiarity with the conventions of schematic drawings of the type commonly seen in elementary physics texts and handbooks of shop practice.

The final test, **Electronics Information**, consists of 20 items asking simple questions about electricity and electronics. Most of the questions require only practical knowledge of the subject, but the more difficult, such as those shown in Figure 2.1-d, draw on knowledge of principles that would have been learned only in formal study.

2.5. METHODS OF ANALYSIS

To investigate differences in performance on the ASVAB tests among the various subgroups defined by the background classification, we use the technique of multivariate analysis of variance. This technique provides analysis of variance of the background effects and interactions for the 10 ASVAB scores simultaneously and takes into account the correlations among the tests. A description of the application of multivariate analysis of variance to the types of nonexperimental data obtained in the Profile Study may be found in Chapter 6 of Bock (1975). The aim of such applications is to find the simplest linear model that will describe all significant score variation between the subclasses of the sample design. In the present study, the design is generated by the crossing of the classifications Sex, Sociocultural Group, Mother's Education, Highest Grade Completed, Economic Status, and Region. Although the design contains 960 subclasses, the distribution of cases among the subclasses is uneven, and only 766 subclasses actually contain respondents. The remaining 194 subclasses are empty and not included in the fitting of the model. As in most survey data, the cell frequencies in the present study tend to be roughly proportional to the marginal frequencies; the design is therefore not grossly unbalanced.

The model fitting was carried out by the exact least-squares method, using the MULTIVARIANCE program of Jeremy Finn (1978). The program calculates best (minimum variance) estimates of the effects included in the model. The estimated effects tell us how much various combinations of background classes can be expected to contribute to the test scores. To give a simple example, the analysis shows that, on average, the fact that a respondent is female adds 9.8 points to her Paragraph Comprehension score relative to that of a male respondent who is identical on all other background factors. The fact that she has some college education adds 46.2 points to her score on this test relative to an otherwise comparable respondent with high school education only. By combining such estimated effects, we obtain the statistics used in Chapters 3, 4, and 5 to display the results of the Profile survey.

To justify this structural, model-oriented approach to analysis, we must satisfy a number of statistical assumptions. These concern, on the one hand, the suitability of the area-clustered probability sample for the analysis of variance technique (which usually assumes simple random sampling) and, on the other hand, properties of the scores produced by the ASVAB tests. We discuss these considerations in detail in Appendix C.

Score Distributions

In certain respects, the "number-right" scores in which test results are traditionally reported are not ideally suited to any form of univariate or multivariate normal statistical analysis. (Our analysis is not based on number-right scores; see below.) It cannot in general be assumed that the distributions of such scores will be normal. Number-right scores reflect the distribution of item difficulties within the test, and tests with too many easy or too many difficult items may exhibit substantially skewed distributions of test scores. In the present study, we are examining groups covering an extremely wide range of abilities and knowledge. The gap between the poor minority group sample with 8 or less years of schooling and the nonpoor majority group with 1 year of college is enormous. It would be too much to expect the ASVAB power tests to yield equally good measurement throughout this range. Measurement with equal precision in such diverse groups could be accomplished only by adaptive testing procedures in which items were selected at difficulty levels suitable for each group.

In fact, some of the ASVAB tests are targeted to an ability range somewhat below the population mean, and thus are less well suited to measurement in the high ability group. Exceptions are the Arithmetic Reasoning and Mathematics Knowledge tests, which are somewhat more difficult. The other power tests tend to be too easy for high ability respondents, and scores in the high ability groups are skewed toward high scores. This is especially true of Paragraph Comprehension, which is intended only as a measure of basic reading competence and is not designed to make distinctions among high levels of reading ability. The speeded tests, Numerical Operations and Coding Speed, are capable of precise measurement throughout the entire range of ability. Even the most able respondents cannot complete all the items on either of these tests in the time allotted. For these tests, the assumption of a normal distribution of test scores within the groups is quite reasonable.

In an effort to improve the distributional properties of the power tests, we have chosen to use latent-trait estimates of ability rather than simple number-right scores. Technically, the scores we use are so-called "maximum a posteriori" (MAP) estimates, computed from item parameters estimated by

Bock's fixed-effect methods (Bock, 1976; Kolakowski & Bock, 1981). The three-parameter logistic response model with guessing parameter set at 0.1 was used. Details of the scoring procedure can be found in Bock and Mislevy (1981). Unlike number-right scores, which show floor and ceiling effects, latent-trait estimates tend to be normally distributed. The improvement is not so great as to remove entirely the skew toward high values in the high ability groups, but the scores on the trait scale are better in this respect than the number-right scores.

Some indication of the shape of the score distributions is conveyed by the histograms in Figures 2.3 through 2.11. These histograms describe the distributions for Arithmetic Reasoning, Word Knowledge, Numerical Operations, and Auto and Shop Information in certain of the sex by sociocultural group by education subclasses. The proportions shown in these figures, computed using the probability sample case weights, represent correctly the populations of persons in these subclasses in the nation as a whole. To simplify the presentation, we have restricted the education levels to those persons who have completed some high school, those who have graduated from high school but have not attended college, and those who have attended or graduated from college. It is in the comparison of these groups that the effect of education on the shape of the distributions is most apparent.

The ASVAB tests are aimed primarily at those who have completed high school but have not attended college, the group that is at present the main source of recruits for the armed services. The items in the tests have been chosen so as to obtain good discrimination among respondents in this ability range. We see from the histograms in Figure 2.4 that, among White male and female respondents, the Arithmetic Reasoning scores fulfill this condition well and have unimodal and essentially symmetric distributions over the range. The Word Knowledge and Numerical Operations tests are somewhat easier for these respondents, however, and there is some piling up of cases on the highest score range, 650 to 700. A certain number of respondents appear to be reaching the test ceiling, that is, answering all items correctly, and thus obtaining the highest possible scale score. This produces a slight skew in the distributions toward the lower ranges where, because the tests have adequate numbers of easy items, the scores are not restricted. In other words, these tests show very little "floor" effect.

The Auto and Shop Information distributions show at all education levels the marked sex differences discussed in Chapter 5.

Among Whites with some college education (Figure 2.5), a larger proportion of the sample is reaching the test ceiling, and the skew of the score distributions is much more apparent. This is especially true of the rather easy Work Knowledge and Numerical Operations tests. Only among the Arithmetic Reasoning test scores of the female respondents, for whom the test is more difficult than for males (see Chapter 7), is the score distribution nearly symmetric at the college level.

For the Arithmetic Reasoning test especially (Figure 2.7), the score distributions of Blacks at the high school level are skewed in the opposite direction. The majority of scores falls below the general population mean of 500, and only a small proportion of these respondents are found in the high score ranges. This effect is somewhat less apparent in Word Knowledge and hardly evident in Numerical Operations. The latter test shows an essentially symmetric distribution in the Black high-school-only education group.

Among Blacks (Figures 2.6, 2.7, and 2.8) another phenomenon appears. There is an indication of bimodality in the score distributions, with a small group of Blacks scoring at levels comparable to the Whites, and a larger group of Blacks clustering at lower score levels. This effect is apparent in the Numerical Operations scores of Black females with some or completed high school education, and in the Arithmetic Reasoning scores of Black males at these education levels.

In the Word Knowledge scores of Blacks, one sees a more general shifting upward of the distributions, combined with a larger proportion of respondents in the highest score ranges. Because these tests are rather easy, any tendency towards bimodality of score distribution that might exist in the population is obscured by test ceiling effects.

The fact that no similar evidence of bimodality appears in the Auto and Shop Information scores of Blacks suggests an effect of education may be involved. The small proportion of Blacks who score in the range of the highest ranking Whites must be those who are participating in and meeting the standards of the educational programs in which Whites are the majority. These would include college preparatory programs in high school and the more demanding courses of study in college. Some of the effects of the different educational emphases and experiences between Blacks and Whites are discussed in Chapter 3.

The results for the Hispanics (Figures 2.9, 2.10, and 2.11) are similar but more complex. For the Arithmetic Reasoning test, Hispanic male respondents show similar evidence of bimodality at the college level. The score distributions for high school and college differ considerably, with a substantial proportion of Hispanic college students falling in the high ranges of the Arithmetic Reasoning scores. The Hispanic females, on the other hand, show only a slight shift of the score distribution toward higher values between high school and college, and only a very small excess of females appears in the highest score category. This is consistent with the impression gained elsewhere in the data analysis (see Chapter 5), that relatively few female Hispanic students pursue quantitative programs in college.

Although there is no evidence of bimodality of the Word Knowledge and Numerical Operations scores for Hispanics, Hispanic males participating in college programs are much more heavily represented than Hispanic females at the high score levels. Other evidence for this conclusion is discussed in Chapters 3 and 5.

Fig.2.3. ASVAB scale score distributions for Whites with some high school by sex

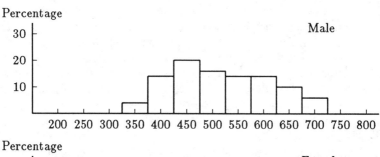

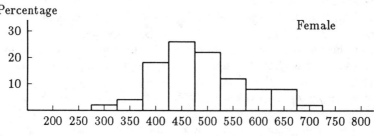

Arithmetic Reasoning

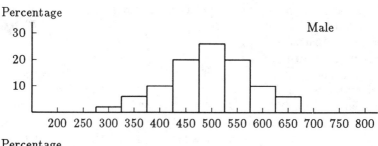

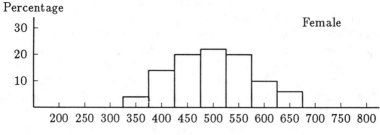

Word Knowledge

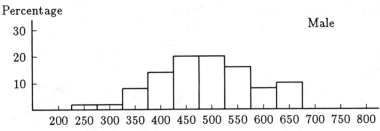

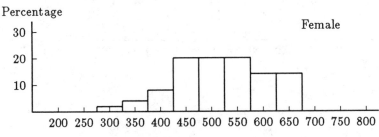

Numerical Operations

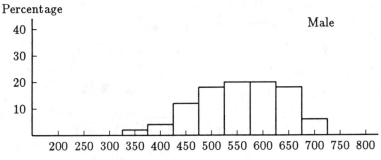

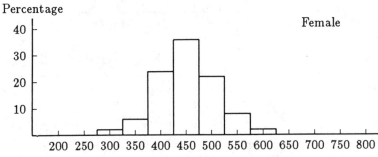

Auto and Shop Information

Fig.2.4. ASVAB scale score distributions for Whites with high school by sex

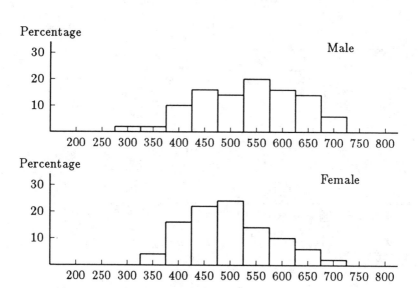

Arithmetic Reasoning

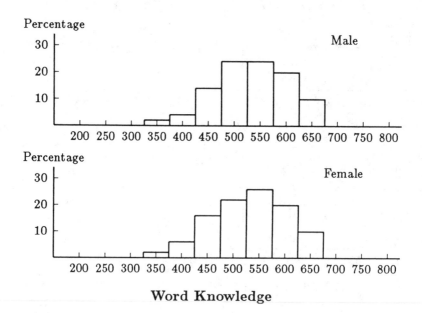

Word Knowledge

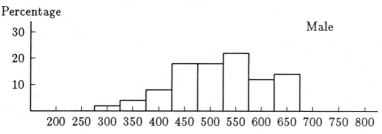

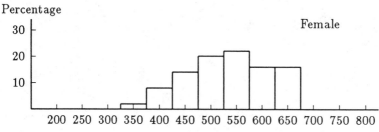

Numerical Operations

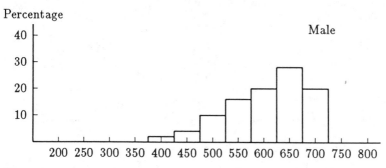

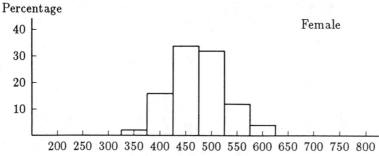

Auto and Shop Information

Fig.2.5. ASVAB scale score distributions for Whites with some college by sex (includes college graduates)

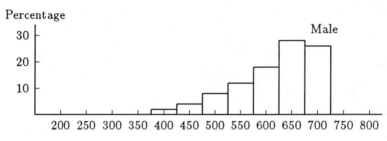

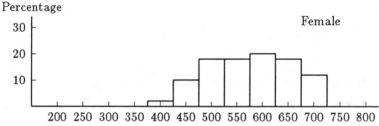

Arithmetic Reasoning

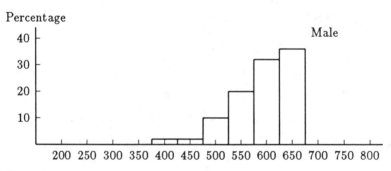

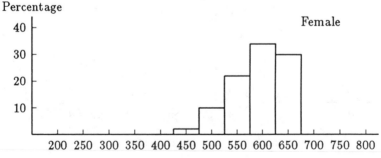

Word Knowledge

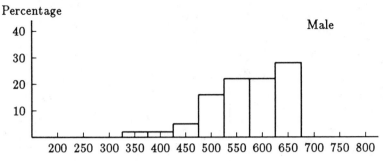

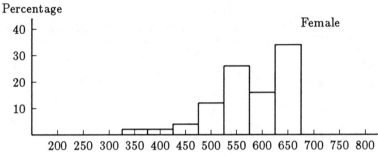

Numerical Operations

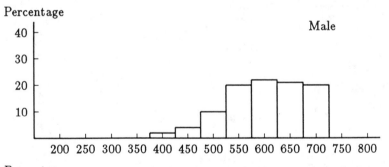

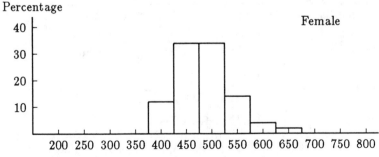

Auto and Shop Information

Fig.2.6. ASVAB scale score distributions for Blacks with some high school by sex

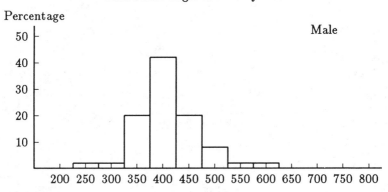

Arithmetic Reasoning

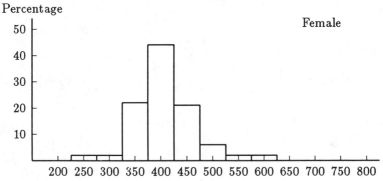

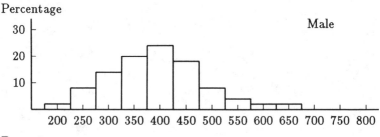

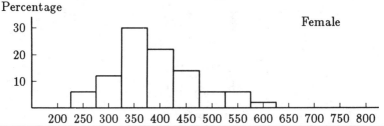

Word Knowledge

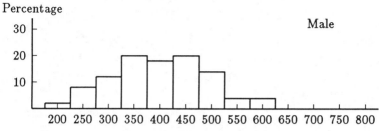

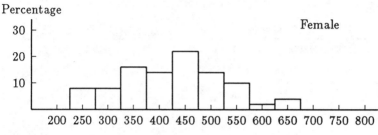

Numerical Operations

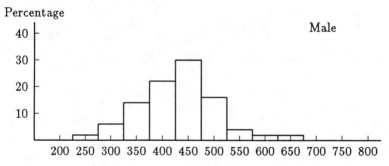

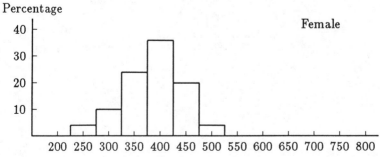

Auto and Shop Information

Fig.2.7. ASVAB scale score distributions for Blacks with high school by sex

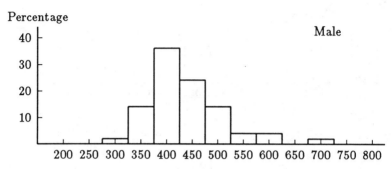

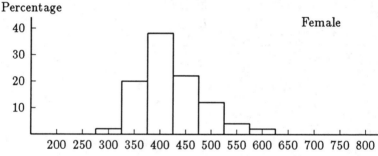

Arithmetic Reasoning

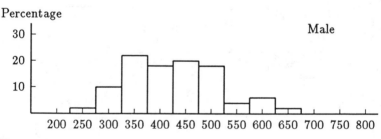

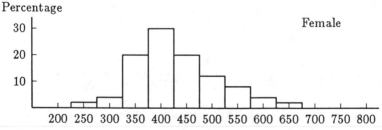

Word Knowledge

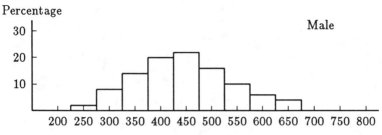

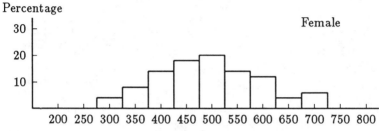

Numerical Operations

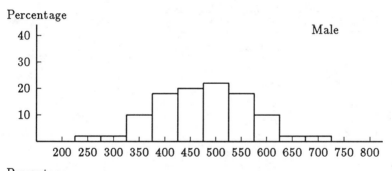

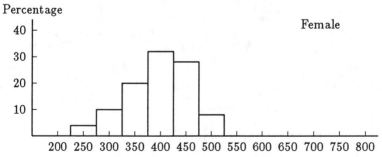

Auto and Shop Information

Fig.2.8. ASVAB scale score distributions for Blacks with some college by sex (includes college graduates)

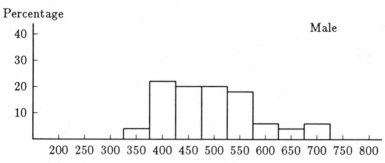

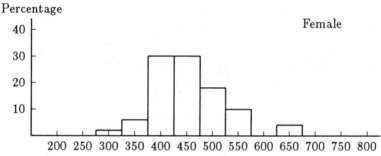

Arithmetic Reasoning

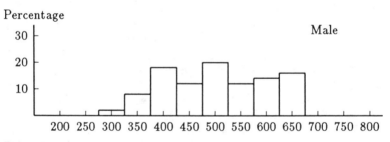

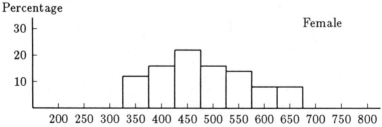

Word Knowledge

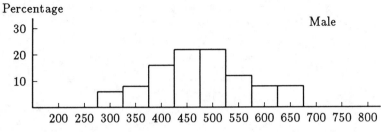

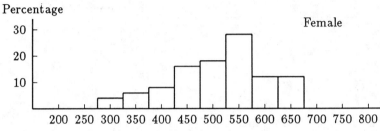

Numerical Operations

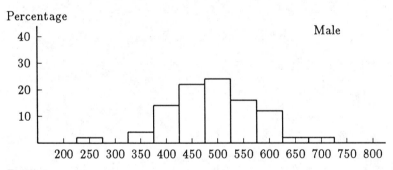

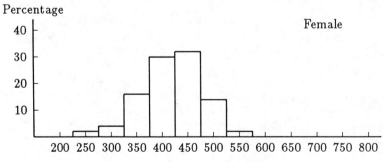

Auto and Shop Information

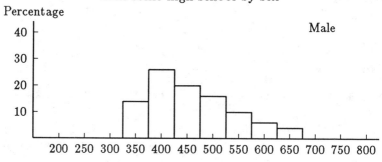

Fig.2.9. ASVAB scale score distributions for Hispanics with some high school by sex

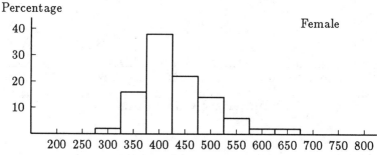

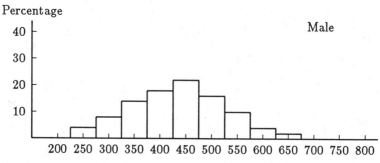

Arithmetic Reasoning

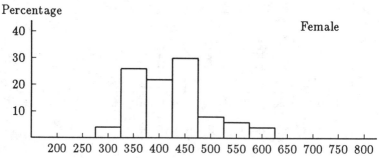

Word Knowledge

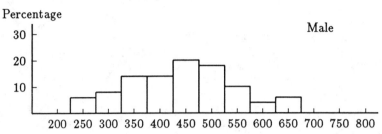

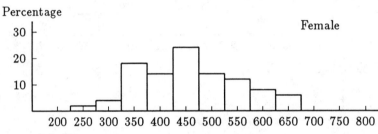

Numerical Operations

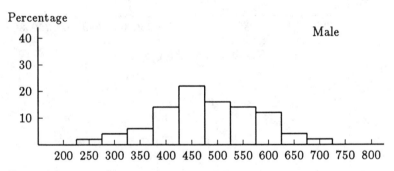

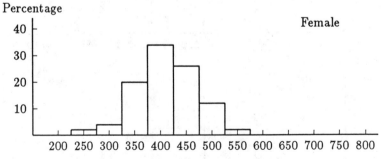

Auto and Shop Information

Fig.2.10. ASVAB scale score distributions for Hispanics with high school by sex

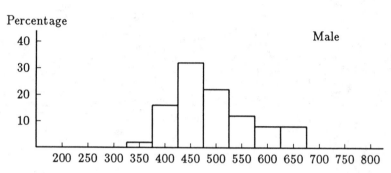

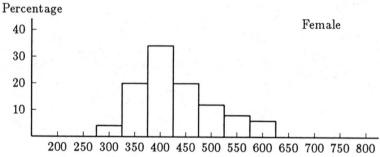

Arithmetic Reasoning

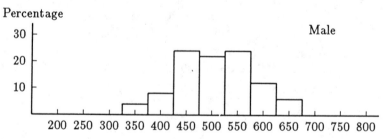

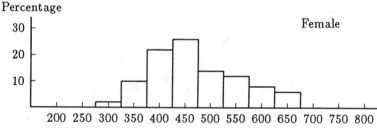

Word Knowledge

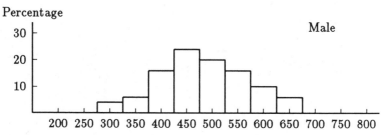

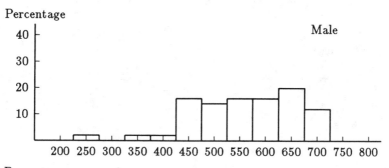

Numerical Operations

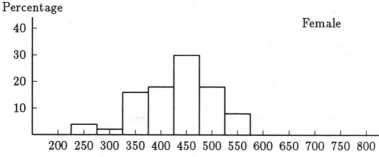

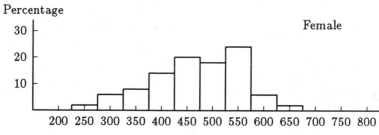

Auto and Shop Information

Fig.2.11. ASVAB scale score distributions for Hispanics with some college by sex (includes college graduates)

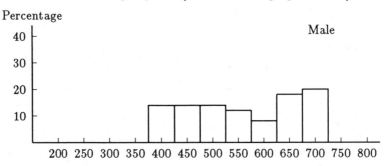

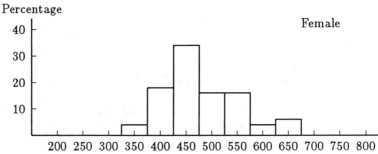

Arithmetic Reasoning

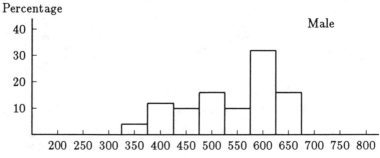

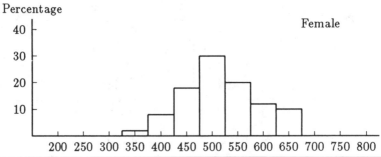

Word Knowledge

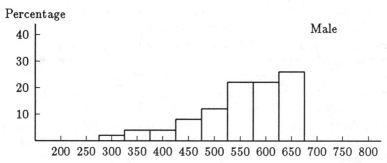

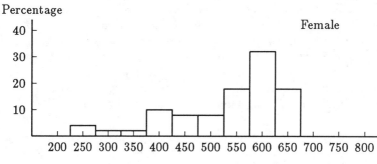

Numerical Operations

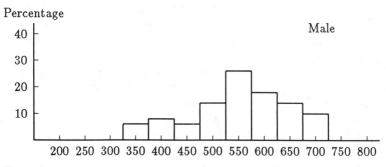

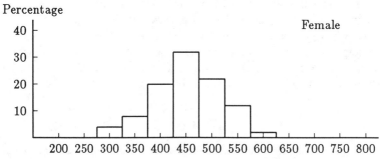

Auto and Shop Information

The tendency of the scores to depart from normal distributions within subclasses of the demographic design is, of course, much more exaggerated in this broad classification by sex, sociocultural group, and education than is the case for the six-way design including socioeconomic class, region, and mother's education. Regrettably, the numbers of cases in the subclasses of the six-way design are too small to allow an empirical assessment of the shapes of distributions. We will proceed on the assumption that the additional classes largely remove the evidence of bimodality seen here, thus bringing the data into closer agreement with the assumption of similar normal distributions within subclasses. If one wanted to answer the question of whether, for example, Blacks pursuing college programs are more heterogeneous in their preparedness than are comparable Whites, a different allocation of sampling resources would be required. That is, the study would have to include many more Black respondents at the college level. The same would be true with respect to possible sex differences in the preparedness and attainment of college-bound Hispanics. With the present data, we must confine ourselves to the analysis and interpretation of the broader aspects of the demographic design.

One effect of the skewing of the score distributions in the high-ability groups is that the variances of the measures are not entirely homogeneous. They tend to be smaller in the high-ability groups. Because the numbers of respondents in these groups are relatively small, however, the lack of homogeneity has little effect on the pooled estimate of the within-cell variance. The estimated variances and covariances of the test scores depend much more heavily on the data from the large groups of respondents who have 9 to 11 years of education or are only high school graduates. For these groups the assumptions of normally distributed test scores within groups and homogeneity of variance more closely obtain. For this reason, and in view of the well-known robustness of analysis of variance techniques to departures from within-cell normality and homoscedasticity, we consider the ASVAB scores analyzed in this study to sufficiently satisfy the assumptions of the multivariate analysis of variance. Most of the effects observed in this study are so large and clearly significant that only gross failures of assumptions could obscure them. In some of the more marginal two-factor and three-factor interactions, however, the conclusions may be more sensitive to the assumptions on which they are made. In these cases, we fall back on the plausibility and interpretability of the result to convince us of its reality. The points at which some doubts about the significance of results may arise are few in comparison with the many clear-cut findings reported in Chapters 3, 4, and 5.

2.6. TESTS OF THE MODEL

The results of the statistical tests on the ASVAB scores are presented in Appendix C. The purpose of these tests is to find the simplest cross-classification by background characteristics that retains all of the useful information in the scores. Technically, the tests identify interactions in the linear model that can be eliminated without significant loss of information when describing the means of subclasses in the six-way classification by background characteristics. (Age effects were analyzed separately; see Chapter 4.) The ways of classification that are involved in each of the retained interactions determine a cross-classification in terms of which the results must be reported.

Fortunately, the highest order interactions that must be retained when describing the Profile results involve only three background characteristics. Two such interactions are significant: years of education by sociocultural group by economic status, and sex by sociocultural group by economic status. Other significant interactions involve only two-factor interactions. They are sociocultural group by region, and years of education by sex. In addition, effects of mother's education are significant, but they do not interact with any other effects.

2.7. INTERACTION DISPLAYS

Because no more than three ways of classification appear in any significant interaction, the margin means that describe the association of the background characteristics with ASVAB test performance can readily be presented in a graphical form, called 'interaction plots." These are displayed in subsequent chapters in the style employed in Winer's (1971) book on analysis of variance. The score values represented in these plots are obtained by adding together the effects that contribute to each subclass. These include, of course, general mean and main-class effects, plus the particular interaction terms represented by the classes that jointly define the cell. As a further aid to interpretation of these plots, each point is bracketed by a standard error bar (plus and minus one standard error), computed from the variances and covariances of the estimated effects that are summed to obtain the subclass values. The variance and covariance factors required in these calculations are given in the extended printout of the MULTIVARIANCE program. To be conservative, we have allowed for the effect of cluster sampling on the estimated error variance by multiplying the nominal standard error by 1.4. This corresponds to a design effect of 2.0, which appears to be a definite upper limit in these data.

Especially in the plot of the sociocultural group by highest grade completed by economic status interaction, the standard errors vary greatly, reflecting the widely differing numbers of respondents in these cells of the design. There are, for example, very few cases with only 0 to 8 years of education in some groups and few with 13 + years in others. For most cells, however, the sample size is large enought to locate the interaction line within a narrow range. All of the standard error bars, long or short, have a two-thirds chance of including the true line. The actual line is drawn through the most likely point—namely, the middle of the two standard error intervals.

We emphasize that these interaction plots are not estimates of the corresponding population marginal means. That is, they are not weighted by the effective numbers of respondents in the other ways of classification. They represent, rather, the effect on test scores that is associated with a respondent's membership in the ways of classification displayed in the plot.

This is not meant to suggest that in surveys such as the Profile study the weighted marginal averages have no practical utility. On the contrary, marginal distributions are essential in calculating overall classification rates in the corresponding subpopulations. For example, the weighted marginal means of the two sexes and the sociocultural groups are shown in Table 2.18.

Suppose a score of 500 or better on Auto and Shop Information was required for entering Vehicle Maintenance School. Assuming a within-marginal-class standard deviation of 100 (a slight overestimate in this case), the percentage of men in the general population represented by the Profile sample who would qualify is 70.2; the percentage of women would be 30.9. Similarly, the percentage of Whites, Blacks, and Hispanics qualifying would be 57.5, 20.1, and 30.9, respectively. Such figures are important in the practical use of the tests for personnel selection, but they do not bear as directly on the question of sources of differences as do the estimated effects in the interaction plots.

In the case of the complex interaction plots, the source of the interaction may be confined to certain variables and to certain subgroups. Some indication of the significant variable can be obtained from the individual F-tests shown in Tables 6-2 and 6-3 in Appendix C. As a convenience to the reader, tests for which the depicted interaction is clearly significant are marked with an asterisk in the various displays in Chapter 3, 4, and 5. In many cases, however, direct inspection of the plot with a view to the possible sources of the interaction in psychological or sociological terms makes clear whether and why the composite null hypothesis is rejected.

TABLE 2.18
Weighted Marginal Means of the ASVAB Standardized Scores
For Men and Women and for Whites, Blacks, and Hispanics

Test	Men	Women	White	Black	Hispanic
Word Knowledge	501	504	522	411	445
Paragraph Comprehension	493	512	520	423	449
Arithmetic Reasoning	515	489	520	420	449
Numerical Operations	490	514	517	430	462
Coding Speed	481	524	516	430	473
General Science	521	483	521	415	445
Mathematics Knowledge	506	498	517	434	451
Mechanical Comprehension	538	465	520	415	452
Electronics Information	537	465	520	417	445
Auto and Shop Information	553	450	519	416	450

3 Sociocultural Differences

The people in the United States have never been homogeneous in historical origin, customs, or language. Distinct communities of work and commerce, celebration and ritual, identity and attitude persist today, long after the original founders have departed. Considering or even distinguishing them all would be such an impossible task that we can justify the broad classification of sociocultural groups specified in Chapter 2. Moreover, the boundaries of most of the smaller ethnic and nationality groups have become so blurred that distinctions among them are not likely to be productive of clear effects in the data. Similarly, and unlike the situation in some other parts of the world, the communal tie of religion has weakened here and no longer strongly influences social and economic life. Thus, there is little justification for including religious affiliation as a category of analysis. In the United States of the 1980s, the important distinction for our purposes is the classification of the respondents in the Profile study as White, Black, or Hispanic according to the criteria specified in Chapter 2. This chapter examines the effects of this classification, which we call "sociocultural group," as it interacts with other background factors to influence ASVAB test performance.

Of the seven background characteristics investigated in the Profile study, sociocultural group is second only to years of education in its association with average levels of performance on the ASVAB tests. Not surprisingly, the average scores increase with educational level for all groups in all tests. As for the association with the respondent's sociocultural group, Whites generally score higher than Hispanics, who score higher than Blacks. Similar, but smaller, effects are seen for economic status: Respondents above the OMB poverty line generally score higher than those below.

These overall effects fail to capture the full pattern of variation in the data, however. When examined jointly, education, sociocultural group, and economic status reveal substantial effects on test performance that are not apparent in each classification separately. These interactions are of interest for the qualitative detail they add to the results. They demand a specific interpretation in a way that the much too general main effects do not.

The phenomenon most difficult to conceptualize, to which we devote much of this chapter, is the expression of sociocultural group membership in test performance in different educational and economic contexts. It is easy to understand how education level and economic factors can affect performance; they measure rather directly the time and resources that go into the development of requisite skills. It is much more difficult, however, to explain the sociocultural group differences when they are considered jointly with the education and economic background. As we search for the origins of these differences in the light of recent research and scholarship, we find compelling reasons for believing that sociocultural context has a much greater effect on cognitive development, and eventually on personal skills and vocational potential, than has previously been recognized. We find support for this conclusion both in the results of the Profile study and in other critical studies of individual differences in cognitive test performance reviewed in this chapter.

The other interaction with sociocultural group revealed in the Profile study is that involving region of the country. Its explanation is essentially historical and relatively straightforward. We discuss this effect in Section 3.2 before attempting the more difficult task of accounting for sociocultural effects on cognitive development generally.

3.1. SOCIOCULTURAL GROUP, EDUCATION, AND ECONOMIC STATUS

The joint sociocultural, educational, and economic effects for each of the ASVAB tests are shown in Figures 3.1a and b. The performance of poor and nonpoor Whites, Hispanics, and Blacks with 0 to 8, 9 to 11, 12, and 13 or more years of education is shown in terms of the standard scores of the total probability sample for each subtest (mean = 500; standard deviation = 100). In interpreting these graphs, we are aided by grouping the tests in four main clusters suggested by the factor analyses discussed in Appendix B. Briefly, we may characterize these clusters as: (a) specialized knowledge (Auto and Shop Information, Mechanical Comprehension, and Electronics Information; (b) verbal skills (Word Knowledge and Paragraph Comprehension; (c) fluent production (Numerical Operations and Coding Speed); and (d) quantitative ability (Arithmetic Reasoning and Mathematics Knowledge). The General Science test shares some of the features of both specialized knowledge and general verbal ability. With the exception of some unusual aspects of the

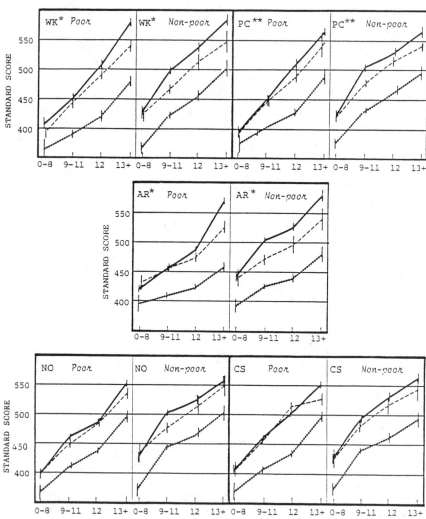

FIG. 3.1a. Interaction of sociocultural group, economic status, and education (highest grade completed).
White ——— Hispanic ------ Black · · · ·
*F > 1.25F(.05)   **F > 1.25F(.01)

Auto and Shop test, the effects of education, economic status, and sociocultural group are essentially the same for all of the tests within each of these clusters.

Specialized Knowledge

The plots in Figure 3.1 for Mechanical Comprehension, Electronics Information, and, in this context, General Science, show very similar patterns of

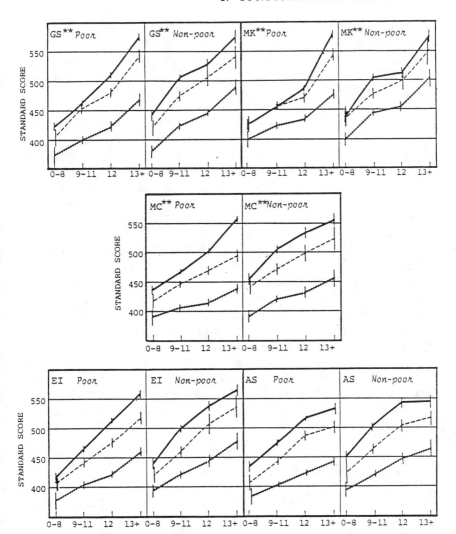

FIG. 3.1b. Interaction of sociocultural, economic status, and education (highest grade completed).
White ——— Hispanic ------ Black · · · ·
**$F > 1.25F(.01)$

interaction. (The exceptional pattern for Auto and Shop is discussed later.) All of the sociocultural groups show obviously improved performance with increasing years of education. But a curious deviation from this pattern becomes evident when economic status is taken into account. Through 12 years of education, higher economic status confers about a 30-point advantage in scores on these particular tests. At the highest educational level (some college), however, an unexpected interaction of sociocultural group and economic status appears: At this level, poor Whites equal and even exceed the performance of nonpoor Whites among respondents with some college education. A number of the other tests in the battery also show this effect, and, to a lesser extent, it is also seen in the Hispanic and Black subsamples.

This interaction has a simple explanation. It is undoubtedly an artifact of using the OMB definition of poverty, discussed in Section 2.4, which in many cases classifies college students below the poverty line when they are living on low incomes independently of their parents. Many young people in college today, especially Whites, declare themselves financially independent of their parents. Consequently, they are assigned to poverty status by the OMB definition when, in many cases, they are from economically advantaged backgrounds. Thus, it is not surprising that the test performance of White respondents with some college fails to reflect their income classification. Low-income Whites with 12 or less years of education, if independent of parents, would probably be working in jobs where their income is related to vocational skills measured by the ASVAB tests. Their test scores would therefore more accurately reflect their actual economic class membership.

In the Black subpopulation with some college, on the other hand, the effect of income status on test performance is different from that of Whites and, to a somewhat lesser extent, from that of Hispanics. For Blacks, this effect is more similar to that at the lower educational levels, suggesting that the income classification of Black college students is a more accurate index of their economic class membership than it is for Whites. Probably a greater proportion of Black college students live with their parents, or those living independently have incomes not greatly different from those of their parents.

Turning to the comparison of nonpoor Whites and nonpoor Hispanics, we find surprisingly similar effects of education on the specialized knowledge tests. In General Science, the scores show an average difference favoring Whites of about 25 points and in Electronics Information, about 30 points. In Mechanical Comprehension, there is very little difference at the lowest educational level, but at 9 to 11 years and above, Whites are about 35 points higher than Hispanics.

Among poor Whites and Hispanics, these differences are about the same or slightly smaller at lower education levels. That the larger differences appear in the some-college groups is another expression of the misattribution of poverty to Whites in this group. Hispanics in college appear to be between Whites and Blacks in their probability of being misclassified as poor, either because they are more likely to be living at home, or because their parents are from an impoverished background. This results in a greater disparity in performance between poor Whites and poor Hispanics at the college level.

Blacks display somewhat different responses to the specialized knowledge tests. Comparing the plots for nonpoor Blacks with nonpoor Whites and Hispanics, we see that in all tests except General Science the disparity in performance tends to increase with education through grade 12. (General Science is more like Word Knowledge in showing a nearly constant difference between Blacks and other groups.) In the still more technical Mechanical Comprehension and Electronics Information tests, nonpoor Blacks show considerably less gain than the other groups in performance between the lowest educational level and grade 12. As a consequence, the 60–point difference in the scores of nonpoor Whites and Blacks seen at the lowest educational level increases to 100 points at the 12-year and the 13 + levels. We interpret this effect as an indication that Blacks are receiving less exposure to this particular type of content in later years of high school. This would explain why, for Blacks, the gain due to completing high school is smaller for these tests than for more general tests such as Word Knowledge or General Science.

The role of formal education in the technical knowledge skills is clarified when we examine the special pattern of Auto and Shop Information scores referred to above. As can be seen in Figure 3.1a, the Auto and Shop Information scores of respondents with some college are on average not much higher than scores of those with 12 years of education. Especially among nonpoor Whites, some college education has no discernible effect on Auto and Shop scores beyond that of high school completion. This trend is similar among poor and nonpoor Hispanics, and among poor Whites. Unlike the effects of General Science, Mechanical Comprehension, and Electronics Information, in these groups, performance in Auto and Shop Information is enhanced very little by higher formal education. We believe that this pattern occurs because auto and shop information is not learned primarily in school. Such information is equally or more accessible to young people who go to work after high school as it is to those in college.

For Blacks of both higher and lower economic status, the influence of education on Auto and Shop Information is different from that of other sociocultural and economic groups. Especially among poor Blacks, performance increases steadily with increased educational level instead of remaining essentially constant after 12 years of education as it does in the other groups. For Blacks, the increase after high school is about as great as the increase between some high school and completed high school. We take this as an indication that, among Blacks, more education is associated with greater access to automobiles and machinery, probably through a connection between more education and greater economic resources. Relative to the Black community as a whole, Blacks who go to college are economically a more select group than are college-bound Whites, relative to the White community. They are more likely to own automobiles and acquire information about them. Whites with some college have no similar advantage over those without college.

Verbal Skills

Although we might expect the English language tests (Word Knowledge and Reading Comprehension) to distinguish the Hispanics from the other sociocultural groups independent of economic status, poor Hispanics are not very different from poor Whites in performance on these tests. (The advantage of poor Whites with some college is another expression of the misclassification of this group mentioned earlier.) Nonpoor Hispanics parallel Whites in verbal attainment but are consistently about 30 points lower except at the lowest education level, where there is no difference. The interesting point is that the difference between Whites and Hispanics on these verbal tests is smaller than the difference for Arithmetic Reasoning, General Science, and the specialized knowledge tests. This suggests that the disadvantage of the Hispanic groups in the applied subjects is not just due to the language barrier, but to lack of exposure to the relevant material. We examine the implications of this observation in a later discussion of linguistic factors.

Surprisingly, it is the Blacks, not the Hispanics, who show the largest disadvantage relative to Whites. But unlike the trend of increasing differences with education between nonpoor Blacks and the other sociocultural groups seen in the specialized knowledge tests, there is a constant difference of about 75 points in the verbal tests between nonpoor Blacks and Whites, and a difference of about 50 points between nonpoor Blacks and Hispanics.

The same is not true for poor Blacks. The difference in the verbal skills of lower income Blacks and their economic peers in the Hispanic and White subsamples increases with education through the 12th grade. This finding is consistent with that of Coleman et al. (1966), who reported that the gap in achievement between Blacks and Whites widened with continuing education. However, the present data indicate that this is the case only for poor Blacks, and only to the 12th grade. The effect of education on the verbal attainment of higher income Blacks is similar to that seen in the other sociocultural groups.

In view of the literature that attributes the scholastic difficulties of poor Hispanics to language factors, this pattern of verbal test performance in which poor Hispanics exceed nonpoor Blacks at all education levels is somewhat unexpected. These results suggest, rather, that language factors may be more salient for the educational performance of Blacks than for Hispanics. In our later discussion of linguistic factors in the test performance of Hispanics, we suggest that common assumptions about language effects in education may be wide of the mark.

Fluent Production

Considering that Numerical Operations and Coding Speed tests require minimal use of the English language, we might expect the performance of Hispanics to be nearly the same as that of Whites at the same economic level. This tends to be true, but more so for poor Hispanics than for the nonpoor. Except for the misclassification effect at the college level, poor Whites and Hispanics are essentially indistinguishable by these tests. Nonpoor Whites, however, show a small 20- to 30-point advantage over the corresponding Hispanics at all but the lowest education level. Apparently, nonlinguistic factors affecting the fluency tests come into play at the higher economic level. We discuss later some work of Ramirez (1973), who suggests that culturally conditioned cognitive styles and motivational differences between Hispanics and Whites affect the relative attainment of these two groups.

Quantitative Attainment

Arithmetic Reasoning and Mathematics Knowledge scores show very similar patterns of education by sociocultural group by economic status interactions. The main source of the triple interaction is again the reduced economic effect at the college level due to the misattribution of poverty status to White students living independently of their parents. As in the other tests, the economic effect at this level is more pronounced in Blacks, amounting to about 25 points, reflecting less likelihood of misclassification.

Scores on these quantitative tests are notable, among nonpoor Whites and Blacks, for the small differences they show between some high school education and completing high school. We believe that this effect is due to the concentration of general courses relevant to Arithmetic Reasoning and Mathematics Knowledge in the first two years of high school. General math, algebra, and geometry are taught to many high school students during these years, especially in middle-class communities. Far fewer students take the more specialized mathematics courses offered in the last two years of high school. For this reason, the gain in quantitative test performance of persons who complete high school as opposed to those who do not is less than for the other tests that are not as dependent on the high school curriculum. Word Knowledge, for example, reflects more general intellectual attainment garnered from many sources both in and out of school. As a result, verbal attainment increases steadily with education but without any close relationship to the high school curriculum. Indeed, word knowledge tends to increase throughout life, but mathematics knowledge does not.

Persons with some college have a definite advantage in responding to the quantitative tests. Those who go on to college tend more often to take a full 4 years of high school mathematics and are generally exposed to it again in the first year of college. Consequently, the increase in performance for the 13+ group is substantial for these tests. The data suggest that more advanced mathematics education does not impact broadly the high school population, but rather tends to be concentrated on the college bound.

For the technical knowledge tests such as Mechanical Comprehension and Electronics Information, on the other hand, the relevant high school courses are typically offered in the last two years of high school. The effect on these tests of completing 4 years of high school is more marked, and substantial score differences between educational levels are seen in Figure 3.1b.

Sociocultural Group and Economic Status Differences in Relation to High School Attendance

Paragraph Comprehension, Arithmetic Reasoning, General Science, Mathematics Knowledge, and, to a lesser extent, Numerical Operations and Word Knowledge all show a curious form of interaction in the contrast of nonpoor Whites and Blacks with the other groups. This interaction is especially apparent in the school-related context of Arithmetic Reasoning, Numerical Operations, General Science, and Mathematics Knowledge. For these tests, the difference between respondents with 9 to 11 years of education and those with 12 years is smaller for the higher income Whites and Blacks than for the other groups. The result is a perceptible "step" in the middle of the curves for those groups. No such step is seen in Coding Speed, Auto and Shop Information, or Electronics Information; it appears only to a lesser extent in Mechanical Comprehension. For the school-related tests, nonpoor Whites and Blacks with some college also show a relatively sharp increase in performance over those with no more than a high school education.

A plausible explanation for this phenomenon is the effect of selective dropping out of high school. If less able students in the Hispanic groups and in the poor White and Black groups are more likely to drop out of high school before graduation, then the groups that retain most of their members through the 12th grade will be less select and score relatively lower on the tests. Moreover, propensity to drop out differs among sociocultural groups: Current estimates are that the school dropout rate of Hispanics is substantially higher than that of Blacks. The dropout hypothesis therefore explains some of the differences in the achievement patterns of Hispanics and Blacks. It does not, however, explain the difference in achievement between the Black and the White groups.

The widespread practice of ability grouping (tracking) to facilitate instruction in school may play a part in the latter effect. There is evidence that a disproportionate number of Black (and other minority status) children are assigned to low-ability groups because of schools' reliance on general attainment tests to determine ability to learn (Brown, Carter, & Harris, 1978). Because minority-status children generally do not perform well on such tests, they tend to be placed in low-ability groups where standards of achievement are low. In fact, ability grouping often begins even at age levels where learning-readiness test scores are not available. Rist (1973) observes ability grouping as early as kindergarten before school personnel and teachers have any valid basis for determining ability to learn. Grouping in these early years appears to be strongly determined by children's physical appearance and verbal behavior. Similarly, Haskins, Walden, and Ramey (1983) report considerable ability grouping in kindergarten and first-grade classrooms based on teachers' informal observations of the children. Some researchers conclude from classroom observation that, because of the adverse effect that ability grouping has on the type of instruction low-ability children receive, separation of lower and higher ability students can defeat the purpose and logic of intraclassroom ability grouping (Felmlee & Eber, 1983; Haskins, Walden & Ramey, 1983). By the same token, early ability grouping tends to establish a pattern of reduced expectations and cumulative educational deprivation for minority children, the pervasive influence of which is convincingly demonstrated by Pedersen, Faucher, and Eaton (1978). They present longitudinal data showing that teachers' expectations and attitudes toward children are correlated with the growth of children's verbal facility and the attainment of self-concept.

The practice of ability grouping impinges on all children who are not identified with the majority culture, but its impact appears greatest on Blacks. The majority of Black children begin school without having assimilated many of the facts, attitudes, values, and standards of behavior that organized education assumes. As a result, they appear slower to learn and are assigned to lower ability groups in which less achievement is expected, less effort is demanded, and less content is covered. The cumulative effect of this practice, compounded by other factors we discuss later, inevitably leaves Blacks in the disadvantaged position we observe in the society-wide comparisons of the Profile study.

Linguistic Factors in Hispanics' Achievement

Because Spanish speakers are the largest linguistic minority in the United States, it is essential to assess impact of language problems on the vocational potential of the Hispanic sociocultural group. We have seen in Figure 3.1, however, that the performance of nonpoor Hispanics in the *nonlanguage* tasks—Coding Speed and Numerical Operations—is somewhat lower than that of the comparable White group. This suggests that their lower average performance on language tasks may be attributable not only to linguistic factors but to other cultural factors as well. This impression is reinforced when we note that, among all the Hispanic subjects who took the ASVAB tests, only 85 requested that the instructions for taking the test be presented in Spanish (see Appendix A). Moreover, the performance of Hispanics on the Paragraph Comprehension test is not much different from their performance on the nonlinguistic tests. We doubt, therefore, that the lower scores relative to Whites in the vocationally significant mathematical and technical tests can be attributed primarily to language. Other factors, probably similar to those affecting Blacks, must also be operating.

Neither is the higher performance of the Hispanic groups relative to non-poor Blacks at each education level consistent with the long-standing assumption that the language skills of Hispanics hinder their educational attainment; one might have predicted that Hispanics would show lower performance than Blacks. In 1953, Anastasi and Cordova observed significantly lower intelligence test scores for Puerto Rican children than majority test norms would predict. They concluded that although the low socioeconomic status of these children contributed to their lower scores, "a solution to the language problem would seem a necessary first step for the effective education of migrant Puerto Rican children" (Anastasi & Cordova, 1953, p. 17). The present data indicate that the same cannot be said of the Hispanics in 1980: The language problem does not loom as large as it did in 1953.

There is continuing controversy about the extent to which bilingualism affects cognitive performance (Carter, 1970; Garcia, 1980; Cuevas, 1984). Cummins (1979) theorizes that a balanced proficiency in two languages can be highly beneficial to the child's cognitive development. But trends in the acquisition of English by Spanish-speaking children in kindergarten and first grade, observed by Garcia (1980) in a national study of English–Spanish bilingualism, suggest that Spanish-speaking children show a decline in Spanish-language ability and a gain in English-language ability by first grade. The Spanish-language ability loss is thought to result from the monolingual educational curriculum. Thus, proficiency in one language appears to displace rather than supplement proficiency in the other.

Depending somewhat on their country of origin, many Spanish-speaking young people in the United States appear to take Spanish for granted and focus their language learning on English. Fernandez, Espinosa, and Dornbusch (1975) report that Chicano high school students believe that learning English is very important for school performance and vocational prospects. Portes, McLeod, and Parker (1978) found that the educational, occupational, and income aspirations of immigrant Mexicans are more strongly determined by their knowledge of English than is the case for immigrant Cubans. These investigators surmise that greater familiarity with American society, through personal experience or that of friends and relatives, makes the Mexican immigrants more aware than the Cubans of the importance of English for status attainment. Their research indicates that, as we might expect, the strong motivation to develop English-language skills among Hispanics stems largely from economic concerns.

Turning to the question of why the Hispanics uniformly exceed the Blacks in the verbal skills tests, we point out that first knowledge of a foreign language does not compete with the learning of formal English in the way that first knowledge of a nonstandard English would. Thus, we could believe that the English learned by Hispanics is actually closer to "school English" than that acquired by many Blacks, and that continued everyday use of the

Black vernacular interferes with the learning of more formal English in a way that Spanish does not. Stimulus similarity effects of learning inhibition would predict such a result. If this is the case, the relatively higher attainment of the Hispanics on the verbal tests could be attributed in part to their having learned more formal and precise English skills.

It may also be the case that, if a substantial proportion of the Hispanic respondents in the Profile study are indeed bilingual, their bilingualism may have actually facilitated their verbal test performance, particularly on the Word Knowledge test. Of the words included in this test, 69% have Spanish cognates (Foster, 1981). Foster, a professor of Spanish, notes that most "high-class" English words have Latin roots that appear in the everyday language of Hispanics. The linguistically aware speaker of Spanish taking the Word Knowledge test would therefore have clues to the correct alternative—clues that are available to relatively few Whites and to even fewer Blacks.

The fact that a slightly higher percentage of the Hispanic respondents refused to take the test than was observed for the other groups (see Section 4.1) also helps explain these findings. It is likely that Hispanics with the poorest English skills are not included in this sample, and that the average performance observed for this group is slightly increased, especially on the tests that depend heavily on English language knowledge.

To decide between alternative hypotheses about the Hispanics' language performance relative to Whites and Blacks or about the impeding or facilitating effects of bilingualism would require knowledge of the language development of individual subjects. The necessary information is not available in the Profile study. The data suggest only that conventional ideas about English language as related to Hispanics in the United States may need revision.

Minority Group Effects

That Blacks should show less benefit of education in their responses to the specialized knowledge tests than to other tests is somewhat puzzling. The effect seen in Figure 3.1 agrees, however, with other research indicating that Black males, when responding to vocational interest inventories, express less interest in scientific, technical, and mechanical fields than do White males. Black males tend to be more interested in artistic, health and welfare, and business–clerical fields and in general show a more restricted range of occupational interests (Sewell & Martin, 1976; Williams & Whitney, 1978). As early as 1941, Witty, Garfield, and Brink found that Blacks' vocational interests tend to be more "people oriented," whereas the interests of Whites are more "thing oriented." Bray and Moses (1972), who tested this early hypothesis by examining the majors of Black and White college freshmen, found that Blacks tend to major in the social sciences, education, and health fields, whereas White freshman favor the biological and physical sciences. Attempting to account for these findings, Sewell and Martin (1976) suggest that the restricted range of vocational interests expressed by Blacks is the result of Black adolescents' tending to aspire to occupations in which they more often observe Black role models. Talented young Blacks appear to choose careers elsewhere because they see few examples of successful Blacks in the scientific and technical occupations (Johnson, 1984). Garfinkle (1975), in his examination of the occupations of Black workers between 1962 and 1974, confirms the paucity of Blacks in these "thing-oriented" occupations relative to the more "people-oriented" fields.

In contrast, Hispanics are proportionately more represented in scientific and technical fields than Blacks, and their better prospects of entering may explain the greater benefit of education to this group's performance on the specialized knowledge tests. There is evidence that more Hispanics than Blacks select courses related to these occupational areas: Sells (1980) reports that, in 1978, 25% of the Hispanic students in California were enrolled in mathematics courses leading to calculus, whereas only 20% of the Blacks were similarly enrolled. Moreover, Fernandez et al. (1975) report from a sample of San Francisco high school students that about half of the black students in 10th grade were performing at less than the 6th-grade level in mathematics, whereas only 17% of the Chicanos were performing below this level. Thirty-three percent of the Chicanos, compared to only 18% of the Blacks, received high grades in mathematics.

Similar statistics obtain outside the classroom. Wilson and Portes (1980) report that in the Miami area, Cubans own 40% of the construction business and employ large numbers of their community in these businesses. Role models for Hispanics in the skilled trades are not lacking in the Southeast.

At a more general level, we have more to say about many of these topics when we survey theories of sociocultural group differences in cognitive test performance in Section 3.3. Before beginning that discussion, however, we examine another sociocultural group interaction in the Profile data that these theories should account for.

3.2. SOCIOCULTURAL GROUP BY REGION EFFECTS

We observed in Chapter 2 that there are no statistically significant three-factor interactions of sociocultural group, economic status, and region. Neither is there any evidence of two-factor interactions of economic status and region. This means that the amount by which the test scores of the nonpoor groups exceed those of the poor is not noticeably different in the four regions of the country. Although, as we saw in Section 3.1, the effect of the economic status classification differs somewhat with years of schooling and sociocultural group, the general advantage of the nonpoor subjects over poor is about 20 points for any of the ASVAB tests.

The differences between sociocultural groups interact substantially, however, with the classification by residence at 14. Figure 3.2 shows the performance of the sociocultural groups in the Northeast, Southeast, Midwest, and West in terms of the standard scores of the national probability sample. (For a list of the region assignments of the states, see Table 2.6.) Although the patterns of these interactions show similarities when the tests are grouped by specialized knowledge, verbal skills, fluent production, and quantitative skills, these distinctions are less helpful in discussing the region effects and are not used in this section.

Regional Effects on Hispanics' Achievement

By far the most conspicuous interaction of sociocultural group and region is that in the Hispanic subsample. Unlike Hispanics elsewhere in the country, those of the Southeast region equal Whites on 7 of the 10 subtests (i.e., Arithmetic Reasoning, Word Knowledge, Paragraph Comprehension, Numerical Operations, Coding Speed, Mathematics Knowledge, and General Science); they are only moderately below Whites on the remaining tests. Whites show somewhat higher average scores in the specialized knowledge areas of Electronics Information, Mechanical Comprehension, and Auto and Shop Information.

The performance of Northeast Hispanics, on the other hand, is more similar to that of Blacks on all the tests. The substantially lower performance of this group of Hispanics on the Numerical Operations and Coding Speed tests suggests that linguistic factors may not be the only variable in their lower attainment relative to Whites. This is not the case in the Midwest and West, where the performance of Hispanics is nearly identical to Whites on these nonverbal tests. Perhaps benefiting from better reading instruction in that region, Hispanics of the Midwest are also equal to Whites in performance on the Paragraph Comprehension test.

Owing to the absence of any historical antagonism between Hispanics and Whites in the Midwest, the Hispanics of that region are more fully integrated into schools and other community institutions than in the West. In the urban Midwest especially, social class has a greater influence on vocational attainment than ethnicity. Alvarez (1976) observes that Mexican–Americans migrated to the Midwest and Northwest to escape the caste-like status they experienced in the Southwest. He points to industrialization and the religious, ethnic, and political heterogeneity of the Midwest as factors attenuating discrimination against Mexican–Americans. The status of Hispanics in this region tends to be more a condition of lower class than of lower caste as

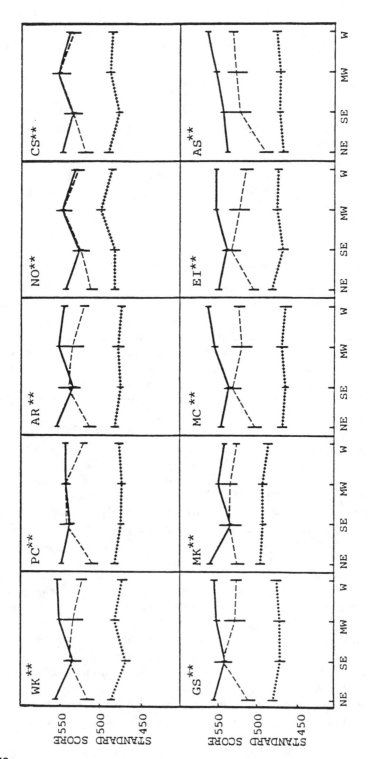

FIG. 3.2. Interaction of sociocultural group and region of residence at age 14.
White ——— Hispanic ------ Black · · · · · ****F > 1.25F(.01)

76

in the Southwest. The stability of their tenure in the Midwest community may also account for this pattern because unlike the situation in the Southwest, travel between the central United States and Mexico is not as convenient. Moreover, the Midwestern Hispanic community, composed of Cubans, Mexicans, Puerto Ricans, and other Central and South Americans, is itself more heterogeneous. This greater diversity relative to the largely Mexican community of the West could also account for some of the observed regional difference in test performance.

Hispanics in considerable numbers in each of these regions are nevertheless isolated in many ways from the majority culture. Many tend to persist in traditional cultural patterns rather than becoming bicultural. Ramirez (1973) has reviewed studies showing that, among Mexican–Americans, those who can be considered bicultural are more successful than the less assimilated at all levels of education from kindergarten to graduate school. The relative attainments of Hispanics in the Northeast, Southeast, and West seem to reflect something of their different national and social origins. The Puerto Ricans who predominate in the Northeast are often from a rural and agrarian background. In the Southeast, the Hispanics are mostly Cubans who came to the United States in the early 1960s after the revolution. In many cases they were skilled, well-educated business people and professionals (Wilson & Portes, 1980). With assistance from the public sector, including local-, state-, and federal-funded educational programs, they were able to reestablish themselves economically (Pedraza-Bailey, 1982). It is their children who appear in the Profile sample.

The Mexican–Americans in the West, on the other hand, generally have come to the United States with fewer skills and economic resources. They are not faring as well economically as the Hispanics of the Southeast. Their children have a record of high rates of school dropout, and educational programs designed to facilitate adjustment in the United States have suffered from insufficient funds and fluctuating levels of community support. Thus, it is not surprising to observe the considerable differences in the relative performance of Hispanics and Whites in the West as compared to the Southeast. The one exception is the Auto and Shop Information test. On this test, western Hispanics do about as well as or better than those in the other regions. Apparently, the automobile-centered majority culture of the West, particularly California, extends to the minority Hispanic culture. Perhaps the "low-rider" clubs can take some credit as well.

We have not attempted in the present study to analyze the performance of the Hispanic respondents by national origin. Eitelberg and Doering (1982), however, have examined the average Armed Forces Qualification Test (AFQT) scores of self-identified Mexican-American, Puerto Rican, and Cuban respondents included in this sample. The AFQT is a composite measure derived by combining scores of the Word Knowledge, Paragraph

Comprehension, Arithmetic Reasoning, and Numerical Operations tests of the ASVAB. It is one of the criteria used by the armed services to determine eligibility for enlistment. Although not identical to the individual test scores we have analyzed to this point, the AFQT is highly correlated with the separate test scores, especially in the school-intensive skills. Eitelberg and Doering report that the Cubans in the sample achieve an average standard score on the AFQT of 494, Mexican–Americans achieve an average score of 448, and Ricans Ricans achieve an average score of 444. These scores are very similar to the pattern of scores we see for Hispanics in the various regions where the different Hispanic groups tend to predominate.

Regional Effects in Blacks' Achievement

Blacks in the Northeast and Midwest are similar in their performance on all of the tests except Numerical Operations and are at a higher level than Blacks in the Southeast and West. This result generally confirms the earlier finding of Coleman and his colleagues (1966) that Blacks in the Northeast are achieving at levels higher than those in other regions. The present data indicate, however, that Blacks of the Midwest are doing just as well and even exceeding those of the Northeast on the basic arithmetic calculation of the Numerical Operations test.

Blacks in the Southeast fail to exceed those in other regions on any of the tests, but are significantly lower only in Word Knowledge and perhaps Coding Speed. The earlier disadvantages of Blacks in this region seem much reduced in these data. In particular, they differ little from the Blacks of the Southwest.

Unlike the regional effects observed for Hispanics, there is no region where the performance of Blacks approximates that of the White groups. The data reveal clearly the pervasiveness of Black youths' lack of preparation for successful competition in the meritocracy. The factors that contribute to this failure, including ability grouping in schools, will be elaborated in later sections.

3.3.   SOURCES OF SOCIOCULTURAL GROUP DIFFERENCES

The young people included in the Profile sample were born or attained formal school age during an era of unprecedented efforts to provide equal educational opportunity to all American children. There was a national resolve to eliminate the educational handicaps that prevent minority-status children from participating fully in the economic life of our society. If these good intentions had actually translated into effective action, we might have expected some positive effects to show in these Profile data. From this perspective, the findings of this survey are encouraging with respect to the performance of Hispanics and low-income Whites, but are disappointing with respect to Blacks. In view of the considerable amount of time, energy, and resources focused on the problem of Black children's failure to benefit from schooling during the '60s and '70s, how can we explain this lack of progress? Why are the differences between Blacks' and Whites' average skill development observed by Coleman et al. (1966) still at about the same level? Some answers to these questions are suggested in the subsequent sections of this chapter. We focus first on the general process of status attainment, then consider the elements of the process in which Blacks and Whites may differ, and finally suggest how and why these differences contribute to variations in Blacks' and Whites' educational attainment and, we would predict, in their occupational attainment as well.

The Process of Status Attainment

No one would dispute the economic advantage that attends high educational attainment in our society. Persons with more education obtain higher status jobs and generally earn more money than those with less education. Sociologists have attempted to develop a multivariate model of status attainment to explain the educational and occupational achievement process among White males and females (Duncan et al., 1972; Jencks et al., 1972; McClendon, 1976; Sewell & Hauser, 1975; Treiman & Terrell, 1975). Essentially, it is a five-stage model in which mother's and father's education, income, and occupational status, and the individual's ability (indexed by IQ), explain scholastic achievement. All background variables and scholastic achievement determine the influence of significant others (i.e., mother, father, teachers, best friends); all of the preceding variables affect the individual's level of ambition; and, finally, educational attainment and occupational status are determined by all previous variables in the model. Although the goal of much of the work on status attainment has been the development of a model valid for the entire society (Blau & Duncan, 1967; Sewell & Hauser, 1975), comparisons of the educational attainment process of Blacks and Whites have shown that this model does not provide as good an explanation of the attainment process for Black Americans as it does for White Americans (Kerckhoff & Campbell, 1977; Porter, 1974; Portes & Wilson, 1976).

Portes and Wilson (1976) observed differences in the educational attainment process of Blacks and Whites, particularly in the order of effects delineated by the model. Socioeconomic status variables, mental ability, and academic performance—variables appearing early in the model—were found to predict strongly overall White educational attainment. For Blacks, however, the strongest influence on educational attainment was observed for variables appearing later in the model—namely, self-esteem and educational aspirations. Similarly, Kerckhoff and Campbell (1977) report that family socioeconomic status is a much more important influence on the educational attainment process of Whites than of Blacks. These investigators conclude that the results for Whites often appear much more orderly and predictable (p. 25).

A similar model of status attainment has guided much of the thinking about factors that lower the school performance of minority-status children. The "cultural deprivation" theory is an example. Bloom, Davis, and Hess (1963) described culturally deprived students as: "the students whose early experience in the home, whose motivation for present school learning, and whose goals for the future are such as to handicap them in school work. This group may also include those who do not complete secondary education" (p. 4).

As this description suggests, these investigators believe that family background variables exert a strong influence on the entire educational attainment process. The specific focus of their work was the determination of what early experiences resulted in these negative effects, and how these experiences mediated scholastic achievement.

But findings of Portes and Wilson (1976) and Kerckhoff and Campbell (1977) suggest that early experiences in the home may not be quite as critical to Black children's educational attainment as previously thought. Both of these reports suggest that the educational attainment of Black students may be determined more by what happens to them once they enter the school system than by what they bring to the system. They do indicate, however, that IQ test scores significantly predict the educational attainment of both Blacks and Whites, although in each study the effects for IQ are stronger for Whites than for Blacks. Family background factors and associated early experiences may therefore be important to Black children's educational attainment to the extent that they mediate general verbal ability.

IQ Scores and the Educational Attainment of Black Children

Children from the lower socioeconomic levels of our society typically achieve lower intelligence test scores than those from the middle class (Golden, Birns, Bridger, & Moss, 1971; Hall & Kaye, 1980; Jones, 1954; Lesser, Fifer, & Clack, 1965). Investigators who have compared the intelligence test performances of different ethnic groups from both high and low social classes report significant effects within economic strata. Black children typically achieve lower average scores than their White peers when social class is controlled (Nichols & Anderson, 1973; Scarr, 1971; Sitkei & Meyers, 1969; Trotman, 1977).

As Anastasi (1982) points out, IQ is the general designation of scores derived by tests designed to assess a number of different cognitive skills, such as the ability to manipulate abstract symbols, verbal facility, numerical facility, and other such specific skills thought to be necessary to succeed in a particular culture. Because most of the current intelligence tests were modeled after the original Binet Scale developed for purposes of assessing the nature of children's learning difficulties in the school setting, IQ tests today assess verbal facility primarily and, to a lesser extent, numerical facility and reasoning skill (skills required in most school curricula). The score obtained from such a test is used to index both previous learning experience and to predict subsequent scholastic achievement. To the extent that it does the latter, the IQ score is thought to indicate "ability" or potential to benefit from future training in cognitive tasks.

Because a positive correlation exists between intelligence test performance and school achievement (Cleary, Humphreys, Kendrick, & Wesman, 1975), Black children's lower average IQ scores were early seized upon as major factors contributing to lower scholastic achievement. Not realizing that both of these variables could be reflecting the same cultural differences, many researchers believed that if Black children's IQ scores could be raised, then their school achievement would also rise. Thus in testing intervention programs designed to eliminate Black children's academic handicaps, they used performance on standardized intelligence tests to evaluate effectiveness (Horowitz & Paden, 1973). Because Bloom (1964) had reported that IQ was relatively stable after the preschool years, it was assumed that if gains in Black children's IQ scores could be effected by intervention programs early in life, these gains would carry the child to higher educational attainment, and ultimately, higher occupational status.

Although some of these programs succeeded in boosting Black children's IQ scores, the investigators were disappointed to find that the increments were not maintained past the first few years of public school attendance. These experiences prompted Jensen (1969) to theorize that the failure of the programs to produce lasting changes in Black children's IQs could be explained on genetic grounds. According to Jensen (1969, 1973, 1980), the Black and White subpopulations in the United States differ in the frequency of certain unknown but behaviorally predisposing genes that substantially account for the typical one-standard-deviation disparity between their mean IQ scores.

His reasoning is based primarily on research that shows substantial heritability of IQ scores within homogeneous populations. Although heritability can be defined in more than one way, it is basically an index expressing the proportion of the total population variation of individual differences for a given measurable trait that can be attributed to genetically determined differences in constitution. Nonzero heritability of a trait implies higher positive correlation of the trait among more closely related persons, and numerous empirical studies of IQ scores have in fact shown that, as family relatedness increases, similarity in IQ scores increases to the expected degree. Erlenmeyer-Kimling and Jarvik (1963) reviewed 52 studies of IQ scores of related and unrelated persons reared together and apart and found the median correlations to increase with relatedness in the degree predicted by quantitative genetic theory. A more recent review published by Bouchard and McGue (1981), including many additional studies, gave much the same result, but with somewhat lower estimates of the coefficients of correlation than were previously accepted. The studies reviewed by Bouchard and McGue show a median correlation of first-degree relatives reared apart is about .23. Although these correlations are necessarily attenuated somewhat by the unreliability of the IQ measures, they are also likely to be strengthened by similarities of the environments in which separated family members find themselves. All things considered, the data reported in the literature suggest a heritability for IQ in the range of 50 to 60%. This would mean that 50 to 60% of the total variance in IQ seen in a population is due to heritable genotypic differences. However, 40 to 50% of variation remaining leaves ample room for environmental influences to affect responses on these tests.

Although students of genetics would agree that these findings indicate appreciable heritability of IQ within homogeneous cultural groups, they also agree that the typical methods and assumptions of genetic analysis regarding psychological test scores do not apply to comparisons of mean levels of performance between reproductively distinct populations (Bock, 1974; Thoday, 1969). Standard models of quantitative genetics deal exclusively with variation within populations; intergroup comparisons of behavioral traits are problematic because, insofar as there is any environmental component in the trait variation, there is no basis for inferring the quantitative effect of environmental influences on the population mean. Jensen, in particular, violates this principle of genetic analysis when he extrapolates models of genetic variability and transmission derived from analysis of within-group variation of the trait (IQ score) to account for between-group differences in the population means. As a result, his conclusions regarding the genetic basis of differences between Blacks and Whites in IQ have no factual basis. Careful examination of this problem (Bodmer & Cavalli-Sforza, 1971) finds no grounds for Jensen's conclusion that racial and ethnic differences in intelligence are genetic in origin. In fact, there is good evidence to the contrary, as we shall see.

In order to justify between-group comparisons for genotypic IQ based on test scores, it is necessary to show that, within the two populations, environmental factors affect the development of intelligence in the same way, and that complete identity in the distribution of the environmental variables exists between populations (Scarr, 1975). Even if the first point were conceded, the socioeconomic variability observed between Blacks and Whites, as well as differences in cultural patterns, does not allow the second point. Intelligence tests performance is influenced not only by ability to apply memory and reasoning to a problem, but also by familiarity with the cultural forms in which the problems are couched. Researchers now recognize that the intellectual and social isolation of Blacks in this country over more than 100 years has either given rise to, or resulted in the maintenance of, substantial cultural differences between the White and Black populations. These differences are reflected in the way children are oriented to the social and object environment, modes of communication, and tolerance for varying levels of sensory stimulation (see Hale, 1980, for a review of this literature).

The proof of the correctness of this conclusion is in research showing that when Black children are reared in the majority culture, they achieve average test scores on IQ tests comparable to those of the White population. Scarr and Weinberg (1976) report that when Black children with at least one Black parent are adopted by middle-class White parents in the first year of life, they achieve an average IQ of 110. Of course, some might argue that since the Scarr-and-Weinberg sample contained a large portion of biracial children (i.e., children with one White parent and one Black parent), these children's White ancestry contributed to their higher performance. However, Moore (1980), in a similar study, reports that for Black children adopted by middle-class White parents, there are no differences in average IQ score between Black children who are the offspring of two Black parents and those who had one White and one Black parent. The average full-scale score in the Wechsler Intelligence Test for children (WISC) was 118 for the former group, and 116.5 for the latter.

Moore's (1980) study was specifically designed to determine the influence of the cultural environment on Black children's intelligence test performance, when socioeconomic status is controlled. She compared the WISC performance of two groups of adopted Black children: one group adopted by Black middle-class families ($N=23$), another group adopted by White middle-class families ($N=23$). Both groups of children had been adopted from the same two agencies, and both groups of parents had met the agencies' stringent placement requirements. There were no significant differences between Black children placed in the two kinds of adoptive homes in terms of biological mothers' health and prenatal care. All of the children were similarly healthy at the time of birth and were comparable in the number and quality of preadoption placements, and in age at placement (about 15 months for both groups).

In Moore's study, there were two differences between the Black children in the White homes and those in the Black homes. First, the average educational attainment of the biological mothers of the Black children placed in Black homes was significantly lower than that of the biological mothers of those placed in White homes. However, 15 of the biological mothers in the former group were still in school when their babies were born, and it was impossible to determine from agency records how much more schooling they actually obtained after the birth of their children. Second, biracial and "full Black" children were not normally distributed in the two kinds of adoptive placements. There were more biracial children in the White homes ($N = 14$) than in the Black homes ($N = 6$). However, discussions with the social worker who made all placements for the two agencies indicated that this was not the result of the agencies' attempt to effect any type of environment-genotype correlation. Rather, this particular distribution of biracial and "full Black" children among the two adoptive placements was consequent to the Black parents' preference for a child who would resemble themselves in physical appearance.

Just as there was no significant difference in the WISC full-scale IQ of biracial and "full Black" children in the White adoptive homes, there was no significant difference in the average performance of the biracial and "full Black" children in the Black adoptive homes. Biracial children averaged 105.7; the "full Black" children average 102.9. The average full-scale WISC IQ of all the Black children in the Black adoptive homes was 103.6; for the Black children in the White homes, 117.1. The 13.5-point score difference between these two groups of adopted Black children is of the magnitude observed between Black and White children in the general population. While the advantages of a middle-class rearing environment for Black children's intellectual performance are demonstrated in the scores of the Black children in middle-class Black homes, the advantages for Black children's test performance that come with rearing in a middle-class home of the majority culture are even greater. These data suggest the importance of the cultural component to Black children's IQ test performance, as well as the influence of a social class component.

Taken together, the findings of Scarr and Weinberg, and of Moore, indicate that when Black children are reared by parents in the majority culture, they obtain IQ test scores comparable to, if not greater than, their White counterparts. Further, both biracial and "full Black" children benefit similarly from rearing in advantaged White homes.

To further explore the effects of racial genetic differences on individuals' intelligence test performance, Scarr, Pakstis, Katz, and Barker (1977) analyzed the relationship between estimates of degree of White ancestry obtained for a large sample of Black and White children based on blood group markers (i.e., genetically determined antigens on red cells that have been found to be reliable markers of population differences) and their IQ test scores. Jensen (1973) hypothesized that there would be a correlation of approximately .50 between degree of White ancestry and IQ based on his estimates of the effects of genetic differences between Whites and Blacks for IQ test scores. However, Scarr et al. report no significant correlations between their estimates of degree of White ancestry and children's scores on five different intelligence tests. The highest correlation found between these estimates and test performance was .13. This is very strong evidence that the mean difference in IQ scores of the Black and White populations does not arise primarily from genetic sources.

Genetic differences between groups are much more evident in characteristics that are adapted to climatic differences, such as skin color and hair form, than in behavioral or other physiological characteristics. Average intellectual attainments of populations that have been historically distinct are mostly expressions of their particular institutions and cultures and are transmitted by imitation and instruction within the family, school, and community.

Additional evidence of the influence that social–environmental factors can have on intelligence test performance within populations has been provided by Schiff, Duyme, Dumaret, and Tomkiewicz (1982) from an adoption study in France. These investigators designed their research to address directly the question raised by Jensen in 1969—"How much can we boost scholastic achievement and IQ scores?" They identified a sample of French school children ($N=32$), abandoned at birth, whose biological parents were both unskilled workers, but who were adopted by upper middle-class families within 4 months of birth. The adopted children's IQ scores were determined by the administration of an individual intelligence test—the French version of the Wechsler Intelligence Scale for Children (WISC)—and a group intelligence test, the ECNI, which, according to the investigators, is widely used in the French school system. The school records of the adopted children were also examined to determine their scholastic achievement. The effects of the change in the adopted children's social class membership on their IQ test scores and on school achievement were estimated by comparing their performance to that of children of unskilled workers in the general French population, which had been obtained in two previous large scale studies. An internal control group was also developed that consisted of the half-siblings of 20 of the 32 adopted children who had been reared by the working-class biological mother they shared.

Schiff et al. (1982) report that the change in social class membership of the adopted French children increased their IQ scores by 14 points (about one standard deviation) over what would be expected if they had been reared by their working-class biological parents. The mean score observed for the adopted children on the group intelligence test was 106.8; for their half-siblings, 95.1; for children of unskilled workers in general in France, 95.1; and for biological children of upper middle-class families in general, 110. The mean WISC score of the adopted children was 110.6 as compared to a mean score of 94.2 for their half-siblings on this individually administered IQ test, and an average WISC score of 100 observed in the French population generally.

The scholastic achievement of the adopted children was assessed primarily in terms of school failure rate. School failure was defined as either having to repeat grades or placement in classes for slow learners. The school failure observed for the adopted children was 4 out of 32; for their half-siblings 16 out of 32; for children of unskilled workers in general, 16.5 out of 32; and for the biological children of upper middle-class parents in general, 4 out of 32. Therefore, these investigators concluded that the change in social class membership of the adopted children reduced their probability of school failure by a factor of four.

The Schiff et al. (1982) study is particularly well designed and executed. It provides very clear evidence of the significant influence of social variables on IQ test performance within populations, where the estimate of the heritability of IQ is in the 50 to 60% range. However, the findings of Schiff et al. are not surprising. Quantitative genetic theory recognizes that environment can influence the average expression of traits even when they are highly heritable within populations. As a case in point, Bock (1974) cites the example of average stature in European, American, and Asian populations. He notes that in these populations, measures of stature have a heritability estimate almost identical to that of IQ scores. Yet, the mean stature of all three of these populations has increased nearly one standard deviation in two generations—an increase comparable to the observed difference in measures of intellectual ability between Whites and Blacks in the U.S. population. The increase in average stature of the Japanese since World War II is even more dramatic. This demonstrates that environmental influences (presumably better nutrition in the case of growth in stature) can substantially change the mean of a highly heritable quantitative trait. Noting the parallels between the heritability of stature and of general intellectual ability, Bock (1974) goes on to observe that: ". . . nothing now known about the determinants of general verbal ability should induce us to rule out a similar trend in the average ability of the U.S. Black minority as it moves out of years of segregated life and into the majority educational, linguistic and cultural environment of the United States" (p. 595).

In short, the bulk of the evidence currently available does not support genetic explanations of the observed differences between Black and White children's IQ. The explanation for the average differences in Black and White children's IQ and in school achievement must be sought elsewhere.

The Schools and Black Children's Achievement

The theory that formed the basis of early school intervention programs is based on the assumption that experience in early infancy and childhood has a lasting effect on the individual (i.e., persists throughout the course of development). However, Clarke and Clarke (1976) and Brim and Kagan (1980) have compiled evidence from a variety of areas to demonstrate that this is not entirely true. These investigators conclude that the effects of early experience (both positive and negative) are not permanent, but that over the life-course, individuals change as a result of continual interaction between their capacities and their changing environments.

From this emerging view of a dynamic process of human development has come a new understanding of why Black children's IQ scores can diminish with public school attendance. The public schools have generally been unable to provide continued support for these children's intellectual development at the level provided by high quality preschool programs (Ramey & Haskins, 1981). Two decades ago educators recognized that the public schools were failing to educate Black children adequately, but it was assumed that the problems were with the children, not with the schools. Now it is becoming more apparent that the major problem in Black children's scholastic achievement is that public schools are not attuned to their particular needs as learners. The majority of Black children may come to the school context with skills, attitudes, and achievement orientations that are different from those of middle-class White children (Cole & Bruner, 1971). These differences are interpreted as fixed deficits by many school personnel. The importance of cultural relativity for determining educational potential is generally recognized by theorists, but has not been sufficiently understood in the public school system. In the case of poor Black children, in particular, teachers do not believe that the children can master higher level skills and therefore do not provide the same level of exposure to new materials, encourage independent exploration, or require mastery at the level they do for children viewed as more able (i.e., middle-class White children) (Haskins, Walden & Ramey, 1983).

IQ tests can be useful in providing an assessment of the scholastic skill development of Black children for purposes of diagnosis and remediation. However IQ test scores are most often used to relegate Black children permanently to inferior positions in the school curriculum. When IQ scores are used to set limits on the type of education children receive, with teachers providing instruction limited to the level of the child's IQ and making only modest attempts to provide intellectual growth experiences, it is not surprising that IQ and subsequent educational achievement are so strongly correlated. There is evidence that, from kindergarten on, teachers make assessments, either formally or informally, of what each child can learn. They then teach to this level, which results all too frequently in Black children remaining behind their more advantaged peers as the schooling process continues (Rist, 1973).

Hall and Kaye (1980) present data that address this point. Citing results from a longitudinal study of 900 Black and White lower and middle-class boys, ages 6 to 9, who were administered tests of memory, intelligence, learning, and transfer over a 4-year period, they conclude that at age 6 Black and lower-class children are behind their White middle-class peers in intellectual functioning and information processing. However, the Black and lower-class children, although they fail to "catch up," continue to progress at the same rate as middle-class children. These investigators interpret their findings to mean that at age 6 Black and poor children show a developmental lag in intellectual functioning behind their more advantaged age mates. They conclude, therefore, that formal school training should not be required of the former group until they are ready, so as to avoid poor achievement and an associated negative attitude toward school.

However, a plausible alternative interpretation of their findings is that, because at age 6 Black and poor children have lower test scores than their more advantaged peers, teachers do not provide them with educational stimulation sufficient to support an acceleration of skill development to the point of "catching up." According to this view, teachers are, in effect, delaying training of these children. The negative affect that these children develop toward school may not be due to frustration in trying to master school-intensive skills, so much as to frustration with the teachers' failure to provide appropriate instruction and exposure (Rist, 1973).

Scarr (1980), in commenting on the research presented by Hall and Kaye (1980), disagreed with their recommendation that formal school training should be delayed for Black and poor children until their underlying intellectual ability catches up to that of advantaged Whites. She points out that this results in their falling further behind in academic skill development. Since Black and poor children show developmental lag, Scarr recommends that they be given intensive training in basic verbal and numerical skills from kindergarten on (even if they do not get training in music, art, or recreational sports) to allow for the possibly longer time it will take them to master these skills. Certainly Black children must have these basic skills as prerequisites of the more complex abilities that will permit them to become competitive in the world of work. Scarr's recommendation is a reasonable one in light of the current findings.

Fernandez et al. (1975) report from their study of high school students that Chicanos and Blacks have a higher self-concept than expected for students low in achievement. These investigators attribute this finding to the fact that teachers set lower standards for students who enter high school with below average test scores and reward them with grades and praise for minimal achievement. As a result, the students assume that they are making appropriate progress in school because they do not get feedback to the contrary. To illustrate the problem of school standards for these young people's achievement, these investigators report that even though Black and Chicano students had low skill levels at high school entrance, teachers did not provide them with assignments sufficient to challenge them. The students with the lowest achievement scores were also more likely than other students to say that the assignments were "just right" for them. In contrast, Asians and Whites, who tended to have higher achievement scores, more often reported their assignments were too difficult. Further, among the students with low achievement scores, those who indicated that they spent 15 minutes or less on homework per week were as likely to report that they completed their homework as often as not. These investigators conclude that high standards were not being communicated in these schools to low achieving students.

Mackler (1977) has reviewed a number of studies of minority status children, particularly Black children, who are successful in school and/or score high on IQ tests. These studies all come to similar conclusions. In one of them, McCable et al. identified school children living in East Harlem (New York City) who had full-scale WISC scores of 112 or over, a verbal scale score of 110 or over, and a performance scale score of 115 or over. From nine elementary schools in this area, achievement test scores were obtained for 67 children who met these standards from the 2nd through the 4th grade (37 Black children; 23 Puerto Rican children; and 7 White children). Despite these children's high IQ test performance, their achievement was well below what would be predicted. An example of their underachievement is seen in their performance on the Stanford Achievement Test. Of the 67 children, 21 were 1 or more years above level, 21 were less than 1 year above level, 2 were on grade level, and 23 were below grade level. According to Mackler (1977), the clinical summary of this group states that ". . . though well-endowed, well-behaved, and receptive to intellectual stimulation, the children's performance was below their capabilities. Both teachers and parents were too easily satisfied by the children's modest attainment. . . . Parent's interaction with the schools was limited. . . ." (p.11).

According to this point of view the diminished skill development in Black children is the result of cumulative educational deprivation. Ogbu (1978) concludes that many schools fail to prepare Black children for desirable adult roles to the same degree as White children because the schools passively accept the cultural stereotypes that pervade American society. The education by sociocultural group interactions in the Profile data support the conclusion that Blacks are not receiving the same benefits of education as Whites, and the literature implicates the schools and other institutions in the community in this condition of undereducation.

This assessment reflects the situation current at the end of the 1970s, but it does not take into account trends in achievement of Whites and Blacks during this period. Evidence of change in relative levels of attainment in a number of school subject matters over this period has been investigated by Burton and Jones (1982). Using test scores of national probability samples of children ages 9 and 13, as collected by the National Assessment of Educational Progress, they examined differences in average percent correct responses of Whites and Blacks to test items in writing, science, mathematics, social studies, and reading. Between 1970 and 1980, differences between Whites and Blacks declined significantly in all of these subject matters, except for isolated instances in science in 1970 and 1972. The decreasing differences were highly consistent, occurring in both of the 5-year intervals in which the tests were administered, and equally in the 9- and 13-year-old age groups.

Although these reductions in the gap between the scholastic performance of Whites and Blacks are modest in size relative to the size of the difference, the fact that they seem to be continuing is reason for optimism concerning the eventual equalizing of educational opportunity and attainment. There is nothing in these data to support those who allege that efforts during the 1970s to enhance access to quality education have failed; on the contrary, there is every indication that Blacks, and presumably also other sociocultural groups, will improve their relative standing in school attainment if progress of education in the United States continues during the 1980s.

3.4. SUMMARY AND CONCLUSIONS

The Profile study presents an accurate and detailed picture of average vocational test performance in 1980 of the three main sociocultural groups in the United States, namely, Whites, Blacks, and Hispanics. For the 10 tests of the Armed Services Vocational Aptitude Battery it reveals how performance of these groups varies with educational level, economic status, and region of the country. Relative to the total range of test scores, variation from these sources is large, and its very existence prods us to attempt an explanation of the differences seen in the graphical summaries of Figures 3.1 and 3.2. As we have discussed in Section 3.3, theories as to the origin of these differences already exist in the scholarly literature. In the present section we review our conclusions that three of these theories have little or no support and suggest a fourth theory that we believe to be closer to the truth.

Genetic Endowment Theories. In Section 3.3 we documented the fact that books and articles can still be found that invoke theories of more and less favorable genetic endowments as the explanation of behavioral differences between exclusive populations. But we also cited four independent studies—the results of which clearly exclude this possibility for measures of general ability.

One of these studies demonstrated that estimates of the proportions of the genetic makeup arising from the source populations are uncorrelated to general ability. Such correlation is a necessary consequence of a genetic theory of population differences in the trait, and failure to find it effectively rules out the theory.

But perhaps more telling are the cross-fostering studies, also referred to in Section 3.3, in which children from disadvantaged social groups are adopted at an early age into middle-class White families and raised totally within the White sociocultural context. Such children are found to have the same average scores on general intelligence (IQ) tests as children in the White population. The same has been found to happen when lower-class White children are adopted and raised in middle-class homes: Their average scores are at the level of the middle-class population and not at that of the working-class population into which the children were born. These studies show that the demonstrable tendency of performance on IQ tests to be partly heritable within homogeneous populations fails to explain the differences in average performance between exclusive populations. Such differences appear to be concentrated in that part of IQ variation that is controlled by environmental factors.

Formal Models of Status Attainment. Although formal quantitative models have been constructed to account for variation in educational and occupational status, their interpretation is questionable when they use an IQ measure as an explanatory variable. Even when these models successfully describe relationships between status and other variables—without explaining the source of the IQ test performance differences, they do not identify the ultimate causes of the sociocultural group differences. We must therefore seek elsewhere an explanation for the differences we see in the Profile data.

Linguistic Theories. Another theory cogently argued in the literature is what may be called "the linguistic hypothesis." Some researchers suggest that because most test performance and much of school attainment depends upon proficiency in middle-class English, differences observed between sociocultural groups reflect disparities in the quality of language (Bernstein, 1961). There can be no denying that the major sociocultural groups have their distinct variants of English, but it is not clearly established that these differences are important in scholastic attainment or test performance.

The Profile data provide some insight into this question. Insofar as differences between the White and Hispanic groups are concerned, the Profile data suggest that a linguistic factor is involved to some extent. The evidence is the almost complete lack of differences between these groups on the Numerical Operations and Coding Speed tests. Proficiency on these tests is largely independent of language; the cognitive operations required by the tests can be performed in whatever language is convenient for the examinee without interfering with correct response. Only when we examine the tests that require English language proficiency, such as the Word Knowledge and Comprehension tests, do we see a notable difference in the performance of Hispanics and Whites. But the size of the difference is surprisingly small—

less than the difference between Whites and Blacks on these tests. The indication is that the linguistic factor is not a salient determinant of the ability of Hispanics to respond to tests in this battery. Larger differences are seen for such tests as Electronics Information, Mechanical Comprehension, and Auto and Shop Information that require more specialized technical knowledge.

The Profile data therefore suggest that a difference in educational emphasis is more important than the language factor in determining the performance of Hispanics on these vocational tests. The majority of Hispanics have not yet moved into those types of occupations for which specialized technical knowledge is a prerequisite, and their preparation is more limited in these areas. Further evidence for this conclusion is the fact that in the Southeast region, where Hispanics participate more broadly in the economy and enjoy a greater variety of occupations, differences between Whites and Hispanics are almost nonexistent on all of the tests. The Profile data lend some support to the linguistic hypothesis vis-à-vis the White and Hispanic populations, but implicate educational effects equally or more so.

With respect to average performance of the White and Black sociocultural groups, however, there is little if any evidence of a language effect. Differences between the group means for the non-language Numerical Operations and Coding Speed tests are almost as large as those for the tests that place heavy demands on language proficiency. As we have seen, there is an extraordinary uniformity in the gap between average performance of Whites and Blacks on the ASVAB tests. It appears at all education levels, for both poor and nonpoor economic classes and in all regions of the country. It is not purely a regional effect reflecting differences in urban and rural backgrounds. In fact, performance of Blacks varies less across the 4 regions of the country than does that of Whites and Hispanics. It is not limited to lower education groups but also appears among the participants of the Profile study with 13 or more years of school. With minor exceptions, the difference in means between Whites and Blacks is the same for those classified "poor" as it is for those classified "nonpoor."

Early Deprivation Theories. These latter observations bear on yet another theory of group differences to be found in the literature—the theory of cultural and educational deprivation, especially deprivation in the first 6 or 8 years of life. This theory holds that the scholastic performance of disadvantaged children is impaired in the earliest years of schooling and becomes even more noticeable later because of the cumulative effect of generally slower rates of learning.

We have already noted that subsequent researchers have questioned the deprivation hypothesis in its original form and have suggested that levels of educational achievement are affected throughout a person's formative years. Gains in early childhood will not necessarily be retained later; nor is it impossible that educational deficits will be made up.

Moreover, the Profile data do not seem to be in accord with an early deprivation theory. First, if the disparity between Whites and Blacks is due to educational and economic impoverishment, then it should be smaller for the nonpoor group than for the poor. In fact, the difference tends to be larger for the nonpoor. If there is a deprivation effect, it must therefore be affecting poor Whites more than Blacks. Second, we should see reduced differences between Whites and Blacks in the nonpoor 13 + (some college) groups. We would have to expect that Blacks in this more educationally select group are relatively less deprived than, for example, those who have no more than 8 years of education. But again, the differences tend to be largest in the college group and smallest in the 8-year group, so that if there is a deprivation effect, it is acting more on Whites than on Blacks. The pattern of average scores for the sociocultural groups at these four educational levels does not suggest a deprivation effect, unless the term is used so broadly as to be synonymous with uniformly lower levels of scholastic attainment and test performance.

The Community Norm Theory. We believe that the differences seen in Figures 3.1 and 3.2 between the mean scores for Blacks and Whites have a simpler explanation, hinted at in the studies referred to in the final paragraphs of Section 3.3. These studies show that children from the urban Black communities who display relatively high verbal IQ scores (110 or better) do not have levels of school attainment comparable to children of this IQ range from White middle-class communities. The difference in attainment, which is too large to be attributed to regression to the mean for a highly reliable test such as the WISC, suggests rather a lack of standards and challenges that stimulate a higher level of attainment. Schools are charged with teaching those kinds of knowledge and skills that the child cannot learn spontaneously from his surroundings outside the school. They do this by setting standards of performance, especially performance on tests, and challenging the pupils to reach those standards with the aid of the instruction and learning resources that the school offers. To the pupil it appears that the standards are set by the classroom teacher, and in part they are, but no one teacher can make demands on his or her pupils that too greatly exceed those of other teachers in the school. This is because the school is a kind of social system characterized by norms and expectations for student attainment and behavior that largely determine the instructional activities and performance standards of teachers. These points have already been made by Brookover, Beady, Flood, Schwietzer, and Wisenbaker (1979). All members of the school social system participate in the development and maintenance of the school's normative climate and find ways to constrain performance demands from individual teachers that are perceived as inappropriate according to existing norms.

Similarly, no one school can set standards of attainment too far above those of the community in which the school functions. Unless the school is highly selective in admitting students, the community norm will prevail, and the higher standards will not be met. This situation seldom arises, however, because teachers and principals of local schools seldom strive to set an exceptional standard. Moreover, economic exigencies bar schools from attempting to rise much above the community norm. Meeting higher standards requires extra expenditures for better qualified teachers and enhanced instructional materials and facilities. In the face of limited budgets, it is more often the lowest tolerable standard that is met rather than an ideal and seemingly utopian goal. So the compromise between cost and quality is made more or less on the same terms from year to year, the status quo maintained, and the historically prevailing standards perpetuated.

The effect of school standards will be most clearly seen in knowledge and skills that are learned primarily through formal schooling. A good example in the ASVAB test is Arithmetic Reasoning. Most of us know how to do quantitative problem solving only because we have been taught specific strategies and algorithms for their solution. We do not learn to compute volumes and solve ratios and proportions in casual activities outside of school. So it is this sort of test that shows especially large sociocultural group effects and increasing differentiation of the groups at higher levels of education. The same is true of the other specialized technical knowledge tests.

This is not to say that learning outside the school is not also subject to social norms. Each family implicitly or explicitly sets standards for many of the aspects of attainment and behavior of its children. As we see in Chapter 6, the mother necessarily plays a prominent role in this process. But because children influence and are influenced by their peers, no one family can enforce a standard too high above that of the community. Indeed, many families may have no clear conception of a standard other than that which emerges by an informal consensus out of the typical behavior patterns of friends and relatives. (See Blau, 1981, for a discussion of the significance of the social milieu of families as distinguished from SES, for children's scholastic achievement).

If we view individual behavior as largely an adaptation to the demands of a person's immediate social environment, we realize that children whose horizons are limited respond primarily to the norms of the community in which they play their part. These norms determine most of their speech, conduct, interests, aspirations, and motivations. The average effect of such determinants of behavior can be greatly different in communities that, for historical reasons, have been separated from the majority culture by barriers of communication and cultural interchange for many generations. In the United States the major sociocultural groups, and perhaps to a lesser extent the smaller ethnic communities, have existed under conditions that have encouraged the development of different norms.

In the case of a test such as Coding Speed, for example, it must be this broader social process, involving all of the community and not just the schools, that explains the difference in performance between Blacks and Whites. The Coding Speed test, which has no formal educational content beyond the ability to recognize words and numbers, is mainly an exercise in organizing and performing a simple task as rapidly as possible. The examinee's level of motivation is critical, as is his or her typical pace of doing any sort of paper-and-pencil task. That Blacks and Whites with 13 or more years of education should differ considerably in their average performance on this test can only be understood as differences in norms in responding to this arbitrary kind of task. Blacks and Whites must interpret differently the test instructions to mark the items "as fast as you can."

Although we have cited studies that cast doubt on a rigidly interpreted theory of early deprivation as the source of the sociocultural group differences, we would also take the somewhat similar position that a community standard, once internalized by a particular person, is not easy to change. Thus, the most dramatic effect of change of standards is seen in the cross-fostering studies discussed above, in which children were moved entirely out of one community and into another early in life. To effect such a change in an older child would require more than a short-term intervention. In young people and adults such a change would be even more difficult. This would explain why the average performance of Blacks in the service training schools, discussed in Appendix B, is in accord with their lower average scores on the ASVAB tests. The training school is a kind of intervention, but it is too limited to make a profound change in habitual modes of responding to training and instruction.

The community norm theory also helps us to understand the regional differences in the ASVAB test performance of the Hispanics. The different groups of Hispanics in the United States, having migrated from different parts of Latin America, and having brought with them norms typical not only of different countries but also of different economic strata, maintain typical levels of average response because of the inertia within communities that makes institutions function in much the same way from one year to another. The differences reinforce themselves: Higher levels of attainment bring the resources that make such levels easier to maintain; lower levels deprive communities of the skills and leadership needed to create a higher standard.

If the community norm interpretation of sociocultural group differences is correct, it would suggest that schools have a special role to play in raising community standards. The school is the main interface between the larger society and the local community. It is the avenue by which young people can be introduced to a broader view and higher aspiration. It can challenge the community to a more stringent standard—if not in the present generation then in the next, as the youth begin to take their place in the work and leadership of the community. The response to such initiative may be quite slow, measured in decades and generations, but the ultimate consequences in terms of the economic health of the nation and the well-being of all of its people are so great that that effort has to be made. And the effort must especially be made in those communities where for too long very modest levels of attainment have been accepted as the norm, with little hope or belief that they can be changed.

Just such an effort has been underway in the Atlanta, Georgia public schools since about 1972. Alonzo Crim, the superintendent of Atlanta public schools, outlined a plan in 1981 that he projected would help pupils in this public school system to achieve at the national norm in basic numerical and verbal skills by 1985. Crim described this as a "bold goal" in view of the fact that the great majority of the students served by the Atlanta public schools are Black and poor; the school system is perceived by the larger community as low-achieving; and the pupils in the system have scored well below the national norms on standardized tests of achievement since the testing program was introduced into the system. Central to the plan that Crim advanced is the development of what he terms a "community of believers" in the ability of children to meet this goal (i.e., a change in the community norm of student achievement), which he views as a critical step in building pupils' commitment to learning and attainment. With the support of students, parents, educators, business persons, members of the clergy, the media, and the citizens-at-large, Crim reported steady progress toward the 1985 attainment goal between 1980 and 1982 (Crim, 1981, 1983) and achieved this goal in 1983—2 years early (personal communication). The remarkable gains seen in the academic achievement of Atlanta public school children in a 10-year period attest to the significant influence of the community norm on student achievement and to the role that educators can play in helping to upgrade the norm of achievement that characterizes the communities that their schools serve.

That these and similar programs of educational enrichment aimed primarily at disadvantaged children are beginning to have a positive effect is documented at the end of Section 3.3. Analysis of surveys of school achievement carried out during the 1970s by the National Assessment of Educational Progress reveals that differences between Whites and Blacks ages 9 and 13 are steadily decreasing. If these trends can be maintained by consistently applied programs to raise community standards and enhance the quantity and quality of education, the sociocultural group differences seen in the Profile study of 1980 should decline substantially over the next 10 or 20 years.

4 The Effects of Mother's Education and Respondent's Age and Education

The educational, cultural, economic, and regional influences examined in the previous chapter ultimately affect vocational potential through factors in the developing child's immediate environment. In this chapter we argue that mother's education, which is among the best predictors of the cognitive characteristics of her offspring at maturity, is the most important of these factors.

In addition, we also attempt to disentangle the effects of the respondent's age and education on the development of the skills assessed by ASVAB. To a great extent, increasing years of education are confounded with increasing age because legal requirements for young people's school enrollment and attendance tend to create educational cohorts from birth cohorts. But, because of differences in grade promotions and individual decisions to leave school prior to secondary school graduation, educational cohorts and birth cohorts in the Profile are not identical. We therefore have some information in the data about age and education that enables us to estimate them separately. Our analysis of age effects is based primarily on summaries of the Profile study showing the test performance of persons of different ages who have completed the same number of years of schooling.

4.1. MOTHER'S EDUCATION

Most of the previous research on the influence of family-background variables dealt with intellectual ability and employed IQ tests, which measure mainly general verbal skills. The Profile data go considerably beyond this, however, and also measure more specific attainments. We are therefore able to examine the effects of one of the most important of the family-background variables, mother's education, on a wide range of skills.

Results of the Profile Study

Although we find highly significant main effects of mother's education for each of the ASVAB tests, we find, somewhat to our surprise, only weak interactions with the other background variables. Earlier research literature would suggest appreciable interaction effects between mother's education, sex, and sociocultural group (Featherman, 1980; Laosa, 1983). But we have found only minor effects, involving most prominently Auto and Shop Information, and to a lesser extent the other specialized knowledge tests. For most of the tests, mother's education has only the highly regular main effects plotted in Figure 4.1. Generally, as mother's education increases, the mean performance of the respondents increases, but the strength of this trend varies from one test to another.

Fluent Production.   In the two tests where females have an advantage over males—Numerical Operations and Coding Speed (see Chapter 5)—mother's education is seen to have a relatively small effect on Coding Speed scores. For Coding Speed, the mean difference between respondents whose mothers have 0 to 8 years of education and those whose mothers have earned at least a college degree is about 60 points. But having a mother with 16 or more years of education gives only a slight advantage in Coding Speed score over having a mother with a high school diploma. Apparently, there is a limit to the influence that a more favorable family environment can have on this simple performance test.

A somewhat different pattern is seen for Numerical Operations. The performance advantage of respondents whose mothers have college degrees or more education, relative to those whose mothers have no more than an 8th grade education, is modestly larger at 75 points. But unlike the effects for Coding Speed, having a mother with 16 or more years of education greatly enhances respondents' performance on Numerical Operations. A possible interpretation is that the Numerical Operations task, which all children are expected to master, is more sensitive to mother's press for children's scholastic attainment than is the more recondite Coding Speed task.

Specialized Knowledge and Quantitative Skills.   The relationship of respondent's performance to mother's educational level is similar and strong for all the more academic topics—Word Knowledge, Paragraph Comprehension, Arithmetic Reasoning, General Science, and Mathematics Knowledge. The effect is greatest for Mathematics Knowledge, where respondents whose

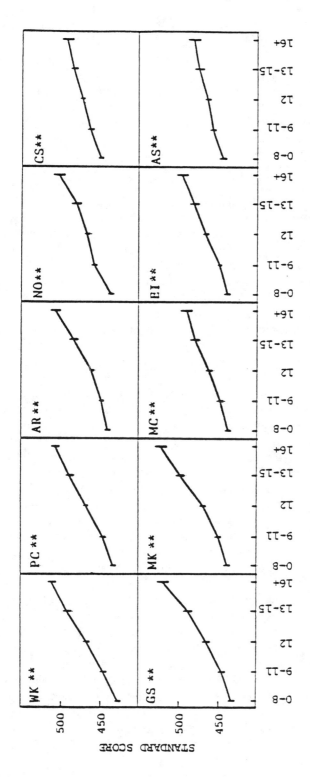

FIG. 4.1. Effects of mother's education (mother's highest grade completed)
$**F > 1.25F(.01)$

mothers have college degrees outperform those whose mothers are in the lowest educational level by a full standard deviation. As mother's education increases from some high school to the highest educational level, there is a steady and substantial increase in respondents' performance on this test.

At the other extreme, the young people's performance on Mechanical Comprehension, Electronic Information, and Auto and Shop Information is not affected nearly as much by mother's education, although the trend is still positive. The least affected is Auto and Shop Information: changes in mother's education are accompanied by only small increases in Auto and Shop Information. Since this subject matter is more likely to be learned through outside experience than in school, the mother's education may not be as important. In other words, mother's education appears to be most important for attainment in school-intensive skills. The effects of mother's education on Mechanical Comprehension and Electronics Information are very similar. For both these subtests, the difference in the performance of respondents whose mothers have a college degree and those whose mothers have an 8th grade education or less is about 75 points.

There is a steady increase in average performance on all the tests with mother's education, but the amount of gain to the respondent is less for the specialized knowledge tests than for the more academically oriented tests. We may be seeing here the effect of the learning ability inherited from the mother and achievement values acquired from her, but not necessarily the direct contribution of knowledge and instruction that the mother could offer in less technical areas where she is likely to have some attainment if she is sufficiently educated.

Note, however, that for the specialized knowledge tests, the mother's education main effect in Figure 4.1 is not a complete description of the variation. There is in addition some degree of interaction with sex and with sociocultural group. The interaction with sex, most apparent in the Electronics Information test, is plotted in Figure 4.2. There is a small but regular tendency for sons' scores to increase more than daughters' as mother's education increases. An obvious, and quite satisfactory, explanation would be the effect that sex-role expectations have on how young people apply the advantage an educated mother brings to the home in the development of these specific skills. Male offspring, for example, with their greater interest in technical material, may be more likely to apply the advantage an educated mother brings to the home to the study of electronics than would female offspring. The size of this interaction seems, however, too small to be of any practical importance.

The interaction of mother's education with sociocultural group, shown for General Science and Auto and Shop Information in Figure 4.3, is more interesting. It appears that performance on these tests is more strongly dependent on mother's education in the Hispanic group than in the other two

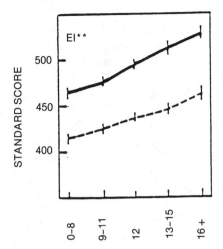

FIG. 4.2. Interaction of mother's education (mother's highest grade completed) and sex. Male —— Female ---   **$F > 1.25F(.01)$

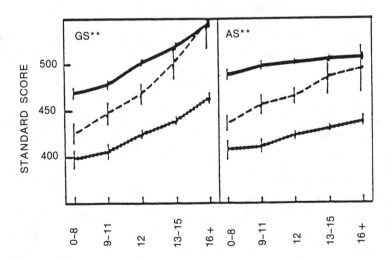

FIG. 4.3. Interaction of sociocultural group and mother's education (mother's highest grade completed).
White —— Hispanic ------ Black · · · ·
**$F > 1.25F(.01)$

groups. The group effect is concentrated mainly in the range from only-high-school education to college-graduate.

Among offspring of mothers with only-high-school education, the Hispanics are about 30 points below Whites, but among those whose mothers have college degrees, Hispanics and Whites perform at essentially the same level; Hispanics are slightly higher than Whites in General Science and Whites slightly higher than Hispanics in Auto and Shop Information. That this effect is seen mainly in the specialized knowledge tests suggests a press for achievement in homes with better educated mothers that is turned more towards scientific and technical pursuits in Hispanic homes than in White or Black homes. This orientation is suggested by Brown, Rosen, Hill, and Olivas (1980), who report that a higher proportion of Hispanic youth who pursue postsecondary educational programs are enrolled in noncollegiate schools than in four-year colleges. In addition, a higher proportion of Hispanics in noncollegiate programs are enrolled in trade and industrial technologies than is true for Whites enrolled in similar institutions. Astin (1982) also reports that a higher proportion of Hispanic students in four-year colleges identified themselves as engineering majors in their freshman year of college in 1971 than was true for Blacks or Whites, though the proportion who actually obtained baccalaureate degrees in engineering was nearly identical to that of White students.

As we have pointed out in Chapter 3, much the opposite is true of Blacks. In the absence of abundant role models in the scientific fields, Blacks from homes with well-educated mothers look more to the nontechnical fields and prepare themselves accordingly. As a result, the trend for increased scores on the specialized knowledge tests with increasing mother's education is weaker among Blacks than among Hispanics and Whites. Compared to the main effect of mother's education, however, the difference in response to the specialized information tests among the sociocultural groups is relatively small.

Summary of Mother's Education Effects. We attach special significance to the fact that mother's education interacts only weakly with the other background factors. We take this as an indication that specific familial effects, genetic and cultural, act in a summative manner with those general effects of school and community that impinge on all subjects. Of course, the mother's educational level is itself a response to both familial and community influences, but the contributions are linear, not multiplicative, and no interaction of the two types of influence appears. That such effects are simply additive justifies in a certain way the separation of the disciplines of developmental psychology, which concentrates on the intra-familial influences, from social psychology and sociology, which concentrate on the extra-familial influences on behavior and attainment. Taken together, the present data indicate that the familial effect indexed by mother's education is greatest on the offspring's academic skills represented in the ASVAB by Word Knowledge, Mathematics Knowledge, General Science, Arithmetic Reasoning, and Paragraph Comprehension. The mother's educational level has a smaller effect on the respondents' achievement on the fluent production items (Coding Speed and Numerical Operations) and on technical skills (Mechanical Comprehension and Electronics Information). The smallest effect of all is seen on Auto and Shop Information. In general, those young people who have mothers with a college degree have developed higher skills in all areas tested than those whose mothers have less education. Young people whose mothers have 8 years or less education show the lowest level of skill development in all areas. While having a mother with some high school increases the offspring's performance, the largest gains are seen among respondents whose mothers have achieved a high school diploma and a college diploma.

The general pattern of the effects of mother's education is consistent with the existing literature on the relationship between mother's socioeconomic status (which uses educational attainment as an index of social status) and her children's general ability (measured, for example, by IQ tests). In the present data, the advantage of having a highly educated mother is pervasive for offspring's performance across all tests. The fact that mother's education has a strong effect on offsprings' Word Knowledge is also consistent with the empirical and theoretical literature. Females' general superiority in language (Maccoby & Jacklin, 1974) is probably amplified at the upper educational levels, resulting in more verbally complex environments for individuals with highly educated mothers. These data generally support Williams' (1976) observations that highly educated parents tend to provide more complex learning environments for their children and encourage academic excellence.

The Process of Mother-Child Interaction

Although there is abundant evidence that the socioeconomic status of the family, as indexed by mother's and father's education, occupation and income, is strongly related to offspring's educational and occupational attainment (Jencks et al. 1972, 1979), the specific factors that mediate the action of this complex of demographic variables remain obscure. One finds in the developmental literature a body of research based on the theory that the effective agent of these macroenvironmental factors is the early mother-child interaction. Much of the effort of developmental psychologists has been to identify in families of different social strata the processes of mother-child interaction that contribute to social class differences in early cognitive development, achievement orientations, values, and learning styles (Chan & Rueda, 1979; Crandall, Preston, & Rabson, 1969; Farran, Haskins, & Gallagher, 1980; Hess & Shipman, 1965; Witkin, Dyk, Paterson, Goodenough,

& Karp, 1962; Wolf, 1964). In large part, their work has been stimulated by the observations that individual and group differences in these aspects of behavior appear early in life, prior to systematic experiences with cultural institutions beyond the family. This suggests that the family is the dominant conveyor of cultural conventions and that mothers, who in all societies are invested with early caregiving, are the primary mediators of children's early development of skills, attitudes, and beliefs. If recent trends continue, the mother's influence in this role can only increase in the United States as the number of children reared in mother-only families grows with the increasing rate of divorce and the rise in the number of children born to never-married women (Glick, 1979). Because of all these influences, cultural variations in mothers' attitudes, beliefs, expectations, and aspirations regarding their children may be expected to leave their mark on vocational test scores in the form of group differences in performance.

Conversely, the socioeconomic status of the family influences the pattern of maternal behaviors that in turn affect children's intellectual and emotional development as well as school success. Family socioeconomic status has been found to be related to the amount, variety, and complexity of the stimulation that mothers provide (Dave, 1963; Jordan, 1978; Tulkin & Covitz, 1975; Tulkin & Kagan, 1972). It is also related to the style of interactions in the home, especially language behavior and maternal control strategies (Bernstein, 1961; Blau, 1981; Streissguth & Bee, 1972), and to maternal teaching strategies (Hess & Shipman, 1965; Hess, Shipman, Brophy, & Bear, 1969). All of these behaviors appear relevant to children's cognitive and affective development, both by shaping intellectual processes and affective modes in children during the early years and by inducing a motivation to learn (Slaughter, 1983: Slaughter & Epps, forthcoming).

Many sociologists aggregate the mother's educational attainment with other indices of family socioeconomic status (i.e., parents' occupational and income attainment) to develop a global index of social class. However, some investigators believe that parental education in general, and mother's education in particular, is the most salient of these sociodemographic variables in determining learning strategies and values related to later school success (Hess, 1970; Jordan, 1978; McClendon, 1976; Willerman & Stafford, 1972; Laosa, 1982). Laosa (1982) theorizes that the high frequency of scholastic failure observed among young people from minority status groups may be explained largely by the fact that their parents, particularly their mothers, have generally completed fewer years of schooling. Laosa's conclusions are drawn from a series of comparative studies of intact Anglo- and Mexican-American families and their preschool children specifically designed to disentangle the effects of culture, parental education, and parental occupation on children's scholastic attainment. His data indicate that the amount of schooling completed by the mother is a major determinant of both the press for verbal skill development in the preschool years, and of the mother-child interaction processes in the home that provide children with the opportunity to master "the forms and dynamics of teaching and learning processes" that have adaptive value in the classroom (Laosa, 1982, p.   800). Neither mother's nor father's occupational status was found to have a significant relationship to any of the parental behaviors examined in the Mexican-American subsamples; in the Anglo subsample, father's occupation was related only to maternal aspirations for the child's educational attainment.

Value orientations and community norms appear to underlie many of the differences in socialization observed between families that differ in amount of parental education (Blau, 1981; Kohn, 1977). Slaughter concludes from a review of the literature on parental influences on education (1983) that parental values toward education in general, and achievement in school in particular, are important determinants of their offsprings' motivation to become knowledgeable and, thus perhaps the salient influence on scholastic attainment of young people as they mature. With more education, parents tend to be more vigilant of their children's academic achievement and more likely to consult their children's teachers and principals about their children's progress (Douglas, 1964). Better educated parents appear more attuned to the requirements of upward social mobility, particularly the importance of scholastic attainment, and they consciously prepare and encourage their children and monitor their progress in meeting these requirements (LeVine, 1973).

In addition to transmitting behavioral orientations to her children socially, the mother transmits half her genes to her offspring, and thus influences biologically the behavior of her children. Moreover, there is in the United States and other developed countries considerable assortative mating with respect to intellectual characteristics (Vandenberg, 1972). As a result, the attainments of the mother are substantially correlated with those of the father, and thus provide a convenient and often more accessible index of the father's contribution to both cultural and biological transmission of behavioral traits. For all these reasons, the mother's characteristics are among the best predictors of the characteristics of her offspring at maturity.

Socialization and Mother's Education

Erickson (1968), having observed considerable differences in the childrearing practices of diverse cultures, concluded that there is a logic to socialization of children based on the group's understanding of what the child is to become and where he or she will find a livelihood. Parents' social values learned in the surroundings in which they grew up, and their concepts of competence based on personal experience or that of friends and relatives, will determine what they believe the child can achieve and how they may help him or her to realize the goal. It is not surprising, therefore, that educated middle-class mothers are able to induce skills and attitudes in their children that give them long-term advantages over lower-class children in competition for position and resources. We have commented on the fact that middle-class families are more attuned to the need for mobility and resource-fulness, and consciously set about preparing their children to meet these requirements.

Referring to the childrearing of university-educated American parents, LeVine (1973) characterizes their practices as an attempt to "rationalize the process of socialization by consciously gearing both ends and means to infor-mation feedback from a changing environment" (p. 516). Levine suggests that educated parents are conscious of the fact that criteria for evaluating behavior are in a constant state of change and that their children will be assessed by different standards than they have experienced. These parents therefore search out information on the emerging selective pressures, relying on childrearing experts as a resource, and self-consciously acting as media-tors of environmental feedback to their children. In rationalizing the sociali-zation process, highly educated parents are attempting to transmit their socioeconomic advantage to their children.

The results of the present study can be understood as an outcome of that process. The strong mother's education effects observed for performance in academic areas, especially in Mathematics Knowledge, Arithmetic Reasoning, General Science, Word Knowledge, and Paragraph Comprehension, indicate that more highly educated parents are rewarded with a high level of skill development in their children. Parents from groups that have not fully parti-cipated in the American "mainstream," however, have less basis for knowing what competencies are or will be required for social mobility in their children's generation. Research also shows that mothers in the lower social strata are not aware that they can influence the development of their children's skills through specific activities (Tulkin & Kagan, 1972). Chan and Rueda (1979) conclude that social class differences in parenting behaviors arise from "inadequate access to knowledge and information concerning the requirements and techniques of socialization" (p. 425). These effects offer some explanation for the difference in response to mother's education seen in different sociocultural groups in Figure 4.3.

Why differential access to this type of information and its implementation exists is not clear. What is clear is that socialization strategies vary among sociocultural groups and that one of the consequences is intergenerational transmission of inequality. There is no question that various sociocultural groups show different levels of skill development. Nor is there any question about the probable consequences of differential skill development for voca-tional prospects. However, whether or not persons in low-scoring groups can be helped to develop greater levels of skill through providing more edu-cational and vocational information to parents, and to mothers in particular, is an open question. We remain optimistic that low-achieving individuals in these groups can be helped to develop competitive skills through better counseling of parents and children, programs to broaden vocationally relevant experiences, and more instruction in basic skills. While some may argue that such efforts have been tried and have failed, they should be reminded that these earlier programs were generally poorly conceived, based on erroneous assumptions regarding the nature of the problem and the efficacy of different interventions, and hastily implemented (see Horowitz & Paden, 1973, for a critical review).

A direct and promising strategy would be greater exposure to a variety of occupations. Isolated, poor, minority status young people would profit from this increased exposure, especially if accompanied by clear discussions of the necessary skills for success in these occupations. It is now believed that one factor contributing to the lower academic achievement of poor and minority status young people is their failure to perceive the relevance of specific school subject matter for their later occupational prospects (Ogbu, 1978). Generally, teachers do not have the time, or do not take the time, to demonstrate the relevance of academic subject matter. Family members are less likely to be able to perform this function effectively because, with their limited educational and occupational experiences, they do not have the first-hand experience or specific knowledge to do so. While better vocational information and counseling may not eliminate variations in skill development, it seems a reasonable and efficient strategy to attenuate the differences.

4.2. AGE AND EDUCATION

The analyses discussed in Chapters 2 and 3 do not include age as a background factor because the addition of another factor would have made the design unmanageably large and spread the data too sparsely over the smallest subclasses. Thus, the effects of highest grade completed are not distinguished from those of age in these discussions. Clearly, most subjects with some college will be older than those with less than 12 years completed and so on. The increase in test performance with increasing years of education seen in Chapters 5 and 6 could thus be equally well interpreted with respect to increasing age. To distinguish age from education effects, we must examine the test performance of persons of different ages who have the same number of years of schooling.

In this investigation we take advantage of the fact that mother's education interacts only in a minor way with other background factors. It justifies the collapsing of that classification so that age can be added. By ignoring mother's education, we can fit a model similar to that represented in Table C-2 in Appendix C, but also include age, age by sex, age by sociocultural group, age by highest grade completed, age by poverty, and age by sociocultural group by highest grade completed. The multivariate tests indicate that all but the triple interaction of age, sociocultural group, and highest grade completed are significant. We therefore fitted a model including all age-related terms except the latter.

For present purposes, we are primarily interested in the age by education interaction. Of the six possible contrasts for interaction of the three age groups and four education levels, only four can be estimated. The two remaining contrasts are confounded because there are no subjects with one year of college in the 15–17 age group, and only a few who have completed high school. When plotting the effects of age by highest grade completed, as in Figure 4.4, we therefore omit in the 15–17 year age group the points for 12 and 13 + grades completed

We are justified in examining the age by grade interactions if these two factors do not appear in any significant three-factor interaction. Inasmuch as the most likely candidate—the age by grade by sociocultural group interaction—was not found to be significant, we will assume the triple interactions of age and grade with sex, region, and poverty are also nonsignificant. We therefore proceed to interpret the estimated age effects in respondents with similar amounts of education as indexed by highest grade completed. Effects of all other background factors are eliminated from these estimates.

Age and grade effects on test performance are difficult to interpret because at least four distinct influences are at work to increase or decrease scores:

1. *Average age at grade.* It is well known to educational researchers that children who are more than six months younger than the average age for their grade in school have generally higher scholastic ability than their classmates. This occurs because such pupils include highly precocious children who have been advanced over one or more grades. Generally, these children are not advanced so far that they fall below the average of the class in achievement; in fact, they are usually found near the top of their class in spite of their younger age. For the opposite reason, children who are more than six months older than the average age for their grade in school tend to be below average in ability; they include children who have been held back until they can meet minimal standards for their grade. Because of the age-at-grade effect, we expect a deficit in test performance when an older group is compared with a group that is at the expected age for grade.

2. *Lack of practice and forgetting.* When people of any age leave off formal schooling, they may begin to forget, through lack of practice and disuse, the more academic content of what they were taught. Arithmetic and mathematical skills are particularly susceptible to these

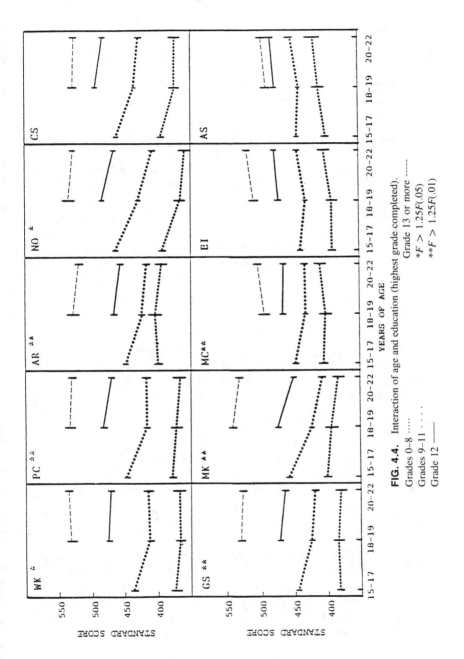

FIG. 4.4. Interaction of age and education (highest grade completed).

Grades 0–8 ⋯⋯

Grades 9–11 ⋯⋯⋯

Grade 12 ——

Grade 13 or more ------

*$F > 1.25F(.05)$

**$F > 1.25F(.01)$

effects because their practice is limited to special occupations. Most students retested on this type of material some years after leaving school will tend to show decreased scores.

3. *Experiential learning.* The converse of 2 above, some skills of a practical nature tend to improve with experience, at least into middle age. Word Knowledge, for example, tends to increase somewhat through the third and fourth decade of life as the cumulative result of contact with language.

4. *Cohort effects.* Changing curricular emphasis and instructional practice may be reflected in differences between average test scores of cohorts who passed through the school systems at different times. The well-publicized decline in nationwide average Scholastic Aptitude Test Scores is believed to be due in part to changes in the curriculum and relaxing of academic standards in the high schools during the 1960s and '70s. These effects can appear as age differences when cross-sectional data are analyzed. But they are really cohort differences that have nothing to do with developmental changes within persons.

Some or all of the above influences may be seen in the results plotted· in Figure 4.4. It is apparent, however, that when these influences are at work, they are acting in much different mixtures in the various ASVAB tests. Among respondents with the same amount of schooling, the Electronics Information and Auto and Shop Information scores appear to be generally benefitting from the experience that comes with age. As we observed earlier, this is the kind of knowledge that is acquired mostly outside of school, so much so that persons with only an 8th grade education can increase their scores over the years from 18 to 22 just as much as those in college. A similar but weaker effect is seen in Mechanical Comprehension.

One reason that experiential learning effects can readily be seen in these types of tests is that they are not criteria for scholastic advancement or holding back. They are therefore not subject to the age-at-grade phenomenon that works in the opposite direction (i.e., produces higher scores in younger persons with the same amount of formal education). This permits gains with increasing age to be clearly seen.

Word Knowledge, General Science, and possibly Paragraph Comprehension also measure knowledge that would be expected to accrue with experience in this age range. But these tests are closely related to criteria for educational attainment, and so would be subject to the age-at-grade phenomenon. The result is consistent with what we see in the plots for these tests: rather small changes, some positive and some negative, between ages within educational levels.

Mathematics Knowledge, Arithmetic Reasoning, possibly Coding Speed, and most prominently, Numerical Operations, appear to combine the age-at-grade phenomenon with the deleterious effects of disuse and forgetting. The older groups at the same educational levels perform more poorly, in some cases much more poorly, than the younger age groups. The contrast with the Electronics Information and Auto and Shop tests in this regard suggests the deterioration of skill rather than continued learning once formal education is terminated. A more optimistic interpretation would be that in these quantitative areas we are seeing cohort effects resulting from improved instruction in mathematics. If the younger groups received better instruction in quantitative skills they might score better on these particular tests. For this to happen in the Profile sample would, however, require a nationwide change of instructional practice in a relatively short time—an unlikely possibility. Lacking any independent evidence for such a change, we might explain these effects more reasonably as the result of knowledge and skills in the numerical and mathematical area not being maintained as well as those in the more verbal and practical topics. This is less true among college level people, and certainly would not be true of young people specializing in these areas, but such people are relatively few and do not much influence the broadly based sample in the Profile study.

The more general conclusion that must be drawn from the mean scores displayed in Figure 4.4 is that, for the most part, test performance tends to be typical of the highest grade completed. With possible notable exceptions in individual cases, most of those young people who drop out of school with not more than eight grades completed, or without graduating from high school, have little opportunity or inclination to improve their abilities in areas represented by the more academic of the ASVAB tests. Even their improvement in the practical areas is small relative to the large differences between education levels.

The deleterious effect on vocational opportunities of lower performance levels of persons who drop out of school will be considerable and will ameliorate little as they grow older. The broader educational implication of the age-by-grade effects would seem to be that efforts toward more complete schooling of all young people who are to any reasonable degree capable of it will benefit both them and the society at large. This is especially true of the Hispanics, who, as we have seen in Chapter 2, have excessively high drop-out rates.

4.3. SUMMARY AND CONCLUSIONS

This chapter deals with two variables influencing vocational test performance that are related by their direct role in the personal development of young people. One of these is the years of education of the mother; the other is the number of years of schooling that a person has completed by a given age.

Mother's Education

Increasing level of mother's education—from grade school only, some high school, completed high school, some college, to completed college—is directly and strongly related to higher scores on all tests in the ASVAB battery. The relationship is stronger for the tests that are more academically oriented, namely, Word Knowledge, Paragraph Comprehension, Arithmetic Reasoning, Numerical Operations, General Science, and Mathematics Knowledge. It is weaker for the tests that assess knowledge acquired experientially, namely, Mechanical Comprehension, Electronics Information, and Auto and Shop Information, and also for Coding Speed, which is a performance task. The implication is that the mother's educational values, if not her direct instruction, prime her children for achievement in areas that are part of, and identified with, school learning. Other types of attainment, while benefiting from better home resources (and possibly heritable potential) contributed by a better educated mother, are less directly affected and do not increase as much with increasing years of education of the mother.

Mother's education shows only limited and very minor interactions with other background factors. In very technical topics such as Electronics Information, there is a slight but significant tendency for sons to benefit more than daughters from increased mother's education. Presumably this is due to sons making better use of mother's contribution to home resources in this male-stereotyped area.

A somewhat stronger interaction appears between sociocultural group and mother's education for two of the tests, namely, General Science and Auto-Shop Information. It is due entirely to improved performance of offspring of Hispanic mothers with education beyond high school. Studies of course participation in higher education suggest that Hispanics who are oriented toward higher education favor technical programs. Those with less academic interests, but whose family backgrounds direct them toward more economically rewarding occupations, frequently choose mechanical and construction trades. These tendencies appear to be more marked in Hispanics than in Whites or Blacks, and thus appear to explain the interaction.

The fact that these interactions are small relative to the overall effect of mother's education, and all other interaction of background factors with mother's education are statistically insignificant, indicates that variables that influence achievement through the mother's contribution to her offspring are largely independent of the broad social and cultural effects on attainment that we have examined in Chapter 3. They are for the most part also independent of the influences of sex of offspring that we consider in Chapter 5.

Studies in the literature that have inquired into the role of the mother in shaping the educational and vocational achievement of her children emphasize the guidance she can provide to the best opportunities in these areas. Better educated mothers are much better informed in this respect than the poorer educated, and their children benefit accordingly. Programs that provide greater counseling and experiences with vocations, both to parents and offspring, have promise for extending educational and vocational opportunities to all segments of society.

Age and Education

Examining mean scores of persons in the age range of 15 to 17 who have completed up to 8 grades compared to those who have some high school, and those in the 18 through 19, and 20 through 22, age groups who have up to 8 grades, some high school, completed high school or some college, we find evidence that performance on some of the ASVAB tests improves with age independent of education and on others deteriorates. As we might expect, it is the school intensive subjects, Mathematics Knowledge, Arithmetic Reasoning, and, most prominently, Numerical Operations, in which the older respondents at the same education levels perform more poorly. Perhaps the most plausible explanation is simple forgetting of facts and loss of skills due to disuse.

Conversely, the knowledge that is acquired and maintained by experience outside of school, represented here by Electronics Information and Auto and Shop Information, improves with age among respondents with the same education. Areas represented by the remaining tests are intermediate between these extremes.

These age by education interactions are not, however, the dominant impression conveyed by these comparisons of respondents classified by age and highest grade completed. The more general conclusion is that, regardless of age, vocational test performance tends to remain near the level of the highest grade completed. In particular, failure to complete high school argues poorly for meeting vocational test standards at a later time through informal learning and experience.

5 Sex Effects

Although women's share in the total U.S. labor market continues to increase, their relative numbers in many occupations remain much different than those of men. Census figures confirm that females are under-represented in the more prestigious and higher paying occupations such as engineering, science, mathematics, business management, and the skilled trades. And they are over-represented in limited-income jobs such as clerical work, elementary school teaching, and nursing. Why this pattern should exist, and the extent to which it is conditioned by personal capacities and preferences as opposed to sociocultural sex-role expectations and proscriptions, are questions that have stimulated much study and controversy.

In a comprehensive review of research on sex differences in behavior, Maccoby and Jacklin (1974) concluded that certain differences in the cognitive performance of males and females are clearly established beginning in early adolescence and increasing through high school. Girls have greater verbal ability than boys; beginning in adolescence and continuing to maturity, boys increasingly excel in visiospatial ability and in mathematical ability. More recent studies have qualified these generalizations on several points: the greater verbal ability of girls applies to fluency of verbal articulation and production, and not to greater work knowledge or verbal reasoning ability; sex differences in verbal fluency and visiospatial ability can be observed prior to adolescence if tests suitable for younger children are used (Bock, Zimowski, & Laciny, 1986); Linn & Petersen, 1985).

Jacklin (1979), however, has warned that these conclusions must be viewed with caution because of the limitations of the data from which they derive; nearly all of these findings are based on samples of White middle-class subjects. She considers the apparent sex-related differences in cognitive abilities, though potentially significant for occupational choices, to be only tentatively established and to require broader verification.

In large measure the present study provides this verification. The Profile data assess sex-related differences in cognitive and vocational test performance in the larger socioeconomic and cultural milieu of this country. These data are, of course, descriptive and cannot be used to address all issues concerning sex differences. In particular, they do not speak directly to the question of causes. But combined with an extensive research literature, they provide a background for theorizing about the origins of sex-related differences in test performance observed in the profile sample.

To put the sex differences in their proper perspective, we must point out that the size of these differences varies greatly among the ASVAB tests. Sex differences for the five cognitive tests, Word Knowledge, Paragraph Comprehension, Arithmetic Reasoning, Numerical Operations, and Coding Speed, are statistically significant but small relative to the size of the differences we have seen between education levels and sociocultural groups. Differences for the technical knowledge tests, General Science, Auto and Shop Information, Mathematical Knowledge, Mechanical Comprehension, and Electronics Information, include some of the larger effects seen in the data. As we shall discuss, the differences are greatest in the tests that require information about occupations that are predominantly pursued by men.

In addition, the classification by sex interacts with education and with sociocultural group and economic status in determining test performance. Thus, while main effects of sex clearly exist (females generally perform better than males in Paragraph Comprehension, Numerical Operations, and Coding Speed; whereas males perform better than females in Arithmetic Reasoning, Auto and Shop Information, Mechanical Comprehension, Mathematics Knowledge, and Electronics Information), these effects are best understood in the context of the interactions between sex and other background variables.

The picture is simplified by the fact that the stronger interactions do not extend beyond sex and education, and sex, sociocultural group, and economic status. The interactions of sex and age, sex and region, or sex and mother's education, are negligible in comparison.

5.1. SEX BY EDUCATION EFFECTS

The interaction between sex and highest grade completed is displayed in Figures 5.1a and b. The performance of males and females with 0 to 8, 9–11, 12, and 13 or more years of education is shown in terms of the standard scores for each subtest (mean = 500, standard deviation = 100). These graphs reveal various patterns of sexual differentiation in test performance by educational level as follows.

Specialized Knowledge. Sex differences in achievement increase with increased years of education for those tests that assess technical knowledge, namely, General Science, Auto and Shop Information, Mechanical Comprehension, and Electronics Information. These areas of knowledge can be described as traditional male specialties where sex differences would be expected.

In General Science, the males in the sample with 0 to 8 years of education score only slightly higher than females; but with some high school and high school completion, the difference favoring males increases to about 35 points, and at 13+, to about 50 points. A similar pattern of increasing differences

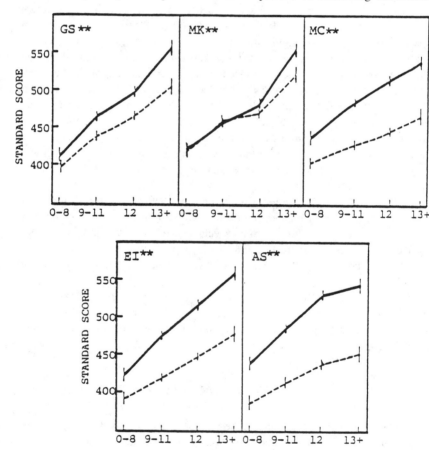

FIG. 5.1a. Interaction of sex and education (highest grade completed). White —— Hispanic ------ Black · · · ·

with education also is seen for Mechanical Comprehension: at the lowest educational level, the difference in favor of males is 30 points; with some college, the males outperform females by more than 70 points. For both sexes, however, Mechanical Comprehension is appreciably less strongly related to educational level than is General Science.

The picture is much the same for Electronics Information, but in both sexes the mean scores are even more strongly related to education than in Mechanical Comprehension. Except for the greater sex difference, the Electronics Information plots look more like those of General Science. We take this as an indication that Electronics Information and General Science depend more on knowledge of technical facts or principles gained through formal

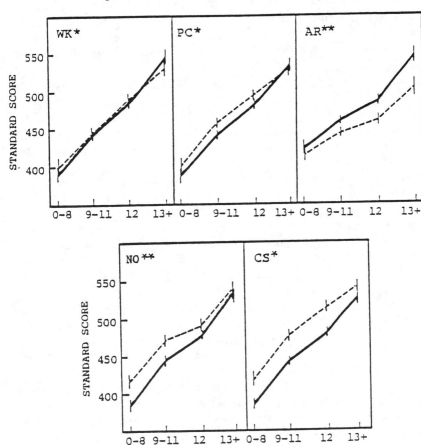

FIG. 5.1b. Interaction of sex and education (highest grade completed).
Male ——— Female ---
*F > 1.25F(.05)
**F > 1.25F(.01)

study, while Mechanical Comprehension contains elements that can be learned by practical experience of mechanical relationships. Women are less in contact with, or less perceptive of, the latter and for Mechanical Comprehension show the least gains with education.

While males achieved higher scores than females on each of these tests at each level of education, the fact that the performance of both males and females increase with education deserves emphasis. In both groups, more education appears to enhance performance, but in General Science, Mechanical Comprehension, and Electronics Information, education at high school and beyond is associated with better performance among males than among females.

The possible origins of these sex differences are discussed in Section 5.3. But one conclusion is obvious: large sex differences occur in those areas that traditionally have been occupied by males. The Auto and Shop Information test, for example, shows the greatest differences between the sex groups at each education level. Males at the lowest educational level out-perform females with similar education by 70 points. Males who have completed high school or have some college are a full standard deviation (100 points) above females at each of these educational levels. As Figure 5.1a shows, male performance on this test exhibits a much greater benefit from education through completion of high school than does female performance. Education beyond high school, however, results in only a small increase in the mean scores for males, while scores for females rise steadily over all education levels.

These results have a plausible explanation in the observation that auto and shop information is highly dependent upon experience. Males at present are much more likely to have experiences in this domain in their jobs and in their hobbies than are females. They are also more likely to participate in the largely male stereotyped auto and shop school electives. The inevitable result is that females' performance on this test is considerably lower than that of males at every educational level.

In addition, correct responses to the auto and shop items require less knowledge of principles than do Mechanical Comprehension and Electronics Information, and, as is clear in Figure 5.1b, performance does not change with college education to the extent that it does in Mechanical Comprehension and Electronics Information among both males and females. By the same token, the greater change in female performance between high school and college probably reflects the greater tendency of females to develop this information from reading or vicarious experience rather than hands-on experience. Hyman, Wright, and Reed (1975) have shown that as education increases, people's seeking of information in general also increases. Having learned less of this material in high school (as Figure 5.1b indicates), better education women have an opportunity to increase their knowledge in this area by reading, greater understanding of mechanical principles, and general experience. Finally, the result could also be explained by women who elect to attend college having wider interests extending even to such traditionally male domains as auto and shop.

As background to these conjectures, the current literature substantiates the common observation that in high school and college a higher proportion of males than females enroll in science courses, such as physics and chemistry, and in shop and mechanical drawing courses (Cook & Alexander, 1981; Erlick & Lebold, 1977; Fennema, 1981; Sells, 1980). Males also show greater interest in science in the early school grades (Fox & Cohn, 1980), and their out-of-school activities more often involve work with power tools and reading magazines such as Popular Science and Popular Mechanics (Erlick & Lebold, 1977). Females generally avoid these knowledge domains in high school and college, doubtless because they do not perceive vocational opportunities in fields where this information is required and do not aspire to careers in these fields. The exception is biology, which is more often taken by women (Marrett, 1981). As a result, the General Science test, about half of which is devoted to biology, shows smaller sex differences than Electronics Information. Generally, the pattern of group means on the ASVAB specialized knowledge tests is consistent with the different patterns of high school and college study typical of males and females.

Verbal Skills.   The second clear pattern in the sex group means involves the Word Knowledge and Paragraph Comprehension tests. In contrast with the increasing sexual differentiation with education seen in the tests of specialized knowledge, differences between the mean scores of males and females are small for the tests that assess verbal ability. As Figure 5.1a shows, the advantage of females over males in Word Knowledge at the lowest educational level is small, becomes smaller at each higher educational level, and ultimately gives way to an advantage for males at the 13+ level. The differences are so small, however, that the statistical significance of Sex by Highest Grade Completed interaction in Word Knowledge is marginal (see Table C.2).

A pattern of increasing similarity in the performance of males and females is also seen in the Paragraph Comprehension test. Females show a larger advantage in this area at the lower educational levels than they do in Word Knowledge, however, and their advantage is nearly constant to grade 12. At 13+, the average scores of males and females on Paragraph Comprehension are essentially the same.

These patterns of sex differences in verbal ability generally confirm previous research findings. As noted above, Maccoby and Jacklin (1974) conclude from their review of the literature that sex differences in verbal ability occur more consistently in early adolescence or at the time of entry into secondary school. The differences between the sexes are found primarily in verbal fluency and reading comprehension, where girls are higher achievers. Verbal fluency is the ability to produce a quantity of verbal output very quickly. In the Word Fluency test of Thurstone and Thurstone (1947), for example, subjects are required to write in five minutes as many different words as possible beginning with the letter "s." From 8 or 9 years of age onward, which are the youngest ages at which it can be successfully administered, this test shows large sex differences favoring females.

The general advantage of females on the Paragraph Comprehension test (which essentially assesses reading ability) at each educational level except the highest is also a familiar finding. The convergence of the scores of males and females at the highest educational level can be attributed to the greater probability that both males and females who pursue education beyond the high school level reach a mastery level of reading skill. It might also reflect the fact that, in recent years, male students have been attaining a slightly higher average score than female students on the Scholastic Aptitude Test (SAT) verbal scale. The difference in favor of males grew from 3 points (on a scale from about 200 to 800 points) in 1973 to 12 points in 1981 (College Board, 1981). At the same time the quantitative score difference favoring males grew from 42 to 49 points. These changes may be due to the larger, and hence less select, group of women who now take the SAT tests. In 1981, 515,708 women and 478,625 men took the tests, and the relative number of women taking the tests has been increasing.

It is also possible that males who remain in school are introduced to a greater variety of subject matter topics than are females and thus acquire a more varied vocabulary and familiarity with a larger range of reading topics. In addition to fulfilling course-distribution requirements for high school and college graduation, male students are more likely to enroll in elective and major courses not typically taken by females, such as science and technical courses. Additionally, differences in hobbies and leisure time engaged by males and females may result in males' exposure to more diverse domains of vocabulary and expository writing than females. Although these observations are somewhat speculative, the fact remains that, in the Profile data, males with more than a high school education show slightly greater Word Knowledge scores than do females with comparable education. For both males and females, the higher the educational attainment, the greater the Word Knowledge and Paragraph Comprehension, but the educational benefit to males' performance in these areas is greater, particularly at the highest educational level.

Fluent Production. A third pattern of performance difference between male and female respondents emerges for the two speeded tests—Numerical Operations and Coding Speed. Figure 5.1b shows that, while the performance of both males and females on both of these tests increases as educational attainment increases, Coding Speed shows a consistent large difference, favoring females, between the two groups across educational levels. A similar pattern is seen in Numerical Operations through grade 12. With some college, however, the scores of males and females are nearly identical.

As we discuss shortly, the difference between the two sex groups in Coding Speed, and, to a lesser extent, Numerical Operations suggests the working of the well-known mental test factor of fluent-production on which females typically excel. Also, female students more often than males enroll in secondary school courses that develop fluency skills such as typing and stenography (Cook & Alexander, 1981; Erlick & Lebold, 1977). But why educational attainment should relate so strongly to performance on these simple tasks is not as obvious. It may be that with increased schooling people develop more efficient test-taking skills, particularly in symbol recognition and short-term memory. Motivational factors and persistence factors may be implicated as well. Since more highly motivated young people are likely to seek more education, such people are also more practiced in the rote manipulation of conventional symbols than are people with less education.

Quantitative Skills. In contrast with those for Auto and Shop Information, scores on the Arithmetic Reasoning and Mathematics Knowledge tests are highly associated with education, especially so when subjects with only high school education are compared with those in college. At the lowest educational levels (0–8 and 9–11), Figures 5.1a and b show no differences between male and female achievement on Mathematics Knowledge and relatively small differences in Arithmetic Reasoning. The amount of increase in male and female scores in the lower educational levels is identical. The performance of the two sexes begins to diverge for subjects with 12 years of education, though the difference in favor of males at this educational level is small, about 12 points. At the highest educational level, the advantage of males over females increases to about 30 points. For Arithmetic Reasoning, on the other hand, a sex difference favoring males is readily apparent among subjects who have completed high school and increases to about 50 points for those with some college education.

In addition to the sex differences in the patterns of education effects in Mathematics Knowledge and Arithmetic Reasoning, the male advantage in Mathematics Knowledge is not as large as that seen for Arithmetic Reasoning. We attribute these differences to the fact that the Mathematics Knowledge test requires the literal application of mathematical rules (see the sample items from this test in Chapter 3), whereas the Arithmetic Reasoning test requires a restructuring of the verbally presented material before an algebraic rule can be applied (Fennema, 1981).

There is no reason to conclude that males and females who have had similar exposure to rules involved in Mathematics Knowledge would differ significantly in their ability to apply them. The equal performance of the two sexes at the lowest education levels, and the higher levels of performance of both males and females with increasing education, support this point. The divergence of males and females in Mathematical Knowledge at the higher educational levels can be explained by sex differences in rule acquisition due to different participation in higher level mathematics courses. In contrast, the form of problem restructuring required in Arithmetic Reasoning is aided by nonverbal thought (i.e., by mental manipulation of images requiring spatial visualizing ability), and the well-documented sex-differences in this ability may contribute to the different pattern of sex effects in these two types of mathematics tests. (We review this evidence in Section 5.4.)

5.2. SEX BY SOCIOCULTURAL GROUP BY ECONOMIC STATUS

Performances of poor and nonpoor males and females in the White, Hispanic, and Black subsamples are presented in Figures 5.2a and b for each of the subtests in terms of standard scores. As can be seen, there are considerable differences in achievement between the income and sociocultural groups on the various tests. In addition, interactions between sex, sociocultural group, and economic status appear as nonparallelism in Figures 5.2a and b. These interactions of sex, sociocultural group and economic status are moderate in size and significant in only four of the ten tests (NO, GS, MK, and EI). Three of the tests show significant sex by sociocultural group interactions only (AR, MC, and AS). The remaining three tests (WK, PC, and CS) do not display any interactions with these factors.

Specialized Knowledge. For the tests that generally show male advantage (i.e., General Science, Mechanical Comprehension, Electronics Information, and Auto and Shop Information), the size of the sex difference in performance is affected by sociocultural group membership, and in General Science, Mathematics Knowledge, and Electronics Information, it is also affected by income level (although the size of the latter effect is appreciable only in Mathematics Knowledge). The main source of the sex by sociocultural group effect is the reduced sex difference in Blacks relative to that in Whites. The sex differences of Hispanics are intermediate between Blacks and Whites, but vary with respect to economic status and are thus mainly responsible for the triple interaction of these factors.

The reduced sex differences in Blacks in these school-related topics (the same is true of Arithmetic Reasoning) can be explained by the encouragement of Black culture, more so than in that of Hispanics and Whites, of women to seek personal and familial advancement through education (Edwards, 1979; Slaughter, 1972). Allen's (1980) analysis of the National

Longitudinal Survey (NLS) data for the High School Class of 1972 provides evidence of the high educational expectation of Black females. This investigation revealed that while the educational aspirations of Whites and Blacks are comparable, the percentages of Black females and White males with goals of higher education are slightly greater than is true of their respective male and female counterparts. Since this is the case, we would expect that, relative to Whites, more Black females enroll in college preparatory programs during high school and participate in more science courses. It is therefore reasonable

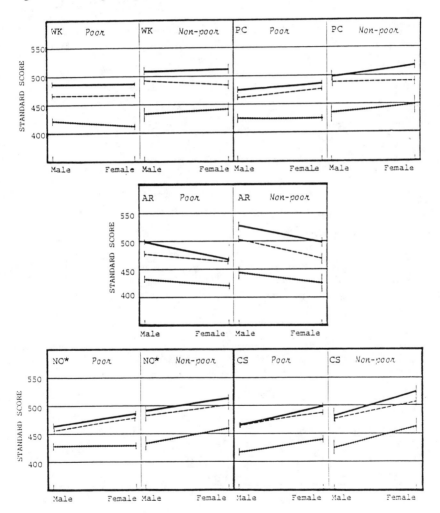

FIG. 5.2a. Interaction of sex, sociocultural group, and economic status.
White ——— Hispanic ------ Black · · · ·
*F > 1.25F(.05)

to expect less sex differentiation among Blacks than among Whites in their knowledge of the specialized knowledge subjects. Black females generally have higher educational expectations than Black males, and a higher proportion of Black females than males in both low and high socioeconomic categories enter college (Thomas, Alexander & Eckland, 1979).

This inference is supported by Marrett's (1982) recently conducted survey of 42 high schools in 36 school districts, which revealed that the science course participation of Black females and males is roughly equal, even in

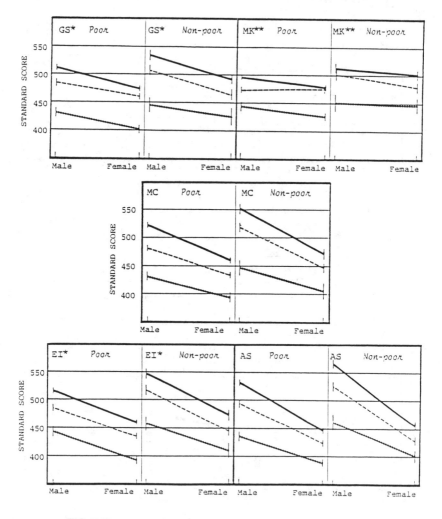

FIG. 5.2b. Interaction of sex, sociocultural group, and economic status.
White —— Hispanic ------ Black · · · ·
*F > 1.25F(.05)   **F > 1.25F(.01)

specialized courses such as chemistry and physics. This is not true of Whites. In the larger context of Black-White differences on these tests, we should note that Marrett also reports the proportion of Blacks of either sex who enroll in these science courses in high school to be considerably smaller than that seen for White males or females. Turner's observations from her 1982 investigation of factors that influence women's science career interests suggest that the educational and career guidance available to Black high school students may be inadequate, especially in portions of the southeast region. Turner notes (1983, personal communication) that about 35% of the high school males and 45% of the females identified by school counselors as probable science majors in college were not enrolled in college preparatory programs of study.

Fluent Production. Of the two tests in which females generally show higher average performance than males (i.e., Coding Speed and Numerical Operations), only the Numerical Operations test provides evidence of significant interaction of sex with economic status and sociocultural group. The interaction is due almost entirely to the fact that poor Black males are essentially equal in performance to poor Black females for this test, whereas this is not true of nonpoor Blacks. The surprising thing is that a similar effect is not seen in the other fluent production tests, Coding Speed. The difference between these two tests is, of course, that NO requires knowledge of elementary arithmetic with mostly single digit numbers (addition, subtraction, multiplication, and division), while the CS requires only recognition of numbers used as labels. Figure 5.2b shows that, where nonpoor Black males are at the same level as poor Black males, nonpoor Black females have profited more from instruction in arithmetic than their poor counterparts. This would seem to be another expression of the tendency of Black females to profit more from better educational opportunities than Black males. The same is not true of CS because that test has so little formally taught content.

Quantitative Skills. Generally, males in each of the sociocultural groups show higher average scores in Arithmetic Reasoning than their female counterparts, regardless of economic classification. However, the amount of difference seen in the scores of the sexes in the various categories of young people is not the same across groups. The smallest sex difference in Arithmetic Reasoning is seen in the poor Black and poor Hispanic subsamples, amounting to about 10 points in favor of males. The advantage of nonpoor Black males is somewhat higher, about 20 points, but less than the 35 to 40 point difference seen in both income classifications of Whites and in the nonpoor Hispanic subsample. Again we speculate that cultural differences, mediated by income level, contribute to the differences between groups in the amount of sexual differentiation in performance seen in Arithmetic Reasoning.

In view of the distribution of the different Hispanic groups in the various regions of the country (Brown et al., 1980), the fact that the highest proportion of poor Hispanics occurs in the West (see Table 2.8) indicates that Mexican-Americans are substantially represented in the poor Hispanic subsample. Since this is the case, the literature indicating cognitive style difference between Mexican-Americans and Anglo-Americans suggests a possible explanation of the reduced sex difference seen for poor Hispanics in Arithmetic Reasoning. These reports suggest that Mexican-Americans who experience more traditional socialization patterns (which is most likely to occur among the poor) differ from Anglo-Americans in the construct "field-dependence/independence." Traditionally socialized Mexican-Americans tend to be less field-independent (i.e., perceptually capable of overcoming an embedded context) than Anglo-Americans (see Kagin & Buriel, 1978, for a critical review), and, Mexican-American females are more field-dependent that their male counterparts. Ramirez (1973) theorizes that culturally conditioned differences in this cognitive style between Anglo-Americans and Mexican-Americans contribute to the latter group's generally depressed scholastic achievement because the American school system assumes a more field-independent style in the formulation of instructional techniques and the development of curriculum materials. A possible link between cognitive style and mathematics achievement, in particular, is suggested by the work of Vaidya and Chansky (1980), who investigated the relationship between relative field-dependence/independence and mathematics achievement. These investigators report that field-independent pupils exceed their field-dependent peers in mathematics achievement, and hypothesize that the relationship exists because "analytic ability required in field-independence and mathematics achievement tests involves perceptual disembedding and developing problem-solving strategies that depend on reorganizing and restructuring the information" (p. 326). A recent large-scale investigation by Gemmill, Bustoz, & Montiel, (1982) of factors that influence the mathematics course participation of highly able Mexican-American adolescents confirms the finding that relative field-dependence/independence as measured by the Group Embedded Figures Test (GEFT) is associated with mathematics achievement, and that Mexican-American youth score more in the field-dependent range than is true for Anglo-Americans. The current literature provides clear evidence that

But care must be taken in interpreting these findings. As Ramirez (1973) has suggested, the significant variable for mathematics achievement may not be cognitive style per se but rather how young people who differ in cognitive style are instructed in mathematics and other subject matter. In other words, the nature of the apparent relationship between culture, cognitive style, and mathematics achievement may not be straightforward.

The current literature provides clear evidence that minorities do not enroll in high school mathematics courses or pursue mathematics-related careers in the same proportions as their White counterparts (Gemmill et al., 1982; Matthews, 1983; National Science Foundation, 1982). A major finding presented by Marrett (1982) from her large-scale survey of minority females in high school mathematics and science courses is that there are far greater sociocultural than sex differences in mathematics participation. Although Black students represented over half of the sample, Marrett reports that they were only one-third of the students enrolled in algebra II, and one-fourth of the students enrolled in calculus. The Black students in this sample were concentrated in lower level mathematics courses, that is, 48.9% of the Black high school students sampled were enrolled in general mathematics courses such as technical math, consumer math, business math, and other introductory level courses. In contrast, only 25.8% of the White high school students were enrolled in similar lower-level courses. Marrett also reports that a slightly higher proportion of the Black females than Black males were enrolled in algebra II, calculus and other advanced mathematics courses, though the proportion of Blacks of either sex enrolled in such courses was considerably lower than that seen for White males or females. One important consequence of lower levels of preparation may be reduced opportunity for sex differences to assert themselves. If so, the lower enrollment of Blacks in advanced mathematics courses generally, would, in large part, account for the lower sex difference in Arithmetic Reasoning seen for poor Blacks, and to a lesser extent, nonpoor Blacks.

The same may be true for poor Hispanics. The fact that Hispanics are considerably underrepresented in mathematics-related professions (see McCorquodale, 1980 for a review), and underrepresented also in science and mathematics majors in college (Astin, 1982), suggests that there may be little differentiation in the secondary school mathematics preparation of males and females in this group. Although McCorquodale (1983, personal communication) reports that a higher proportion of Mexican-American males than females enroll in advanced mathematics courses and Gemmill et al. (1982) report a similar sex effect among highly able Mexican-American students, so few Mexican-Americans of either sex pursue advanced mathematics study in high school and college that sexual differentiation in this subpopulation may be difficult to assess accurately.

In Mathematics Knowledge, the performance of males and females is almost identical in both the poor Hispanic and nonpoor Black subsamples. This suggests that the mathematics training of the sexes in these groups is very similar. However, poor Blacks show as much sexual differentiation in performance, in favor of males, as seen in the two income categories of Whites and the nonpoor Hispanic subsample, amounting to about 20 points. An explanation suggested by Sewell, Farley, Manni, and Hunt (1982) for their finding that Black inner-city adolescent males obtain higher Peabody Picture Vocabulary Test (PPVT) scores than their female counterparts may apply for the sex difference in mathematics knowledge seen here: the home environment of poor youth may not give females the special incentives for achievement that seem to be characteristic of middle-class Blacks. Moreover, home demands competing and interfering with school achievement among poor Blacks may fall more heavily on girls than on boys.

Verbal Skills. The statistical analysis of the Profile data (Appendix C) shows no significant sex by sociocultural group interaction. This result is somewhat at odds with the views of a number of other investigators of language in minority groups. Barral's (1977) investigation of the relative scholastic achievement of foreign-born and native-born Mexican-American students suggested that sex role relative to language may be a factor. Barral reported no significant difference in the school achievement of foreign-born and native-born Mexican-American children; however, home use of English was a significant determinant of females' school performance but not males'. Although this investigator did not advance an explanation of this finding, it is consistent with the fact that females in this group are expected to stay closer to home and are more protected in contacts with individuals outside the family (Murillo, 1976). Kulvesky (1981) reports that the Mexican-American males included in this Texas sample tend to be more Spanish dominant in their oral language with parents, close friends in the neighborhood, and friends in school than is true of females. This suggests that male peers outside the home may also be Spanish dominant. Therefore, though poor Mexican-American males may be encouraged to gain knowledge and experience outside the home (Murillo, 1976), their language experiences may be primarily Spanish. The same may be true for others in the poor Hispanic subsample besides those of Mexican origin.

The lack of any significant sex effect for WK and PC in the Black group also conflicts with the observations of other investigators. Asbury (1973) reports that among first-graders in rural North Carolina, black males scored significantly higher than females in the Peabody Picture Vocabulary Test (PPVT) and the Metropolitan Readiness Test (reading readiness test). Sewell et al. (1982) indicate that poor Black adolescent males in Philadelphia also score significantly higher in the PPVT than their female counterparts. These results would not typically be seen in White children of the same age. In the Profile data, however, there is no evidence that sex differences in the language tests of the ASVAB are any greater in Blacks than in Whites.

5.3. SOURCES OF SEX EFFECTS

From the now voluminous literature on sex differences in cognitive test performance and school achievement, we are able to review here only the main results. We begin with cognitive studies of fluent production and spatial test performance before examining in Section 5.4 the more controversial questions of sex differences in mathematics attainment and those in school achievement among Blacks.

Sex Differences in Fluent Production

Female superiority in verbal fluency, fine motor movements, and tasks requiring rapid perception of details and frequent shifts of attention is universally acknowledged (Anastasi, 1964). It is expressed clearly in the Numerical Operations and Coding Speed tests of the ASVAB, although the difference is reduced at the highest education level. Despite the early discovery of this phenomenon by factor analysts and the appearance of fluent production tests in major test batteries (WAIS, DAT, ASVAB), there has been relatively little research into its causes or consequences. Among the few psychologists that have given it any prominence, Broverman and Klaiber (1969) note that, among male subjects of the same general verbal ability, spatial ability scores and fluent production scores are negatively related. Petersen (1976) confirmed this finding and extended it to females. Although verbal, spatial, and fluent production tests load on different factors (Bock, 1973), the correlations among the factors are such that negative partial correlations of spatial and fluency measures, holding fixed verbal ability, can occur. Broverman and Klaiber advance a hormonal theory, with mediation by brain monoamine oxidase (MAO), to explain the sex differences and individual variation within sexes. More sexually differentiated individuals of either sex (i.e., more somatically masculinized males and more somatically feminized females) are supposed to have lower MAO levels resulting in higher brain norepinephrine, better fluent production, but reduced spatial ability. This theory has not, however, gained much currency.

An alternative explanation for females' advantage in fluent production tests, particularly as reflected in the Numerical Operations and Coding Speed tests of the ASVAB, is that females may be more responsive to the demand for speed in tasks such as these. The instructions to "do the test items as quickly as possible" are obviously interpreted subjectively by each subject. There is some evidence to suggest that females, at least in the early years, are more likely than males to comply with the directions of authority figures such as parents, teachers, experimenters in laboratory situations, and examiners in individual tests administrations (Hertzig, Birch, Thomas & Mendez, 1968; Minton, Kagan, & LeVine, 1971; Serbin, O'Leary, Kent, & Tonick, 1973). Anastasi (1982) suggests that males may be more discriminating in their achievement behavior, choosing to persist in tasks and subject matter that arouse their personal interest. While these hypotheses are speculative and difficult to test experimentally, socially conditioned sex differences in young people's willingness to conform to task requirements and/or motivation to perform certain types of tasks cannot be eliminated as potential sources of variance in the fluency test scores. (For a more recent account, see Bock, Zimowski, and Laciny, 1986.)

Sex Differences in Spatial Ability

That substantial sex differences exist in the ability of persons of equal verbal skill to solve problems that require transformations of visual and tactile images has been known for many years (for reviews see Maccoby & Jacklin, 1974, and Wittig & Petersen, 1979). Some investigators have suggested that these differences in spatial ability offer an explanation for sex differences in arithmetic reasoning such as we have observed in the AR test of the ASVAB. Although no consensus exists as to the nature and significance of the relationship (Benbow & Stanley, 1980; Fennema, 1980; Sherman, 1980), the literature suggests that facility in arithmetic reasoning and also in mechanical comprehension may be influenced by a more fundamental trait of spatial ability. When presented with a configuration of interlocking gears and rods, for example, a person's speed and accuracy in predicting the movement of connecting parts would be facilitated by the ability to manipulate the configuration visually. Without this ability, a lengthy concatenation of verbal propositions would be required to reach conclusions that are obtained immediately by visual imagery. The same may be true for the solution of one- and two-step word problems, such as appear in the ASVAB Arithmetic Reasoning test. As we discuss later, spatial visualization of the configuration may facilitate this type of thinking. In proposing such a connection, however, one must distinguish clearly between the solution of these unstructured problems, on the one hand, and knowledge of mathematical facts or ability to carry out mathematical operations presented formally in arithmetic rubrics or algebraic notation, on the other. Only the former show substantial sex differences.

This distinction helps explain why the Arithmetic Reasoning and Mathematics Knowledge tests loaded on the same factor in the factor analysis reported in Appendix B but do not show the same sex differences. We saw in Figure 5.1 that sex differences in Arithmetic Reasoning appear at all educational levels, while those for Mathematics Knowledge are almost nonexistent except for a minimal difference at the highest educational level. The explanation of this seeming contradiction is that the factor analyses are describing the individual-difference variation within same sex groups, whereas the analysis of group means reveals the often small but systematic effects that make one group of subjects different from another on average. The factor analysis shows that persons who are proficient in Arithmetic Reasoning also tend to be proficient in Mathematics Knowledge, but it takes multivariate analysis of variance to detect the systematic tendency of male subjects to exceed female subjects in Arithmetic Reasoning but not in Mathematics Knowledge.

Other investigators have called attention to this distinction. Sex differences in favor of males appear in the problem-solving tasks but not in the information or operations tasks. Werdelin (1961), for example, studying high school pupils, found better female performance on geometry information items and no sex differences on items that could be solved by well-known formulas or in a step-by-step fashion. But on items that required the solution of problems involving geometrical principles or reorganization of relationships, he found clear male superiority. A study by Armstrong (1980) yielded similar results for the computation and algebraic operations vs. algebraic problem solving. The former did not show sex differences among high school seniors, whereas the latter showed large significant differences favoring males. Eighth grade pupils in this same study, by contrast, did not show sex differences either in arithmetic computation or problem solving. This study corroborates the typical finding that sex differences in quantitative reasoning become marked when adolescent changes become apparent in boys at about age 14. In studies where consistent sex differences in mathematics attainment are not found, such as those of Fennema and Sherman (1977), achievement tests have been used that emphasize mathematical information and content rather than quantitative problem solving.

As early as 1940, it was suggested by Gastrin (1940) that sex differences in geometrical ability could be attributed to the male superiority in the factor of spatial visualizing ability that had been identified in factor analysis of mental tasks in the 1920s and 1930s. McFarlane (1925) found in a set of "practical ability" tests a group factor distinct from general verbal ability and having something to do with judging the relationships between physical objects. She noted that boys surpassed girls on these tests. By 1928, Truman Kelley had devised objective test items measuring spatial ability and had identified by principal component analysis a spatial factor requiring the mental manipulation of shapes.

Spatial tests were prominent in the batteries developed for pilot selection during World War II (Guilford & Zimmerman, 1947). Excellent predictive validities for this type of test have been found in validation studies. Not surprisingly, spatial tests predict skill in engineering drawing far better than do tests of verbal ability (Holliday, 1940, 1943; Slater, 1941). In other practical areas such as shop training and auto mechanics training, spatial tests have good predictive validity (Martin, 1951). The 1974 manual for the Differential Aptitude Tests (Bennett, Seashore, & Wesman, 1974a,b) reported predictive validities of its spatial relations tests of $r = .42$ for drafting, $r = .47$ for shop mechanics, and $r = .69$ for watch repair. Recently, Gibbons, Baker and Skinner (1985) obtained a correlation near .7 between ratings of residents' manual surgical skill and a measure closely related to spatial tests

(Bender Gestalt). Predictive validities of spatial tests have been reviewed by McGee (1979).

In contrast with tests of verbal ability, which show either no sex difference or a slight female superiority, the sex difference in spatial test performance favoring males is one of the most consistent and well-established findings in cognitive psychology. Even simple two-dimensional versions of the tests, such as the Thurstone and Thurstone (1947) item, shown in Figure 5.3, are easier for male subjects, and still greater differences in the same direction are found for three-dimensional versions such as the identical blocks test, an item from which is shown in Figure 5.4 (Stafford, 1961). The distinctive feature of spatial visualization items (which show strong sex differences and load on the spatial visualization factor) is that the problem they pose cannot be readily expressed in verbal form. It can be solved most quickly by directly imagining the appearance of the object after it is turned. Studies by Shepard and Metzler (1971) have found that the time required to decide whether rotated objects, such as shown in Figure 5.5, are identical (and not mirror images) is proportional to the number of degrees that the objects are rotated from one another. This would seem to imply that the subjects are performing an analogue mental rotation in real time. (Subjects who are able to solve these types of items quickly give subjective reports of processing the images in this way.) These results suggest that significant cognitive problems can be solved without verbal mediation and that productive thought can consist of transformation of images rather than recall and relating of propositions. This is not to say that these two kinds of thought cannot take place simultaneously; the introspecting subject can describe an image in terms of features that have descriptors in the language. To the extent that an item presented in the form of a figure can be solved by naming distinctive features, rather than manipulating an image of the configuration as a whole, the item becomes verbal rather than spatial and does not show appreciable sex differences (Zimowski, 1985).

That the human mind is capable of carrying out verbal and spatial thought separately has been substantiated by the remarkable finding that these functions are served by distinct parts of the brain. Studies of brain damaged aphasic subjects (Geschwind, 1974) and of so-called "split-brain" subjects who have undergone sectioning of the corpus calossum and anterior commi-

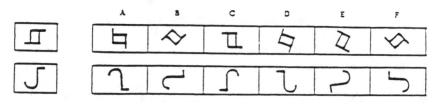

FIG. 5.3.   Two items from the Thurstone and Thurstone Primary Mental Abilities Test (1947)

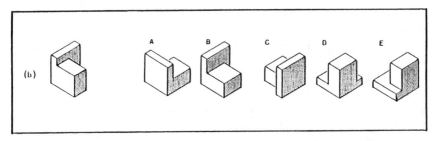

FIG. 5.4. Identical Block Test (Stafford, 1961)

sures to control epileptic attacks (Gazzaniga, 1970; Nebes & Sperry, 1974; Sperry, 1970) confirm that in the vast majority of people the capacity to name objects and utter sentences is the exclusive province of the frontal and temporal lobes of the left hemisphere. The right hemisphere can recognize objects and even transform images but is mute. It cannot name the object but can demonstrate by gesturing or pointing with the left hand that it knows the appropriate use of the object. When a familiar object is placed in the finger tips of the left hand of a blindfolded split-brain subject, the brain receives information only from the projection of sensory nerves in the finger tips onto the right hemisphere. The split-brain subject cannot then name the object but can perform gestures appropriate to its use.

Other evidence supporting this interpretation is seen in cases of brain damage. Lesions in the left hemisphere frequently interfere with speech, but the capacity for spatial problem solving remains intact. Conversely, lesions in the right hemisphere depress spatial ability in most patients without affecting speech (Geschwind, 1970).

Hemispheric specialization of function also explains the finding of Kimura (1967) and others that in normal subjects the right ear, the innervation of which projects most directly on the left hemisphere, has a slight superiority for discriminating speech sounds while the left ear has an advantage for non-speech sounds. Similarly, electroencephalographic studies (Ornstein, 1973) indicate that increased brain activity in the right hemisphere occurs during spatial tests, and in the left during verbal tests.

Bock (1973) suggests that this anatomical separation of function is the source of the verbal and spatial factors in mental test scores. Individual

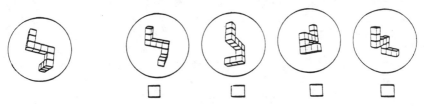

FIG. 5.5. An item from the Vandenberg-Shepard Mental Rotation Test

differences in the vascular and neural architecture of different parts of the brain are commonplace anatomical observations. These differences would be expected to affect differentially the two sides of the brain and produce relatively independent variation in the speed and effectiveness of verbal and spatial thought. Whether this functional specialization of the hemispheres could also account for sex differences in cognition is currently being debated. From studies of brain-damaged patients, McGlone (1980) has presented evidence that the hemispheric specialization of verbal and spatial information processing is less complete in women than in men. In the patients she studied, right hemisphere lesions sometimes affected language in women but rarely in men. Her results have been confirmed in normal subjects by direct presentation of visiospatial and tactispatial problems to the right hemisphere by tachistiscopic projection and tactile stimulation (see, e.g., Witelson, 1976). From an early age, females appear to be less lateralized for verbal and spatial information processing than are males. These sex differences in hemisphere specialization can explain the sex difference in spatial ability on the grounds that the presence of linguistic functions in the right hemisphere competes with spatial thought (Levy, 1984; Bock, Zimowski, and Laciny, 1986). This interpretation will perhaps be clarified as recently developed techniques of monitoring activity at specific sites in the brain, through measurement of local blood supply, improved electroencephalography, or positron emission tomography make it possible to distinguish the cerebal centers of verbal and spatial thought in normal subjects.

Hormonal Influences

That the major sex hormones, testosterone and estrogen, have an important influence on spatial ability is implied by the effect of certain abnormal endocrine conditions that specifically affect this trait. One instance of this phenomenon is seen in subjects suffering from Turner's syndrome. Due to a missing X chromosome, these women are agonadal and exhibit, in the presence of virtually normal verbal intelligence, a striking deficit in spatial visualizing ability (Garron, 1970). In another condition, testicular feminization syndrome, somatic males inheriting an end-organ insensitivity to testosterone are feminized by the low levels of estrogen produced by undescended testes. The subjects have the external appearance of females, are raised and identify as such, and have typically female levels of spatial ability. These cases strongly suggest that testosterone or some other androgen must be present in normal male levels for male-like performance on spatial tasks.

Even clearer evidence of the role of androgens has been presented by Hier and Crowley (1980, 1982), who studied the verbal and spatial abilities of men suffering two forms of hypogonadotropic hypogonadism: an ideopathic (IHH) form in which a developmental defect interfered with the normal stimulation of testicle growth at adolescence, and an acquired form (AHH) in which brain damage or neoplasia affect pituitary function and caused regression of testicle volume after adolescence. Although the verbal abilities of both these forms are normal, spatial ability is depressed below typical male levels in IHH but is near normal in AHH This shows that normal androgen levels are required prior to or during adolescence for male levels of spatial ability to develop; it also shows, however, that once the ability is established in a normal androgen environment, it does not reverse if androgen levels decline. In this respect it is different than other secondary sex characteristics such as laryngeal development, and hair and fat distribution, which revert to female forms in the absence of male levels of testosterone. Finally, Hier and Crowley found in IHH a significant positive correlation between testicular volume and spatial ability, suggesting a dose-response relationship between spatial ability and androgen levels at some period in development.

Other observations on the relation of androgen levels to spatial ability are more difficult to understand. Although the hormonal studies mentioned earlier suggest a direct relation between spatial ability and androgen at low levels, some findings of Broverman and Klaiber (1969) suggested that at high androgen levels spatial ability again declines. The implication is that persons who are hormonally more strongly sexually differentiated are not as adept in spatial tasks as less differentiated persons. This means that the better spatial visualizing females would tend to be less feminized somatically, and the comparable males, less masculinized. This is what Petersen (1976) observed in her study of spatial visualization vs. fluent production in young people from the Fels longitudinal study. In males a more masculine somatotype was associated with poor spatial ability, whereas in females, it was associated with higher spatial ability. More recently, Shute et al. (1983) found a similar relationship in a large sample of male subjects, most in the 20 to 30 year age range, by direct immunoassay of plasma androgens; no significant relationship was found in a similar sample of female students, but this was ascribed to failure to control for phase of the menstrual cycle. These results seem to indicate that there is an intermediate range of androgen/estrogen balance that is favorable to the development of spatial visualizing ability. The fact that there are relatively more good spatial visualizers among males would then be explained by relatively more males falling in this critical range.

How exactly this curvilinear relationship comes about is at present something of a mystery. One possibility is that greater hormonal and somatic differentiation of the sexes is associated with precocious development; that is, persons who mature earlier or more quickly appear to be more sexually differentiated—males have relatively higher androgen/estrogen ratios than slow or late maturing males and are more masculinized—females have relatively lower androgen/estrogen ratios than slow or late maturing females and are relatively less feminized. The theory is that the organization of hemispheric specialization, and especially the development of spatial ability in right hemisphere, does not continue for as long a time in these precocious maturers. Because the period of development of right hemispheric specialization was presumably shorter in males with high plasma androgen indices in the Shute et al. study, the inverse relationship to spatial ability was observed. Similar results might be seen in females if androgens could be more accurately measured.

Although this theory is at present highly speculative, there is considerable evidence, reviewed in Bock, Zimowski, & Laciny (1986), in its favor. Studies by Wilson (1975) and by Levine and Huttenlocher (1985) have established that the profile of higher spatial scores in males and higher fluent production scores in females can, with tests suitable for young children, be observed as early as three and four years of age. This fact, together with the findings of Hier and Crowley (1980, 1982) cited above, strongly implicates early, probably prenatal, androgen influence as the origin of the sex difference in this specific cognitive contrast. Presumably, the developmental precocity of girls, which is apparent in their nearly two year advance in bone age over boys throughout childhood and adolescence (Bock, 1985; Tanner, 1978), and precocity of development of female brain lateralization in utero (Geschwind and Galaburda, 1985), reflects the same influence. If it is this precocity of development that leads to less hemispheric specialization, and if those persons of either sex who mature more rapidly are those that show greater sexual dimorphism at maturity, the kinds of relationships of spatial ability to measures of adrogyny observed by Petersen (1979) and Shute et al. (1983) would be expected.

Family Studies of Spatial Ability

Other evidence of a developmental basis for individual differences in spatial ability comes from family studies, virtually all of which show that proficiency on spatial tests is substantially inherited. Family and twin studies have consistently shown heritability for spatial performance almost as high as that of the more widely investigated verbal abilities and general intelligence. Vandenberg (1967) reviews many of these results. Moreover, factor analytic studies of the heritable variation in batteries of cognitive tests show that the heritable spatial component is distinct from the heritable verbal component (Bock, 1973; Vandenberg, 1975). Although all of these studies have been based on parent and offspring or dyzygotic or monozygotic twins living together, the rather esoteric nature of the spatial trait makes it unlikely that the transmission from parent to offspring could be due to some form of imitation independent of verbal learning. It seems equally unlikely that the environments of monozygotic twins living together could be more similar with respect to sources of the spatial trait independent of the similarity of the verbal environment. [Monozygotic twins are known to spend more time together and to interact verbally more than dyzygotic twins; for a recent review, see Segal (1982).]

Further evidence of genetic influence on the spatial trait comes from observations of bimodalities in the spatial test score distributions. Such a bimodality was first observed in the scores of a spatial test administered to a large sample of young adult male subjects as part of a factorial study of mental ability (Thurstone & Thurstone, 1941). None of the other tests in this study showed any sign of bimodal score distribution—a rare event for any sort of cognitive measure. A similar result was obtained by Bock and Kolakowski (1973) by resolution of score distributions of the Guilford and Zimmerman (1953) spatial visualization test into Gaussian components. Subsequent studies have confirmed the bimodal nature of the spatial score distributions (Ashton, Polovina, & Vandenburg, 1979; Loehlin, Sharon, & Jacoby, 1978; Yen, 1975). These results suggest that the subjects can be classified as "visualizers" or "non-visualizers," corresponding to normal distributions separated by about one standard deviation. In male subjects, approximately equal numbers are visualizers and non-visualizers, but in female subjects, only about 25% are visualizers. This finding agrees with the observations of many workers that in adult subjects about 25% of females score above the male median in tests of spatial ability (Bouchard & McGee, 1977; O'Conner, 1943). The fact that average spatial scores are typically lower in women can be attributed to the smaller number of women who are "visualizers"; those women that have the visualizing trait score just as high on spatial tests as do the male "visualizers."

On the basis of these observed proportions of visualizers among males and females, O'Conner (1943) proposed that spatial visualizing ability is due to an X-linked recessive gene with a frequency of about ½ in the population. Such a trait would be expressed by half the males (whose cells carry only one X chromosome) and $\frac{1}{2} \times \frac{1}{2} = \frac{1}{4}$ of females, who must inherit the recessive visualizing gene from both parents in order to express the trait.

Another consequence of X-linkage of a recessive trait is a characteristic correlation among family members classified by sex. If a test score is influenced by an X-linked recessive gene, then among parent and offspring the correlation of fathers and sons should be zero, that of mother and son and father and daughter should be greatest, and that of mother and daughter intermediate. Between offspring, sisters should show the highest correlations, brothers and sisters the lowest, and brothers and brothers, intermediate. The numerous family studies of spatial visualizing abilities since Stafford's (1961) initial effort have been reviewed by McGee (1979). The results to date are highly variable. Some studies show a pattern of correlation suggestive of sex-linkage (Stafford, 1961; Hartlage, 1970; Bock & Kolakowski, 1973; Yen, 1975; Walker, Krasnoff & Peoco, 1981). Other studies show the pattern suggestive of sex-linkage for one of the tests used but no such pattern for another (Park et al., 1978; Loehlin, 1978). Still others show a distinctly contrary pattern (DeFries et al., 1976; Bouchard & McGee, 1976). On balance, the X-linkage theory does not appear to be substantiated, and a hormonally mediated process similar to that determining other sexually dimorphic traits seems more plausible. The possibility that an X-linked gene is influencing the response to androgens cannot be ruled out, but it might be difficult to detect without a more sensitive method of investigation. One such approach would be to look for linkage between the putative major gene for spatial ability and a marker locus on the X chromosome (Bock & Perline, 1977). This has in fact been attempted with possibly positive results for sex linkage by Goodenough et al. (1977), but the sample size was too small to give any real confidence in the results.

Spatial Ability and Quantitative Reasoning

Smith (1964) and Sherman (1967) argued that the sex difference in performance on quantitative reasoning is due to differences in spatial ability, but lacked supportive evidence. In 1975, however, Hyde, Geiringer, and Yen investigated, in a sample of 45 male and 35 female undergraduates, the relationship between scores on the Identical Blocks test (see Figure 5.4), the Rod and Frame test, the Group Embedded Figures test (Witkin et al., 1962), a mental arithmetic test (Stafford, 1965), and the WAIS Vocabulary subscale. Using the Identical Block score as a covariate, Hyde et al. (1975) were able by the analysis of covariance technique to eliminate the significant difference favoring males both on the mental arithmetic and the Rod and Frame test. This suggests that these differences also arose from the spatial trait. Although a small difference favoring males remained after the covariate adjustment, this is to be expected if the covariate is fallible, as all test scores necessarily are.

In a similar study, Burnett, Lane, and Dratt (1979) examined the relationship between the Scholastic Aptitude Test (SAT) Quantitative Scale and spatial ability as measured by the Identical Blocks test and the Guilford-Zimmerman Spatial Visualization Test. In a group of 183 male and 81 female college students selected for their mathematical ability, they found that males scored significantly higher on both the spatial test and the SAT Quantitative, while females outperformed males on the SAT verbal. Correlations between the spatial tests and the SAT Quantitative in the two groups were substantial ($r = .50, .57$), whereas the correlation between the spatial test and the SAT verbal were comparatively low ($r = .07, .28$). As in the Hyde et al. study, analysis of covariance with the two spatial scores as covariates reduced the sex difference in the SAT Quantitative scores to insignificance.

These studies support the conclusion that the sex differences observed with quantitative reasoning tests arise from the corresponding difference in spatial ability. Only the Fennema and Sherman (1977) study gave mixed results in this connection, but they were using a general test of mathematics achievement (The Scardell Test of Academic Progress, 1972) including many aspects of mathematics knowledge where sex differences are not expected. Indeed, Benbow and Stanley (1980) argue that the Scardell test is not a good measure of mathematical aptitude. On these grounds, the Fennema and Sherman study does not seem a serious challenge to the spatial interpretation of sex differences in quantitative reasoning.

If there is any reason to question the theory, it might be one's difficulty in understanding how spatial items (see Figures 5.3, 5.4, and 5.5) and arithmetic reasoning items draw on any common cognitive function. Arithmetic word problems are, as their name implies, almost always presented in words and not in images. Like many of the items on the ASVAB Arithmetic Reasoning test, they may involve quantities of money, which do not normally have a physical representation. All that can be said is that these items present in an unstructured form and in arbitrary order a number of quantities that must be brought into a configuration that is in one-to-one correspondence with some mathematical formula or algorithm. As Bronowski (1947) has observed, mathematics is a language that communicates those aspects of the world that can be described only in configurations that are not readily amenable to the chains of propositions that make up verbal language. Although some of the items in the ASVAB reasoning test seem more "configural" than others, (for example the item showing the largest sex difference in favor of males is a ratio problem involving the height of two sunlit objects casting shadows), even the unit price and extension problems show sex differences favoring males. From thresholds for these items reported by Bock and Mislevy (1981), one can pick out the items where sex differences are greatest. These differences prove not to be related to the content of the items but to difficulty. Items in the latter part of the test, involving more subtle application of ratio rules, fractions, and interest calculations, show greater sex differences than the simpler items earlier in the test. Either the female subjects are unable to solve these problems or they are too slow in reaching them or give up before completing the test. Sympson and Weiss (1981) report failure to complete all items of the ASVAB Arithmetic Reasoning Test. But perhaps the correct explanation is that arithmetic word problems require active interplay of word and image that puts non-visualizers, in which women are in the majority, at a disadvantage.

5.4. SEX DIFFERENCES IN MATHEMATICS ACHIEVEMENT

The differences in male and female performance on Arithmetic Reasoning and Mathematics Knowledge tests in the Profile data are similar to those found in studies by Centra (1974), Fennema (1980), and Armstrong (1980, 1981). The literature indicates that sex-related differences in mathematics achievement are not consistently found until early adolescence (Fennema, 1974; Maccoby & Jacklin, 1974; Sherman & Fennema, 1977). Generally, adolescence females outperform males in formal mathematical operations, while males show higher performance in unstructured and less formal reasoning tasks (Fennema, 1974). Armstrong (1980) reported from a study of the mathematics achievement of a national sample of 13-year-olds and high school seniors that, while female 13-year-olds achieved higher scores than their male classmates in arithmetic computations, they equalled males in problem-solving ability. Among high school seniors, she found no sex differences in computation or algebra achievement, but observed a large and statistically significant difference, favoring males, in problem-solving ability. Armstrong concludes from this analysis that males and females enter high school with essentially the same level of skill and understanding in mathematics, but during the high school years males surpass females in their ability to solve one- and two-step "word problems."

The disparity in the high school mathematics achievement of the two sexes has been a cause for concern among those responsible for recruiting new technical talent into science and industry. Because mathematical competence is essential in these fields, the relatively small number of women who develop mathematics mastery during the secondary school years has been identified as a critical factor in the persistent underrepresentation of women in science and the technical professions (Sells, 1980; Sherman, 1982; Fennema, 1982; Meece, 1980).

An obvious factor bearing on this problem is the relative numbers of males and females who enroll in advanced mathematics courses (i.e., college preparatory mathematics) in high school. Studies reviewed by Fennema (1982) show considerably fewer females than males enrolled in advanced mathematics courses in secondary school, which suggests that sex differences in mathematics achievement result primarily from females electing to study mathematics less often than males. Supporting this line of reasoning is the finding in the Profile data of higher average scores for males not only in mathematics and mechanical comprehension, but also in electronics information and science knowledge—topics that require a large measure of formal instruction. Although sex differences in these areas of specialized knowledge have not been a focus of psychological research, it is generally thought that the factors contributing to male advantage in mathematics also affect these related areas (Fennema, 1981). Thus, the research findings related to sex differences in mathematics would seem to be supported by those observed in the other specialized knowledge tests of the ASVAB.

Countless variables have been implicated in female attitudes and achievement in mathematics: sex-typing of mathematics as a male domain (Fox, Tobin, & Brody, 1979), sex differences in perceived causes of success and failure (Fennema, 1981; Wolleat, Pedro, Becker, & Fennema, 1980), differential parental expectations of sons' and daughters' success in mathematics (Casserly, 1980; Levine, 1976), sex differences in perceived usefulness of mathematics (Haven, 1971; Sherman & Fennema, 1977), sex differences in self-concept of mathematics ability (Brush, 1980; Sherman, 1980), differential treatment of males and females by teachers and counselors (Fennema, 1980; Casserly, 1980), sex differences in self-confidence in relation to specific tasks (Maccoby & Jacklin, 1974), differential early socialization of males and females for achievement orientations (Rubovits, 1975), sex role orientation (Bem & Lenny, 1977; Nash, 1979), and actual fear of success among females (Horner, 1972). All of these factors tend to work in the direction of reduced female participation in advanced mathematics courses and, thus, in promoting the male advantage in mathematics achievement.

Findings from two recent large-scale investigations question, however, the assumption of differential course participation as a factor in the sex difference in mathematics achievement. The Women in Mathematics project, a survey conducted by the Education Commission of the States (ECS) in the Fall of 1978 with over 1,700 twelfth grade males and females nationwide, and the second Mathematics Assessment, conducted during the 1977–78 school year by the National Assessment of Educational Progress (NAEP) with a national probability sample of 75,000 9-, 13-, and 17-year-olds, show near equality in the mathematics course participation of the sexes (Armstrong, 1981). The Women in Mathematics Project data indicate no significant difference in the proportions of males and females who were taking or had completed courses in calculus, precalculus, trigonometry, geometry, and computer programming. In fact, of the twelve courses covered in the survey, only two showed a significant sex difference in favor of males (probability and statistics, and algebra II), and one showed a significant difference in favor of females (business mathematics). The NAEP study also revealed few sex differences in the mathematics course participation of 17-year-old students. Of the nine courses surveyed in this study, only two showed a significant difference in the proportions of males and females who had studied the course—precalculus and calculus, and trigonometry. The NAEP survey also collected data from the 13-year-olds regarding the number of years of high school mathematics they planned to take. Significantly more males than females planned to take only one year of high school mathematics, but no differences were seen for students planning two, three, or four years of mathematics training.

Nevertheless, sex differences in mathematics achievement favoring males were seen in both studies among 17-year-olds and 12th graders. The males at every level of course participation exceeded the performance of females in solving typical one- and two-step word problems. Armstrong (1981) concludes from this analysis that "It is clear that achievement differences are not solely a function of differences in participation" (p. 371). More recently, however, Pallas and Alexander (1983) examined coursework effects in a prospective study of sex differences in mathematics achievement and came to a different conclusion. Using the data from the Educational Testing Service Academic Prediction and Growth Study (Hilton, 1979), they examined the scores of 6,119 12th grade public school pupils who took the mathematics subtest of the PSAT (SAT-M) early in 1968. Because these pupils were part of a longitudinal study, their quantitative Cooperative School and College Ability Test (SCAT-Q) scores in 9th grade, as well as records of their intervening course-work, were also available. Pallas and Alexander found that, although these pupils entered high school showing practically no sex difference in mathematics attainment, by 12th grade the difference was substantial. Partial regression analyses showed that these differences in math achievement are strongly affected by course enrollment, especially in advanced mathematics courses, and that this effect could not be eliminated by controlling on 9th grade SCAT-Q scores. The analysis indicated that, while not all of the sex differences in 12th grade SAT-M scores could be attributed to sex differences in mathematics course enrollments, the proportion that could be so attributed was large enough to leave little doubt that the differential coursework hypothesis has a basis in fact. The authors suggest that other hypotheses would have to be considered to explain the residual sex difference not attributable to course enrollments. Since recent studies suggest that mathematics course participation is not the only factor in observed sex differences in achievement, there is an obvious need to consider personal characteristics of males and females as learners of mathematics as potential sources of variance in mathematics achievement of the sexes.

Because the perceived usefulness of mathematics does affect mathematics participation and achievement, the near equality in high school mathematics course participation (Brush, 1980; Sherman & Fennema, 1977) of males and females, noted in the Women in Mathematics and NAEP surveys (Armstrong, 1981), suggests that the sex-related difference in perceived usefulness of mathematics may be decreasing. In other words, the task value of mathematics for females may be increasing, at least as indexed by mathematics course participation. It is not clear, however, whether this trend indicates a substantial increase in the proportion of females who are planning careers in science and mathematics-related fields. Matthews (1980) reports from a survey of students enrolled in advanced mathematics courses that twice as many White males (86%) as White females (43%) indicated as an important reason for taking mathematics that "it is important to my career." In fact, a higher proportion of the Black (56%) and Asian (80%) females survey in Matthews' study reported career plans as an important factor in their decision to enroll in advanced mathematics courses than was true for White females. Matthews' data suggest that the increase in females' persistence in mathematics training in high school may be determined more by their plans for higher education than plans to pursue careers in science and mathematics.

A perusal of the literature in this area, guided by the Meece et al. (1982) model of individual academic choice, suggests that success expectancy in mathematics may be a particularly significant factor in the disparities seen between males and females in mathematics course enrollment and achievement. Meece, et al. (1982) assume that the underrepresentation of women in certain courses of study, specifically advanced mathematics, occurs because low success expectancy leads them to choose their training in other areas. However, in view of the considerable differences between the sexes in the affective and attitudinal variables related to mathematics participation that are apparent by junior high school, one may question whether the difference in the programs of study pursued by males and females is, in reality, a matter of choice, which implies selecting from a variety of alternatives after some deliberation. Rather, the presence of sex-role proscriptions, and the socialization process by which they are inculcated, may restrict the educational and occupational options available to women to such a degree that these decisions are more a matter of acquiescence than of choice.

It has been theorized that occupational role choices, and the related educational choices, are so closely tied to fundamental definitions of sex identity that nontraditional choices in these areas may cause considerable identity conflict (Fox, Tobin, & Brody, 1979; Nash, 1979; Rosenberg & Rosenberg, 1978). Nash (1979) suggests that the need for cognitive consistency in sex role identity is a mediator of intellectual achievement, particularly during adolescence when belief in the appropriateness of one's sex role behavior becomes critical for the consolidation of self identity. This view is supported by interviews in which Sherman (1982) investigated attitudes toward sex role and mathematics among girls who, comparable in general ability elected to take varying amounts of theoretical math in high school. The results of these interviews indicated that girls who enrolled in four years of mathematics, more than any other group, showed evidence of sex-role conflict. However, the girls who took four years of mathematics were more ambitious than those who had taken only three years of mathematics, which raised the following question for Sherman: "Did the girls who had taken less math show less ambition because they had resolved aspects of sex-role conflict in favor of renouncing ambition?" (Sherman, 1982, p. 440). This question could not be answered empirically from the data available in this study, but Sherman speculates that this factor did play a role in the girls' decisions regarding mathematics course participation.

Sherman's (1982) findings of greater sex-role conflict among girls who persist in the study of theoretical mathematics is consistent with the work of other investigators who have attempted to identify the salient aspects of adolescence which contribute to sex-related differences in cognitive achievement, particularly mathematics achievement. This research indicates that the formation of heterosexual relationships during this time may be particularly important (Fennema & Sherman, 1977; Nash, 1979). Levine (1976) reports that girls generally believe that boys do not like smart girls, particularly those who excel in mathematics. Sherman's (1982) study confirms this finding and its possible relationship to females' mathematics participation decision and achievement. Fear of peer rejection, in general, has also been identified as an important factor in mathematically precocious girls' decision to not pursue advanced study in mathematics (Fox, 1977). This literature generally questions the extent to which females actually have a choice in their pursuit of various educational programs and careers given their perception of the psychosocial cost of deviation from cultural norms.

There is some evidence to suggest that teachers display lower expectations for females in mathematics achievement than they do for males, and that school counselors actually discourage girls who are interested in mathematics and science careers by advising them against advanced courses in these areas (Haven, 1971; Casserly, 1980; Luchins, 1976). That this may be the case is suggested by Gregory's (1977) finding that teachers refer boys for remedial instruction in mathematics significantly more often than they refer girls. Parsons, Kaczala, and Meece (1982) report a significant relationship between teachers' expectations for a student and the students' self-concept of mathematics ability, regardless of past mathematics achievement (i.e., grades). However, the extent to which teachers' expectations for young people as learners of mathematics are operationalized in different interaction patterns in the classroom was not clear from their investigation.

To summarize to this point, the research literature generally shows that the process of sex role socialization conditions behavior in both social and intellectual areas in keeping with sex-appropriateness. The extent to which a particular task or subject matter is viewed as masculine or feminine reinforces sex differences in performance and development of competence, as mediated by different attainment values, confidence and persistence.

5.5. SEX DIFFERENCES AMONG BLACKS

Our results go considerably beyond previous findings indicating that Black females show a higher level of educational and occupational attainment than

Black males (Edwards, 1979; Jackson, 1973). It is true, in the current sample, that substantially larger proportions of the Black females have completed some college (See Table 2.15) than for Black males. But the test data suggest that the educational attainment differences seen between Black females and males is not the result of the females having uniformly superior skills relative to their male counterparts. Black males, regardless of income level, exceed the performance of Black females in the five specialized knowledge tests (i.e., General Science, Arithmetic Reasoning, Auto and Shop Information, Mechanical Comprehension, and Electronics Information), although the amount of difference in favor of males in the Black subsamples is generally less than that seen for males in other sociocultural-income groups. Poor Black males exceed the performance of their female counterparts in Word Knowledge, equal their performance in Paragraph Comprehension, and outperform the females in their group in both Mathematics Knowledge and Arithmetic Reasoning. Among nonpoor Blacks, females exceed the performance of their male counterparts in Word Knowledge and Paragraph Comprehension and equal males' performance in Mathematics Knowledge, although Black males show an advantage in Arithmetic Reasoning. These data support Ogbu's (1978) hypothesis that Black females show higher scholastic achievement and educational attainment than their male counterparts because they are more motivated to achieve scholastically. In other words, Black females' attainment may be more the result of greater effort and persistence in educational contexts than of higher level skill development as measured by the tests included in the ASVAB. Astin (1982) reports from his analysis of factors affecting minority higher educational progress that "being a woman is positively related to persistence among Blacks, but negatively related among Chicanos and Whites" (pp. 93–94).

Nonpoor Black females' educational motivation appears to be conditioned by the greater family support they receive for educational attainment as compared to males in this group. Blau (1981) reports from interviews with 579 Black and 523 White mothers of Chicago fifth- and sixth-grade children in 1968 that Black mothers generally expressed higher ambitions for their daughters than sons, while White mothers espoused higher ambitions for sons. Both Edwards (1979) and Ogbu (1978) posit that Black families have, historically, invested more of their resources in the education of daughters than sons because the employment opportunities have been more favorable for Black females than Black males. As indicated by Edwards (1979), however, the gap in the educational attainment of Black males and females appears to be closing. Analyzing sex and cohort changes for Black college graduates between 1940 and 1970, Edwards attributes the increase in Black male college graduates to economic advancements for Blacks in recent years and changes in the opportunity structure that portend better occupational prospects of Black males with college degrees.

Similarly, Thomas's (1980) analysis of data from the National Longitudinal Study (NLS) of the High School Class of 1972 revealed that the direct effects of family status on college entry were greater for male and female Blacks than for Whites, and greatest of all for Black males. This suggests that the Black family's investment in the education of males remains more strongly determined by family resources than is true for the investment in females.

5.6. SUMMARY AND CONCLUSIONS

In summary, the analysis of interaction effects between sex and education on the one hand, and sex and sociocultural group on the other, reveals significant sex differences in the vocational preparation of American young people. Males generally exceed females in General Science, Arithmetic Reasoning, Mechanical Comprehension, Electronics Information, and Auto and Shop Information. Females exceed males in Numerical Operations and Coding Speed. The data indicate that, on the average, young American males enjoy a competitive advantage over females for occupations and higher education placements in technical and scientific fields—areas in which females are at present substantially under-represented—because males have developed higher levels of skills required in these areas by the time they leave high school. It is important to note that the average difference in favor of males in these areas varies with educational level, sociocultural group, and income level. These data clearly show that sociocultural group differences in the development of the basic cognitive skills are considerably greater than the sex differences observed within these groups.

The data broadly confirm that sex differences in arithmetic reasoning ability previously observed among White middle-class youth appear also in other social groups, although among Blacks there is a general tendency toward smaller sex differences. In general, sex differences in knowledge of mathematics rules and ability to apply them are much smaller in each of the groups than those seen for Arithmetic Reasoning. In fact, the performance of males and females in the poor Hispanic and nonpoor Black subsamples in Mathematics Knowledge is essentially the same. As is the case for the other cognitive tests, the sociocultural differences in mathematics achievement are considerably greater than the sex differences seen within social groups.

An interesting finding in the analysis of the sociocultural group by sex interaction is evidence that, among poor Blacks, females tend in some respects to be more disadvantaged than males, whereas among nonpoor Blacks, females are relatively more advantaged. We interpret this to mean that stress upon the families of poor Blacks is more disruptive of the school achievement of girls than of boys. Conversely, among Hispanics, the nonpoor females are more disadvantaged with respect to the males than are the poor females. We interpret this to mean that the traditional social constraints of Hispanic culture on girls and women are more rigorous in the middle economic classes.

The sex differences in performance observed for males and females in the Profile sample are primarily in areas that are sex-typed in this society. Whether the sex-typing of particular intellectual and occupational areas as masculine or feminine has evolved from intuitive wisdom about the patterning of abilities of males and females is not clear from the available literature. Mullins (1980) would argue that the evolution of sex-typed occupational areas is the result of social, political, and economic considerations, and is in only a small way an outgrowth of biological adaptation.

There appears, however, to be evidence of a developmental basis for the difference in spatial ability between the sexes. The higher spatial ability of many males might facilitate performance in Arithmetic Reasoning and Mechanical Comprehension, both of which show a male advantage in the Profile data. But it is unlikely to be the cause of the even larger differences in the Auto and Shop Information and the Electronics Information tests. And Petersen (1979) points out, even if there is a developmental factor in spatial ability, the sex differences in this trait could not alone directly produce the large differences between males and females which appear in course selection in high school and college, and occupational choices in adult life. Positive feedback must also be involved.

There are obvious vocational implications of these findings. Because of their greater verbal fluency and greater perceptual speed and accuracy, women have a margin of advantage over men in such areas as instruction of children, translation, redaction, typing, clerical work and clerical machine operation, computer terminal operation, small parts assembly, etc. Because so many women consider only these types of jobs, the supply of labor in these areas is abundant and wages are relatively low. To have access to job markets where supply is smaller and wages higher, women would have to equal or exceed men in the capacities they bring to the occupation. Apart from hard labor and dangerous occupations that command high wages, the professions are the most attractive alternative for those women who are scholastically successful. Professions like teaching, nursing, and, increasingly, law, medicine, and management are entirely compatible with the profiles of attainment we see for females on the ASVAB tests. But the technical professions, engineering and science, find women at an overall disadvantage because of lower attainment in quantitative reasoning. If equality of opportunity is to be realized in these areas, the sociocultural factors that contribute to the disparities in quantitative skills observed between the sexes must be identified and eliminated. Young women must not only have the opportunity to train in mathematics, they must be actively encouraged to do so. Lack of mathematical preparation is one of the main barriers women must overcome if they are to enter the high-paying technical professions in greater numbers.

The sex-related differences in vocational potentials observed in the Profile study must be viewed as the result of a complex interplay of developmental and social factors. Changing patterns of experience will undoubtedly affect the organization of abilities in ways that will alter men and women's profiles of test performance in the future. As modes of socialization change, as women begin to realize the importance of developing mathematical skills for access to careers in engineering and science, the differing vocational prospects for the two sexes that we see now in the Profile data will surely move in the direction of greater equality.

6 Summary and Conclusions

In the spring and summer of 1980, the National Opinion Research Center of the University of Chicago administered the Department of Defense enlistment test—the Armed Services Vocational Aptitude Battery (ASVAB)—to a national probability sample of approximately 12,000 young men and women between the ages of 15 and 23. This battery of tests, in conjunction with other entry standards, is currently used to select personnel for the Army, Navy, Marine Corps, and Air Force and to assign recruits to appropriate military occupational specialities. It currently consists of ten tests measuring knowledge and skill in the following areas: Word Knowledge, Paragraph Comprehension, Arithmetic Reasoning, Numerical Operations, Coding Speed, General Science, Mathematics Knowledge, Mechanical Comprehension, Electronics Information, and Auto and Shop Information. The first six tests measure general cognitive skills, and the last four measure more specialized knowledge relevant to technical vocations.

The ASVAB was administered to this sample in order to obtain up-to-date national percentile norms for the tests and to provide data for an assessment of the vocational preparation of the contemporary youth population. Because the respondents in this study had previously been interviewed as part of the Department of Labor's National Longitudinal Survey of Youth Labor Force Behavior, considerable background information, in addition to the aptitude profile information, was available on each. This study, combining test-score and backround data, called the "Profile of American Youth," provided a unique opportunity to examine the vocational potential of a truly representative sample of American young people. In this monograph we report one such examination of these data.

We estimated the effects of selected background factors on the ASVAB tests by computing scaled estimates of ability for each respondent in the study and subjecting these scores to multivariate analysis of variance. In all tests the scale was chosen so that the mean of the national sample was 500 and the standard deviation 100. The analysis of variance showed that average scores on some or all of the ASVAB tests were related to the background factors—including sex, highest grade completed, sociocultural group, (White, Black, Hispanics), economic status (above or below the OMB-defined poverty line), region of residence at age 14, and mother's highest grade completed. (Highest grade completed for the purposes of this analysis was categorized as 0–8 years, some high school (9–11), completed high school (12), some college (13+), and in the case of mother's education, the additional level of completed college.)

In addition, interactive relationships were found involving the simultaneous effect of more than one factor. Average score differences between sociocultural group and economic status were significantly affected by highest grade completed, by the sex classification and by the region classification (Northeast, Southeast, Midwest, and West). Average score differences between the sexes were affected by highest grade completed, and to a lesser extent by mother's highest grade completed and sociocultural group. The nature and interpretation of these varied relationships among the background factors and the ASVAB scale-score averages are summarized in this chapter.

6.1. THE SOCIOCULTURAL GROUPS DIFFER IN ASVAB TEST PERFORMANCE ACCORDING TO YEARS OF EDUCATION, ECONOMIC STATUS, REGION OF THE COUNTRY, AND TYPE OF TEST

The analysis of the Profile data reveals that sociocultural group differences vary depending upon the educational level and economic status of the respondents, and upon the particular test employed. This means that the interpretation of the observed differences in the test performance of Whites, Blacks, and Hispanics must be qualified with respect to the educational, economic, and vocational context in which they appear. There are, however, a number of generalizations that can be made that simplify this potentially complex picture.

Educational Effects are Strongest for Tests That Measure School-Intensive Knowledge and Skills

At all education levels, the ordering of the average scores for the three sociocultural groups is similar for most tests: the White groups show the highest scores, the Hispanics are intermediate but somewhat closer to the

Whites, and the Black groups are lowest. These results are displayed graphically in Figure 3.1a and b. The differences between Hispanics and Whites depend, however, upon the economic classification and the type of test. For tests such as Word Knowledge, Paragraph Comprehension, Numerical Operations, Coding Speed, and Mathematics Knowledge, the performance of poor Hispanics is not very different from that of poor Whites, especially at the lower education levels. Among the nonpoor, by contrast, Whites clearly perform better than Hispanics at all education levels except 0–8 years, where on the whole there is little to distinguish the two groups.

Blacks score consistently below Whites and Hispanics in all ten of the tests and at all grade levels and economic classes. For tests such as Word Knowledge, Paragraph Comprehension, Numerical Operations, and Coding Speed, the differences between the means for Blacks and those of the other two groups are roughly the same at all education levels, averaging about 50 to 80 score points. For the tests of technical and quantitative knowledge, such as Arithmetic Reasoning, Mathematics Knowledge, Electronics Information, and to a lesser extent General Science and Mechanical Comprehension, the differences between Blacks and Whites increase with increasing educational levels. To a somewhat lesser extent this is also true of the Hispanics, especially poor Hispanics. The differences between sociocultural groups are largest for subjects with some college education.

The conclusion from these observations would seem to be that in topics that must be learned primarily in school, the White and the nonpoor groups, who more often have the benefit of schools that have better instructional resources and maintain higher standards, have an advantage over minority groups and the poor. This phenomenon is much less apparent in topics that are less tied to schooling and more part of daily experience in and out of school, such as Word Knowledge, Paragraph Comprehension, Numerical Operations, and Coding Speed. In these more basic competencies, the differences between the sociocultural groups are about the same at all education levels. The results discussed in Chapter 3 suggest that access to higher quality education has relatively less effect on these very general types of skills.

Poor and Nonpoor Show Similar Performance at the 13+ Education Level Because of an Artifact in the OMB Definition of Poverty

Both the general and specialized tests show the poor to score below the nonpoor at 0–8, 9–11, and 12 grades completed. But at 13+ (some college), the difference between the poor and the nonpoor largely disappears among Whites and Hispanics. This phenomenon is a consequence of the Office of Management and Budget (OMB) definition of poverty, which classifies self-supporting college students as poor even when the family background is one of comparative affluence. The official definition does not truly reflect the socioeconomic origins of the Whites at this education level. Interestingly, the same is not true of Blacks, and for the technical subject matter, is somewhat less true of Hispanics. The likely explanation of this difference is that more of the Blacks and some of the Hispanics who are in college are living at home and are dependent on parents, and are therefore correctly classified in terms of the economic status of their families. Thus the interaction apparent in these data between education level and economic status is a methodological artifact and not of substantive interest.

English Language Limitations of Hispanics Are Not Very Apparent in the Profile Data

Among Hispanics, the data suggest some effect of English language competency, but the size of the effect is surprisingly small. For the non-language tests in the battery—Numerical Operations and Coding Speed—Hispanics and Whites are very similar in performance, and the largest differences are not, as might be expected, in the language tests—Word Knowledge and Paragraph Comprehension—but in the specialized knowledge tests and Arithmetic Reasoning. Thus, the difference in performance between the Whites and the Hispanics would seem to be one of educational emphasis rather than one of English language competence. On the whole the results give a rather optimistic picture of the vocational preparation of Hispanics relative to Whites at both economic levels. Such differences as exist in the test performance of Whites and Hispanics seem to reflect educational emphasis in the Hispanic communities, and they can be expected to change in a favorable direction as trends in education and acculturation continue.

Some of the Test Scores Reflect Prevailing Practices in Mathematics Teaching in American Schools

Yet another phenomenon is seen in those tests where formal mathematics instruction plays a prominent role—namely, Arithmetic Reasoning, Mathematics Knowledge, and to some extent Numerical Operations at lower education levels. For these tests there is a reduced difference between scores of persons who have some high school education compared to those who have completed high school.

As we have pointed out in the discussion of Figure 3.1, this tends to produce a "step" in the plots of average scores vs. education level that is more apparent in these tests than in the tests less dependent on mathematics instruction. We interpret this to be the result of many high school students ending their formal mathematical training at the first and second year of high school, so that less gain is seen in these tests between groups that have completed high school and those that have not. Those students who are college bound, on the other hand, are more likely to continue their mathematics training into the third and fourth years of high school and, therefore, show relatively higher performance on these types of tests both before matriculation and subsequently as they take additional mathematics courses in the early years of college. This observation is consistent with curricular practice in the United States, which treats mathematics beyond grade 10 as largely specialized to the college-bound student.

Blacks and Whites in the Northeast Perform Somewhat Better Than Their Counterparts Elsewhere in the Country

The overall cultural group differences discussed above conceal some interesting differences with respect to the four regions of the United States studied—Northeast (bounded by Maryland and Delaware on the south and Pennsylvania on the west and including Puerto Rico and the Virgin Islands), Southeast (bounded by Virginia and West Virginia on the north and Louisiana, Arkansas and Kentucky on the west, Midwest (bounded by Oklahoma on the south and the Dakotas, Nebraska and Kansas on the west), and West (including all remaining states, the Pacific Trust territories, and the Canal Zone). These were the regions into which subjects in this study were classified according to their place of residence at age 14. This classification is intended to represent the major regional influence on the subject's development, but obviously does so only for those subjects who lived in those regions for an appreciable length of time up to age 14.

Regional effects on the test scores are small, seldom more than 20 scale points, but are statistically significant. The patterns of regional attainment for Blacks and Whites are rather similar. Performance of Blacks and Whites of either economic status tend to be higher in the Northeast, next highest in the Midwest and West, and lowest in the Southeast. But the Auto and Shop Information test is an exception. For this test both the White group and the nonpoor Blacks show progressively higher scores from Northeast to Southeast to Midwest to West, but poor Blacks are lowest in the Midwest. The pattern suggests a perhaps greater involvement of young persons with automobiles and mechanical work as one goes from the East to West across the nation, a trend which roughly parallels extent of automobile use.

The Northeast, as noted, shows higher scores especially in the more academic subjects such as General Science, Arithmetic Reasoning, and Mathematics Knowledge, perhaps reflecting higher scholastic standards in these areas in that region. The West is especially strong both in Auto and

Shop Information and in Mechanical Comprehension, suggesting greater emphasis on practical skills. The Southeast region, both for Whites and Blacks, generally shows the lowest level of performance, although for Blacks the differences between the Southeast and West is small. Blacks generally perform better in the Northeast and Midwest.

The Test Performance of Hispanics is Highest in the Southeast

A quite converse pattern is seen for the Hispanics. The highest levels of performance are in the Southeast and Midwest with both the East and West showing generally lower levels. In fact, nonpoor Hispanics of the Southeast and Midwest perform at about the same level as nonpoor Whites in Paragraph Comprehension, Numerical Operations, and Coding Speed. In General Science, Arithmetic Reasoning, and Word Knowledge, Hispanics of the Southeast perform almost at the same level as the nonpoor Whites. Some of the largest differences between the nonpoor and poor classes occur among the Hispanics, especially those of the Midwest, suggesting that economic factors are more dominant for Hispanics than for either Whites or Blacks.

These effects are easily understood in terms of the origins of the Hispanic populations in these four regions of the country. Hispanics of the Northeast are drawn mainly from lower economic level Puerto Ricans who now reside in the large metropolitan areas of the Northeast in close proximity to the Black populations. Both nonpoor and poor Hispanics are performing at about the same level as Blacks in the Northeast (which is the region of the country where Blacks show their highest performance). In fact, the performance of poor Hispanics in the Northeast is below that of poor Blacks in that region. The Hispanics represented in this sample in the Southeast are largely the children of middle-class Cubans who came to Miami when Castro came to power in the 1950s. They have been largely assimilated into the larger socioeconomic community in Florida, and their performance differs little from that of members of the majority culture in that region. In the Midwest, the higher income Hispanics are well assimilated residents of long standing in major areas such as Chicago and are performing only slightly below the level of the majority culture. Poor Hispanics in the Midwest, however, tend to be new residents and are performing at a level closer to the range of the Blacks. In the West, both nonpoor and poor Hispanics represent persons who have close connections with Mexico and the Spanish language community and perform on these tests at a generally lower level, midway between Whites and Blacks. Moreover, there are smaller differences between nonpoor and poor Hispanics in the West. All in all, these results, especially the regional effects among Hispanics, tend to demonstrate the impact of the cultural background on performance on these types of vocational tests.

Some Blacks Are Performing at High Levels,
But Their Relative Numbers Are Small

Neither the effects of education, those of economic status, or those of region are very revealing of the ultimate origins of the differences in vocational test performance among the sociocultural groups. Blacks, for example, show many education and region effects similar to those of Whites and Hispanics, but their average scores are almost always lower, in some cases by as much as 100 scale points. When the score distributions (shown in Figures 2.6, 2.7, and 2.8) are examined in detail, however, there is some evidence of a distinguishable small group of Blacks, amounting to perhaps 10% of the Black population, whose scores are comparable to those of Whites. We suppose these Blacks to be those who are participating fully in the majority culture as represented in the content of the vocational tests in this study. Unfortunately, the sources of these high-achieving Blacks, who are not accounted for by educational level, cannot be more precisely identified in the present data. For this reason, we have had to rely on studies in the literature for some insight into the reasons for the greater score differentiation seen among Blacks compared to Whites of similar education and economic class.

Evidence from Recent Studies Contradicts the Theory
That Differences in the Average Test Performance
of the Sociocultural Groups Are of Genetic Origin

One unsubstantiated theory that appears from time to time attributes the disparity in cognitive test performance between Blacks and Whites to genetic differences between the subpopulations. It is supposed that there exist genes, as yet unidentified, that are critical for cognitive functioning and, owing to past selective forces, are less widely represented among Blacks than among Whites. The claim is that the substantial differences between mean cognitive test scores of Whites and Blacks in the United States arise from this source. These theories are based, however, on the erroneous assumption that the moderately high levels of heritability that have been found for certain general and special cognitive abilities also account for differences in the average performance levels in socially defined populations.

The clearest evidence that cognitive functioning is influenced by biological inheritance is that identical twins, even those reared separately from near birth onwards, are consistently found to be more similar in levels of cognitive test performance than fraternal twins, and that the performance of early adopted children resembles more their natural parents than their adoptive parents. The bulk of evidence from these types of family study supports the conclusion that genetic effects account for an appreciable part of the individual differences in performance that one sees within populations. Such studies are, however, always carried out within relatively homogeneous social groups, and do not attempt to account for differences between the mean levels of populations.

On the contrary, studies of other quantitative traits, especially those having to do with body size and proportion, show that the average levels of equally heritable physiological traits can change by a comparable amount in only two generations. Mature height, for example, has almost exactly the same degree of heritability as IQ test performance. But in response to better nutritional environments and health care, height has been increasing at about 3.0 centimeters per generation in developed and developing countries. Increases of this magnitude have been occurring in Europe and the United States since the middle of the last century, and have occurred at an even greater rate in Japan and other Far Eastern countries since World War II. Most of the gain is due to increases in leg length, with the result that mature body proportions are also changing. Thus, the stocky build traditionally associated with the Japanese turns out to be an environmental rather than a genetic difference between that population and Western populations. These counterexamples firmly establish the fact that within population heritabilities of quantitative traits, even as high as are found for height or cognitive test performance, do not imply that the differences between the average levels of the trait in socially distinct populations are of genetic origin.

Studies that separate the effects of biological and social inheritance on behavioral indices are difficult to carry out because persons who are more closely related biologically tend to occupy more similar social environments than those who are distantly related or unrelated. As a result, the effects of heredity and environment on cognitive development are thoroughly confounded in most studies. One approach to separating these effects is to examine the relationship between the behavioral measures and biological indicators of genetic similarity. As we have discussed in Chapter 3, one such study carried out by Sandra Scarr (1977) and her colleagues made use of a method whereby the proportions of genes carried by a given person that arose in the European and African gene pools can be estimated from certain minor blood group markers that have widely different frequencies in these populations. If the putative genes for cognitive ability also have different frequencies in these populations, then cognitive test scores should correlate with the proportion of admixture of these gene pools within individuals. Scarr and her colleagues observed no such correlation, indicating that the differences we see in the average test performance of populations in the United States deriving from European and African origins are not substantially of genetic origin.

Another approach to separating biological and environmental effects on cognitive development is to examine the performance of children who as infants have been adopted across sociocultural group or economic class lines. We refer in Chapter 3 to studies of this type carried out by Scarr and

Weinberg (1976) and independently by Elsie G. J. Moore (1980). In both studies, Black children adopted at an early age into White middle-class families were administered standard intelligence tests at several ages during childhood. These children were found to perform at a mean level typical of White children of comparable age, rather than at the lower level typical of such children raised in Black families. Moore's study was especially informative because she compared Black children adopted into middle-class White homes with those adopted into middle-class Black homes. She found that the children in the White homes scored on the tests at a mean level typical of White middle-class children and those in the Black homes scored at a mean level typical of Black middle-class children. There was nothing in the backgrounds of these children to suggest that the observed differences could be attributed to selective placement by the adoption agency. Rather, the difference appeared to be due to the cumulative effect on children of being reared in homes and neighborhoods with different exposure to and emphasis on the kinds of knowledge, skills, and task orientations that are required for successful performance on certain cognitive tests.

The conclusion from the Scarr and Moore (1982,1986) studies is that when Black children are adopted into White middle-class homes at an early age and raised completely within that environment, their performance on cognitive tests is indistinguishable from that of White children of the same age. The similarity of this effect of the sociocultural environment on behavioral development with that of improved diet and medical care on physiological growth and development is indeed striking. In both cases, variation of the traits within population is substantially heritable, but the cumulative impact of a change in nurturance is nevertheless seen as an increase in the average level of the population in a measure of overall growth, cognitive on the one hand and physical on the other. These adoption studies, and the evidence of intergenerational increase in stature in developing countries, suggest a resolution to the longstanding "nature-nurture" controversy in the study of human behavior. Both influences act simultaneously; but whereas hereditary effects are easily seen in individual differences, environmental effects are more clearly expressed in differences in the average levels of traits between generations and between populations.

A Community Norm Theory Seems to Be the Best Explanation of the Sociocultural Group Differences

Although the studies cited above demonstrate the effect of the sociocultural environment on cognitive test performance, they do not give any indication of the processes by which these effects occur. In our review of the literature in Chapter 3, however, we cite several theories of how such processes might operate. One such theory is contained in the formal mathematical models of status attainment that attempt to account for variation in general measures of school achievement similar to the ASVAB tests. The explanatory (exogenous) variables in such models typically include father's occupation, income, and social status, and the child's general ability as indexed by an IQ score. These variables are supposed to affect the child's ambition for attainment and ultimately his or her other school achievement. As bases for causal explanation, however, these models are questionable. Because cognitive measures such as IQ scores are, as we have seen, influenced by the sociocultural group and economic class in which the child is raised, these models would seem to describe relationships among effects rather than responses to ultimate causes. Thus, the formal status attainment models do not seem to offer the type of explanation we are seeking.

Neither do the other prevailing theories of social and economic group differences—namely, the linguistic minority and early deprivation theories—seem adequate to explain the results of the Profile study. Deficits due to lack of proficiency in the majority language do not account for differences in the non-language tests of the ASVAB, nor in the pattern of results of the other tests in light of their language content. Similarly, effects of early deprivation do not explain the increasing differences between Blacks and Whites at increasing education levels through some college.

A more satisfactory explanation is simply that the communities represented by the present more-or-less exclusive sociocultural subpopulations in the United States maintain, for historical reasons, different norms, standards, and expectations concerning performance within the family, in school, and in other institutions that shape children's behavior. Young people adapt to these norms and apply their talents and energies accordingly. These norms are so much a part of the fabric of the face-to-face community setting in which family, relatives, friends, and acquaintances interact that the standards of the larger society—represented here by norms of test performance—cannot easily displace or alter them. Although the task of raising standards of test performance is traditionally assigned in the abstract to schools, actual schools in the United States are responsible first to their communities, only secondarily to states, and only indirectly to the nation. Thus, norms of the immediate community tend to be perpetuated, even when the result is the range of group differences such as that seen in the Profile study.

There is ample reason to believe, however, that many schools could work toward a higher standard than that which currently prevails. But the process of raising standards involves the whole of the communities that these schools serve, and must extend to parents, families, social groups, and every institution in which members of the community participate. Moreover, the community norm is part of the cultural transmission from one generation to another, and the process must work on the scale of decades, not just years. Only steady and consistent efforts over an extended period of time can produce significant changes in the community norm and the educational standards it determines.

6.2. MOTHER'S EDUCATION AND YEARS OF FORMAL SCHOOLING ARE STRONG PREDICTORS OF VOCATIONAL TEST PERFORMANCE

Mother's education (Mother's Highest Grade Completed), discussed in Chapter 4, differs from the other factors investigated in this study in that it is largely a within-family influence on the performance of the children. It stands apart from the broad social variables of educational level, sociocultural group, economic status, and region of the country, which act much less directly. This may explain why mother's education, shows only weak interaction with any of the other background factors.

Mother's Education Is Strongly Associated with Better Test Performance, But Interacts Very Little with Other Background Factors

Mother's education shows a strong and direct association with test performance, especially in those tests which depend upon language and instruction (Word Knowledge, Paragraph Comprehension, General Science, Arithmetic Reasoning, and Mathematics Knowledge). As might be expected, the tests that are less related to formal learning and language depend much less strongly on mother's education. These include Coding Speed, Auto and Shop Information, Mechanical Comprehension, and Electronics Information. The mother's educational variable is of interest primarily to the extent to which it shows how family background characteristics are reflected in test performance. For Word Knowledge, for example, the difference in average scores between children of mothers with only 8 or less years of education versus those with college degrees is about 60 scale points. This difference is not as great as the direct effect of the young person's own education, which amounts to nearly 150 scale points, but it indicates the close association between the intellectual attainments of the mother and those of her children. In large-scale studies where a wide range of education levels is represented, mother's education is an effective indicator of the family's contribution to children's attainment.

**Among Persons of Different Ages Who Have the Same Number
of Years of Education, Some Test Scores Increase with Age,
Some Decline, But for the Most Part Levels of Performance
Remain About What They Were at the End of Formal Education**

Although age and highest grade completed tend to be confounded in the
Profile data, there is enough variation in age within the highest grade completed groups to enable us to draw some conclusions about age effects
independent of schooling. The supplementary analysis of the Profile data discussed in Section 4.2 reveals that performance on tests such as Arithmetic
Reasoning and Numerical Operations, representing intensive, school-learned
skills, tends to decline after a person completes formal schooling. Performance on test content that is learned mostly by experience, such as Auto and
Shop Information and Electronics Information, tends to improve after school.

These effects are small, however, compared with the general tendency for
the level of performance on all tests to remain near their levels at the end of
schooling. The analysis confirms the impact of formal school completion in
channeling the vocational opportunities for American youth.

6.3.   SEX DIFFERENCES VARY MOST STRONGLY
WITH THE TYPE OF TEST

As we have shown in Chapter 5, the size, and in some cases the direction, of
the differences between males and females vary greatly from one ASVAB test
to another. In particular, men and women have distinctly different profiles of
both general ability and special knowledge. Under present conditions of education, women are at a competitive disadvantage relative to men in tests
requiring technical knowledge and quantitative skills; they have an advantage
in tests requiring fluent and accurate information processing and use of
language. Studies in the educational, psychological, and physiological literature suggest that these differences result partly from sexual specialization of
education and experience, and partly from biologically intrinsic differences.

**Men and Women Differ Most in Knowledge of Topics
That Are Traditionally Specialized by Sex, But the Effect
Is More Apparent in Whites and Hispanics Than Blacks**

Typical of the sex differences where average scores of men exceed those of
women is performance on the Auto and Shop Information test. Among nonpoor Whites and Hispanics, the average scores of male respondents exceed

those of female respondents by slightly more than 100 scale points. The sex differences for Blacks of either economic status are considerably smaller for this test, amounting to not more than 50 scale points. They are also smaller for poor persons in all subgroups.

This pattern of attainment suggests that with greater access to automobile and shop experience, it is the young men who benefit most. By circumstance or choice, women do not participate in study or activities that bring them into contact with this kind of information. Among Blacks, poor Whites and Hispanics, auto and shop information is less available or less exploited by both males and females and the sex differences are smaller.

Similar patterns of greater male attainment appear in the Mechanical Comprehension and Electronics Information tests but are not as pronounced as in Auto and Shop Information. The largest sex difference for these tests is about 75 scale points. Still smaller but significant sex differences in favor of males are also seen in the General Science and Arithmetic Reasoning tests, but the interactions with sociocultural group and economic status are diminished. Although Blacks show larger sex differences on General Science and Arithmetic Reasoning than is the case with Auto and Shop, Mechanical Comprehension, and Electronics Information, these differences are still less than the sex differences shown by Whites on the same tests.

Neither the Word Knowledge nor the Mathematics Knowledge test shows consistent or statistically significant sex difference.

Women Excel in Reading Comprehension and in Tasks Requiring Fast and Accurate Responses

Patterns of female advantage are seen in Coding Speed, Numerical Operations, and Paragraph Comprehension. In Coding Speed, females exceed males by about 50 scale points, with the size of the difference slightly greater among Whites than among Hispanics or Blacks. A similar pattern is seen in the Numerical Operations test, but the sex difference is reduced to about 25 scale points. However, very little sex difference is apparent on this test for poor Blacks, even though nonpoor Blacks show the same 25 scale-point advantage of females over males as do the other groups. Females also score higher on Paragraph Comprehension, but the sex differences favoring females are even smaller and are virtually absent for poor Blacks. The results suggest that the cultural and educational disadvantages that impair the test performance of poor Blacks fall more heavily on females relative to males than is true of nonpoor Blacks or the other groups.

Female performance on Numerical Operations, Coding Speed, and Paragraph Comprehension may be explained by psychological research that shows women to be uniformly superior to men in so-called "fluent-production" tasks. These are tasks in which an overlearned response must be made quickly and accurately. Numerical Operations is a speeded test in which the subject is required to perform as many simple 1-digit computations as possible in a fixed length of time. Coding Speed is a similar test in which the subject must look up code numbers of words in a table and mark them on the answer sheet. The Paragraph Comprehension test is a measure of basic reading comprehension. Although the time allotted to this test is not especially short, an element of reading fluency may also be involved that helps account for the sex difference. It has been suggested that women react more positively than men to these types of repetitive tasks and thus perform better. But the few studies that have investigated this phenomenon are far from definitive.

The present study confirms that a pattern of male advantage for quantitative and technical tasks and female advantage for fluency tasks, which has heretofore been seen in studies of White secondary school and college students, is general to all sociocultural groups and economic levels. It is especially significant that the Arithmetic Reasoning test shows sex differences in favor of males while the Mathematics Knowledge test does not uniformly do so. This suggests that Arithmetic Reasoning, which requires the solution of "word problems" using numerical quantities, is in some important respect different from the Mathematics Knowledge test, which asks only for facts about mathematics and the execution of formal algebraic rules. There is a substantial body of evidence that males consistently exceed females in the ability to visualize relationships and movements among two- and three-dimensional figures and objects. It has been conjectured that the solution of arithmetic word problems is facilitated by visualizing the quantities and relationships involved. The contrasting sex differences of the Arithmetic Reasoning and Mathematics Knowledge tests in this study support that conjecture.

As we discuss in Chapter 5, there is also considerable evidence in the literature that the difference in male and female ability to visualize spatial relations is influenced by physiological differences between the sexes. In particular, males in whom the normal hormonal changes of adolescence are pathologically absent have levels of spatial ability similar to those of females. The connection between spatial ability and quantitative and configural problem solving is a possible source of the sex differences seen in the Arithmetic Reasoning and Mechanical Comprehension tests.

Some Sex Differences in Test Performance Increase with Education; Others Decrease

When sex differences are examined as a function of the respondents highest grade completed, it is found that for Auto and Shop Information, Mechanical Comprehension, Electronics Information, General Science, and Arithmetic Reasoning, the differences between the sexes increase with increasing education. This is interpreted as another expression of the principle seen in the interaction of sex differences with sociocultural group and economic status for Auto and Shop Information—namely, that where there is greater opportunity for exposure and experience in those areas where males generally perform better than females, males benefit more from such exposure and thus increase the disparity of performance between the sexes. With the increasing specialization that comes with education, men and women also become more specialized in sex-typed knowledge and skills that lead to different profiles of average vocational test scores. At lower educational levels, experience and instruction are more common between the sexes and sex differences in test performance are not as large.

In the fluent production tasks (measured by the Numerical Operations and Coding Speed tests), where females score higher, sex differences remain almost constant as a function of level of education. This suggests that sex differences in fluency are due to differences between men and women that are not much influenced by education. In Paragraph Comprehension, the sex difference favoring females remains about the same until subjects have completed 13 or more years or schooling. At this point, both men and women have mastered simple reading tasks and the test no longer differentiates between the sexes. The Word Knowledge test shows no sex difference at any grade level, and the Mathematics Knowledge test shows a sex difference in favor of males only at 13+ years, where the greater tendency of men to take mathematics courses in college finally has an effect. This is in contrast with Arithmetic Reasoning, which shows steadily increasing sex differences in favor of males from the 9th grade.

Differences in the Vocational Test Performance of Men and Women Affect Their Vocational Opportunities

The implications of these patterns of sex differences for vocational choice are well known and widely discussed. The disadvantage to females that results from their lower performance in technical areas such as Auto and Shop Information, Mechanical Comprehension, Electronics Information, and General Science is reflected in the relatively small numbers of women who enter the technical fields. The parity between men and women with respect to Word Knowledge and Paragraph Comprehension is reflected in the relative equality of men and women in the literary and writing fields. And finally, the rather marked advantage of women in the fluent production tasks, which are so much a part of clerical work such as business machine operation and word processing, suggests one of the reasons why women largely outnumber men in these fields. The present study gives a more complete account of these vocationally relevant sex differences than has previously been available.

6.4. DIFFERENCES IN TEST PERFORMANCE OF YOUNG PEOPLE AT THE SAME LEVEL OF EDUCATION IN DIFFERENT SOCIAL AND ECONOMIC GROUPS SHOW THE NEED FOR MORE COMPREHENSIVE STANDARDS OF EDUCATIONAL ATTAINMENT

The Profile data reveal striking disparities between sociocultural and economic groups on all tests. These disparities between groups exist even when persons of the same educational level are compared. In Chapter 13 we argued for differences in community attainment standards as the correct explanation of group test scores differences. Some sociocultural groups are more conscious than others of the main avenues of vocational opportunity, and of the kinds of preparation needed to take advantage of them. They know the .importance of language and mathematics skills, and of familiarity with the scientific and technical concepts on which so much of our economic life depends. Young people from communities with a higher achievement standard have a marked advantage on tests designed to predict occupational success.

Everyone would benefit from the diffusion of higher achievement standards. The disparity between social groups would be reduced and the nation's human resources would increase. The social and economic cost of personal failures would decrease, and more skill and talent would be available for every aspect of craftsmanship, technology, art, and science. To believe that levels of attainment in diverse social groups can be influenced by a shared commitment to higher standards is far from utopian. At the end of Chapter 13 we cited the evidence from the school achievement surveys of the National Assessment of Educational Progress to show that differences between Blacks and Whites at ages 9 and 13 lessened during the period of educational restructuring in the 1970s. This trend is unmistakable and applies to almost all of the important school subjects at these age levels. If it continues through the 1980s and 1990s, we can look forward to much reduced differences between advantaged and disadvantaged young people at the end of this century. Quite possibly, smaller differences will then prevail between the sexes as well as between sociocultural groups. Moreover, if the high standards which presently exist for some are spread to all, this society will benefit from future generations that have broader potential for productive and creative lives than any that have gone before.

Appendix A
Sampling Method

The two civilian samples for the Profiles study were selected by standard area probability methods. These methods involve the random selection of progressively smaller units (counties, census blocks or enumeration districts, dwelling units, and individuals) to obtain a representative national probability sample. Stratification was introduced at several stages to insure a sufficient number of individuals from both urban and rural areas and from all geographical Census Divisions. Special procedures were employed to insure the inclusion of college students and persons living in group quarters.

Selection of the civilian samples comprised several steps:

- Random probability selection of 202 geographically dispersed county-size areas (primary sampling units)
- Selection within each primary sampling unit of nine census blocks or enumeration districts
- Listing the addresses of dwelling units within each selected census block or enumeration district
- Probability selection of a sample of the listed dwelling units
- Completion of a screening interview with an adult in each selected dwelling unit to locate youth eligible for the survey

In the fall of 1978, NORC interviewers screened approximately 81,000 households and located some 14,000 eligible youth, all of whom were scheduled for a baseyear (1979) interview. In screening for the supplemental sample, the number of Hispanic and Black youth located in the households selected for screening exceeded the number required in the sample design.

Therefore, it was necessary to select a subsample of these individuals for baseyear interviewing. Table A.1 shows the 714 cases deleted by subsampling. The remaining Hispanic and Black cases received greater caseweights to compensate for the deleted cases.

Tables A.1 and A.2 show the number of individuals located in screening, selected for a baseyear interview, interviewed, and tested in the cross-section and in the supplemental sample.

The military sample was selected from personnel files provided by the Department of Defense. Before selection, the files were stratified by the four Military Services and by five world-wide geographic regions. Females were oversampled at a rate six times that of males in order to produce approxi-

TABLE A.1
Cross-Section Sample Youth Located in Screening, Selected by Baseyear Interview, Completed Interview and Completed Profile Test

Design Cohort	Located in Screening	Out of Scope	Selected for Interview	Completed Interview	Completed Profile Test
Males:					
Hispanic....................	249	5	244	216	195
Non-Hispanic Black	386	7	379	347	332
Economically disadvantaged non-Hispanic, non-Black	189	5	184	203[d]	188
Other.......................	2,599	39	2,560	2,238	2,107
Total.......................	3,423	56	3,367	3,004	2,822
Females					
Hispanic....................	248		248	228	218
Non-Hispanic Black	451	13	438	404	388
Economically disadvantaged non-Hispanic, non-Black	180		180	198[d]	186
Other.......................	2,620	41	2,579	2,277	2,152
Total.......................	3,499	54	3,445	3,107	2,944
TOTAL	6,922[a]	110	6,812	6,111[b]	5,766[c]

[a] Screening interviews were completed in 91. 2% of the occupied dwelling units selected for screening.

[b] Interviews were completed with 89.7% of those selected for baseyear interviews.

[c] Profile tests were completed by 94.4% of those who completed a baseyear interview.

[d] A number of individuals who had not been identified as economically disadvantaged at the time of screening and selection for interview were reclassified after their interview. This accounts for the apparent discrepancy between the number selected and the number interviewed in this design cohort.

TABLE A.2

Supplemental Sample Youth Located in Screening, Selected for Baseyear Interview, Completed Interview and Completed Profile Test

Design Cohort	Located in Screening	Out of Scope (Ineligible)	Deleted by Subsampling	Selected for Interview	Completed Baseyear Interview	Completed Profile Test
Males:						
Hispanic	1,015	26	161	828	730	668
Non-Hispanic Black	1,318	42	50	1,226	1,096	1,043
Economically disadvantaged non-Hispanic non-Black	887	28	1	858	744	697
Total	3,220	97	211	2,912	2,570	2,408
Females:						
Hispanic	1,060	16	205	839	750	695
Non-Hispanic Black	1,502	31	298	1,173	1,076	1,041
Economically disadvantaged non-Hispanic non-Black	1,073	28	0	1,045	899	846
Total	3,635	75	503	3,057	2,725	2,582
TOTAL	6,855[a]	173	715	5,969	5,295[b]	4,990[c]

[a] Screening interviews were completed in 91.9% of the occupied dwelling units selected for screening.

[b] Interviews were completed with 88.7% of those selected for baseyear interviews.

[c] Profile tests were completed by 94.2% of those who completed a baseyear interview.

mately equal numbers of males and females in the final military sample. Table A.3 shows the distribution of NLS baseyear respondents and Profile subjects by sex and Military Service.

A.1. CLUSTERING OF THE SAMPLE

The selection processes just described produced a geographically clustered (rather than randomly distributed) national probability sample. Clustering reduces the costs of contacting and interviewing the sample members in large-scale surveys because fieldworkers can be dispatched to a smaller number of sites than would be the case if the geographic distribution of the sample were random. Despite the clustering, every individual in the target age range in every part of the country has a chance of entering the sample. For a variety of reasons, however, the selected individuals have differential probabilities (i.e. unequal chances) of selection. To compensate for this a system of weighting is employed whereby the sample is once again made representative of the target population. (See Frankel & McWilliams, 1981, for a detailed description of the weighting scheme.)

Although clustering does not bias the sample, it does affect how the data

TABLE A.3
Military Sample Baseyear Interview and
Profile Test Completed Cases

Service	Completed Interview	Completed Profile Test
Males:		
Army	352	320
Navy	212	182
Air Force	163	151
Marine Corps	96	85
Total	823	738
Females:		
Army	224	208
Navy	68	59
Air Force	131	121
Marine Corps	34	32
Total	457	419
TOTAL	1,280[a]	1,158[b]

[a] Interviews were completed with 71.5% of those selected for baseyear interviews.

[b] Profile tests were completed by 90.5% of those who completed a baseyear interview

must be treated to assess the statistical significance of results and to construct confidence intervals. Cluster samples show less internal sampling variability but possess greater standard errors than simple random samples of the same size. However, because the amount of reduction in variance can be estimated, the effect of clustering can be allowed for in statistical inference.

One of the more potent sources of the clustering effect is the selection of all persons in the eligible age range within each household. Of the 12,686 respondents to the Year 1 NLS interview, 4,197 came from households with one respondent, 4,304 from those with two, 2,154 with three, 948 with four, 305 with five, 60 with six, and 718 from other size households. Some of those from multiple-respondent households are siblings, some are spouses, some unrelated. Nevertheless, to the extent that they share a common environment, common heredity, or exhibit correlated mate selection, there will exist within-household (intraclass) correlation that can reduce the effective sample size.

In the present analysis, however, the young people who took the ASVAB tests are assigned to different background subgroups if they are not of the same sex or are at different education levels according to highest grade completed at the time of interview. The probability that two members of the same household will appear in the same subclasses of the analysis (and, by virtue of their similarity in test performance, bias downward the estimated error variance) is therefore considerably reduced. For this reason, we believe that the cluster effect has only a minor impact on our analysis. We discuss the correction for clustering in Appendix C.

A.2. THE INTERVIEWS

In the spring of 1979, NORC conducted the first round of interviews for the NLS. The interviews covered a variety of background factors that influence the vocational prospects of young people entering the labor market. These interviews provided the demographic information used in the present study.

Extraordinary measures were taken to locate and gain the cooperation of the young people for the initial interview. As can be seen in Tables A.1, A.2, and A.3, this effort met with considerable success: of the 6,812 respondents selected for the cross-section sample, 89.7% completed first year interviews. The interview completion rate for the supplemental sample of 5,969 Blacks, lower-income Whites, and Hispanics was 88.7%. In the sample of 1,793 persons selected from the military (with oversampling of women), the completion rate fell to 71.%, largely because of difficulty in reaching service personnel on remote assignment. Because the military sample constitutes only a small fraction of the total sample, however, this lower completion rate has little effect on the broad comparisons made in this study. For these purposes, the overall interview completion rate of 87.0%—higher than is typical in large-scale surveys other than the Census—is quite satisfactory.

A.3. RECRUITMENT OF RESPONDENTS AND TEST ADMINISTRATION

Because this was the first attempt to administer a battery of tests to a large-scale national probability sample, there was little experience to suggest how difficult it might be to convince respondents, on an entirely voluntary basis, to devote three and one-half hours of their time to taking the ten ASVAB tests. Obviously, this would be a far greater imposition on the respondents than the hour or so for the NLS survey interview. Moreover, to simulate as closely as possible the standard conditions under which the ASVAB was administered to military applicants, the battery was to be administered to groups of about ten respondents meeting in the same room at the same time, thus requiring the young people to travel at least a minimal distance to a testing site and increasing the total time they must invest.

The project staff realized that many respondents would participate in the study because they would be interested in receiving their test results or might consider taking the ASVAB good practice for other tests. Others, however, would probably require a monetary incentive to participate. A pretest conducted in the spring of 1980 indicated that a satisfactory rate of participation could be obtained by paying an honorarium of $50. Therefore, because a high response rate was critical to the validity of the overall results, several incentives were used. Participants received copies of their test results, information to interpret the scores, a brochure containing vocational and educational information, and an honorarium of the same amount as proved effective in the pretest.

The participants were first informed of the testing project in a thank you letter sent in May 1980 after the completion of the 1980 NLS (Year 2) interview. In June of that year, a formal request for participation was sent to the young people or to the parents of those under 18 years of age. This letter contained an attractive brochure announcing the "Profile of American Youth" and conveying the national importance of the project. The letter explained that participants would receive an honorarium of $50, an informative brochure, and a report of their own scores, but that their individual scores would not be released to anyone else. The letter indicated that an NORC interviewer would contact them soon to answer any questions they might have and to arrange a convenient time and place for the testing.

Responsibility for contacting respondents was delegated to some two hundred field teams consisting of two persons, one of whom acted as examiner during the testing sessions and the other as the test proctor. Both workers participated in the job of locating and encouraging members of the NLS sample to take the tests. On average, each team was responsible for approximately sixty participants, the names, addresses, and telephone numbers of whom were supplied by NORC. The first action of the fieldworker was to send a letter to each participant on his or her list or, in the case of subjects less than 18 years of age, to the parent or guardian, informing them that they could expect a call from the interviewer some time during the following week. In the majority of cases, the youth could be reached by telephone, but in some instances the interviewers had to call on people at their residences. Participants who had been identified in the 1979 interview as primarily Spanish-speaking were sent letters in Spanish and contacted by bilingual interviewers.

Inevitably, there were some individuals on the roster of 12,686 participants in the 1979 interview who could not be located and tested. But as Tables A.1, A.2, and A.3 testify, the numbers were surprisingly small. Of 12,686 to be tested, only 349 could not be located. They had moved and left no forwarding address or were totally inaccessible. Another 16 were deceased, and 61 of those who were located could not be tested for reasons of health, because they were incarcerated, or for other miscellaneous reasons. Finally, another 346 were located but refused to take the tests. The fieldworkers made substantial efforts to convince them that they should cooperate, but undue pressure was not exerted for fear of alienating them from cooperation in the remaining interviews in the longitudinal study.

In all, 11,914 respondents took the ASVAB. Most were tested in groups of about ten. The testing sites arranged by the fieldworkers typically were meeting rooms in hotels or motels, schools, libraries, or government buildings. About 700 respondents were tested individually. Whatever the site, the testing conditions and the times allowed for each test (measured by stop-watch), were exactly those prescribed for Military Entrance Processing Station (MEPS) administration of the tests. There was one minor departure from standard procedure: for 85 respondents with limited ability to read English the instructions for marking the answer sheet were translated into Spanish. Individual items on the test and the instructions prior to each of the ten test sections, including the practice items, were not translated. Insofar as any of the tests required verbal ability, it was ability in the English language that was measured.

A few participants, 36 in all, had some sort of physical impairment of vision, motor control, etc., that made it possible for them to complete the test only with some modification in the prescribed conditions. For purposes of the present analysis, these respondents are excluded because the difficulty of the test is altered and the scores do not have comparable meaning when standard conditions are not adhered to. This leaves 11,878 respondents who completed the test under standard conditions and who constitute the sample for purposes of the present study. In all, the test completion rate of 93.63% is excellent, considering the exigencies of testing a population-wide sample.

Appendix B
The Tests

The literature on vocational testing in general, and on the ASVAB in particular, is too extensive to survey fully here. In this appendix we give a brief introduction to the general subject and summarize some of the more important studies of the ASVAB.

B.1. THE RATIONAL FOR VOCATIONAL TESTING

Perhaps the best general reference on the subject of vocational testing remains *Appraising Vocational Fitness by Means of Psychological Tests*, by Donald Super and John Crites (1962). (But see also Bray & Moses, 1972.) These authors point out that the use of objective tests to select a number of employees (or recruits) from a larger pool of applicants is justified by a considerable accumulation of empirical studies going back to the 1920s. These studies show, almost without exception, that objective test procedures of employee selection are more economical and superior to the traditional alternative—namely, discretionary judgments based on an interview, references, and possibly school grades. The problem with the traditional procedures is their lack of uniformity, consistency, and objectively, and the ever-present biases and prejudices to which arbitrary judgments are subject. The superiority of objective test methods is established by studies of the "validity" of the tests—that is, the power of the selection tests to predict one or more criteria of job success.

Ideally, a validity study consists of (1) administering the vocational selection tests to a random sample of subjects from the applicant pool, (2) using a test score or combination of the test scores as a prediction scale for a specific job, (3) putting the sample of applicants on the job and, after some period of training or work, obtaining a quantitative measure of job performance or success, and (4) examining the empirical relationship between the selection scale (predictor) and the performance or success scale (criterion).

Usually, the relationship between predictor and criterion is sensibly linear, and the predictive power can be expressed simply as the correlation coefficient between the predictor measure and the criterion measure. This correlation is called the "validity coefficient" of the selection instrument. If, as is usually the case, the predictor and criterion or some one-to-one transformations of them have an essentially bivariate normal distribution in the population, the practical value of the scale for selecting employees can be expressed by calculating the expected proportion of employees who will exceed a certain criterion score if they are above a certain selection score. Under the stated distributional assumptions, this proportion depends on the validity coefficient and the selection ratio, that is, the proportion of applicants who must be taken on to fill the available jobs. If the selection ratio is unfavorable to the employer in that a large proportion of applicants must be hired, then the validity coefficient must be high in order for the selection scale to be useful. If the selection ratio is favorable and only a small proportion of the applicant pool is to be hired, then even a low validity coefficient will substantially improve the probability of selecting a successful employee.

These relationships are illustrated by Figure B.1. The scale of measurement of the prediction (on the abscissa) and of the criterion (on the ordinate) is assumed to be in standard units (mean = 0; standard deviation = 1). The percentage of subjects above any specified criterion score or selection score can be set by choosing the normal deviate corresponding to that percentile point of the normal distribution. Then by use of the table of the bivariate normal distribution (National Bureau of Standards, 1959)—or in the case of Figure B.1, by a computing approximation—these deviates and the correlation coefficient will determine the expected proportion of those who will fall above (or below) the criterion score when their selection score is below the cutting point. (These proportions are also given in Taylor & Russell, 1939). Of the four groups of applicants to be assigned, two represent successful predictions, i.e., those simultaneously below both the selection and the criterion cutting scores. The other two groups represent two types of errors of misclassification: Type 1 errors represent those persons who exceed the selection score but fail to surpass the criterion score; Type 2 errors represent those who fall below the selection score but above the criterion score. Obviously, Type 1 errors are more the concern of the employer because they represent losses due to hiring an unproductive worker. Type 2 errors are more the concern of the applicant who, because of misclassification, is erroneously excluded from employment when in fact he or she is capable of the work. We see in Figure B.1 that, as the selection ratio becomes increasingly favorable to the employer, the Type 1 error is decreased at the expense of the Type 2 error. In other words, if the employer has only a small fraction of applicants to select, he can be fairly sure of selecting the right ones even with a selection test of modest validity. He will, of course, have passed over many applicants who may have done just as well, but since they cannot all be hired, the only rational course for the employer is to select employees from among those applicants who have the least risk of failure.

In specific situations the monetary benefits attributable to selection testing can be calculated: Maier and Fuchs (1973) for example, estimate the savings due to reduced training failure among Armed Services enlistees at 330 million dollars annually.

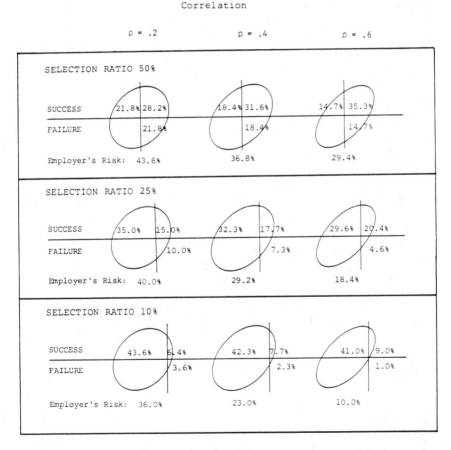

FIG. B.1. Employers' risks (percent of job failures among hired applicants) for various predictor validities (ρ-.2, .4, and .6) and selection ratios (percent of applicants hired)

The validation studies required to assess the error rates of a selection test are, perhaps not surprisingly, difficult to carry out in their ideal form. The greatest impediment in most cases is the impracticality of putting the entire sample of applicants on the job and observing who succeeds and who does not. Often the selection test is used to screen the validation sample so that only those applicants above a certain score level on the predictor are hired. This makes it impossible to know with certainty the true distribution of selection and criterion scores in the population or to estimate directly the validity coefficient. There exist, however, certain statistical approximations to test validity in this situation based on the theory of truncated normal distribution from the censored sample. In particular, a validity coefficient "corrected for restriction in range" can be calculated as an approximation of the true coefficient for an unselected sample. These approximations are reasonable satisfactory, but they place greater demands on the distribution assumptions than would an analysis of complete data—especially so when the initial selection is severe and the adjustment in the validity coefficient is large.

There is occasionally an opportunity to examine the validity of selection tests in an unselected sample. An exemplary instance is a field validation study, carried out in 1953–54 by *Colonel S. E. Jacobs* (Retired), of the Examen Calificacion de Fuerzas Armadas (ECFA)—a Spanish language version of the AFQT. This test, along with a measure of English language knowledge and a non-language test of reasoning ability, was administered to a complete age cohort of male Puerto Ricans. Without regard to the selection scores, and excluding men only for medical, moral, or psychiatric reasons or legal deferment, the entire cohort was inducted and constituted as a special class in the training center at Tortugero. To prevent the wide range of aptitude among these recruits from becoming too apparent and having an adverse effect on training, these inductees were assigned in a balanced manner with respect to ECFA scores to designated companies, platoons, and squads by the investigating team, not by the training camp cadre.

Although some of these subjects, primarily from the low range of ECFA scores, could not adjust to basic training and had to be discharged, 528 completed sixteen weeks of basic training, including English language instruction. At the end of training, these men were administered a soldier performance test including demonstrations of physical proficiency as well as knowledge of equipment and procedures. In addition, each of the platoon sergeants, all experienced Puerto Rican soldiers, rated the troops in his platoon on a specially designed form. The trainees were also tested on their ability to comprehend and speak English and were rated on this criterion by their platoon sergeants.

Correlations between the pre-training and post-training measures from the study have been reported by Shenkel, Leedy, Rosenberg and Mundy (1957) and also by Bock (1975). Table B.1 shows the test intercorrelations calculated from a one-third random sample of the 528 cases as presented by Bock (1975). In comparison to other validation studies, this study produced very high relationships between the selection and criterion measures. The ECFA predicted soldier performance with a correlation of .71, and the English language pretest predicted posttest performance with a correlation of .93. Typical of subjective ratings as opposed to objective criteria, the corresponding correlations with the platoon sergeant's ratings of soldier performance in English language fluency were lower at .55 and .69, respectively.

TABLE B.1
Correlation of Basic Training Predictors and Criteria for
A Sample of Puerto Rican Inductees (Bock, 1975)

	Criteria			
Predictors	Soldier Performance Test	English Fluency Test	Soldier Performance Ranking	English Fluency Ranking
Examen Calificacion de Fuerzas Armadas	.71	.79	.55	.71
Highest Grade Completed	.69	.76	.51	.71
Non-language Reasoning	.67	.69	.50	.62
English Fluency Test	.70	.93	.56	.69

This range of correlations, indicating a high degree of validity for predicting success in basic training, is comparable to or higher than the validities for the ASVAB corrected for restriction of range discussed in the following. It gives us considerable assurance that the corrected figures from studies with restricted range are substantially accurate. Studies that do not report such corrections when the sample has, in fact, been selected on the predictor can seriously underestimate the validity coefficient.

B.2.   VALIDITY OF THE ASVAB

Typical validity coefficients for the ASVAB may be found in the report by Atwater and Abrahams (1980). Aptitude composite scores were used to predict success in six Navy technical schools. Uncorrected and corrected validity coefficients for the schools were as follows:

	Uncorrected	Corrected
Air Traffic Controller	.45	.79
Aviation Support Equipment Technician	.19	.40
Basic Electricity and Electronics[1]	−.10	−.18
Signalman	.26	.48
Signalman-2	.37	.62
Basic Submarine	.27	.44

[1] The correlations are negative because the criterion measured time to complete training rather than final course grade.

This is only one of many studies of the validity of the ASVAB tests and composites for predicting success in Service training schools. Vitola, Mullens, and Croll (1973) reported corrected coefficients with Air Force training school grades ranging from .21 to .86 for airmen in 46 different technical schools. Sims (1978) found for ASVAB Forms 6 and 7 corrected coefficients in the range .22 to .83 with a median of .60 for performance in 38 Marine Corps schools. As is typical of such studies, the correlations for skills that require assimilation and use of information are considerably higher than those for a mostly physical skill. Validity coefficients are also higher when the criterion measure is itself some kind of paper-and-pencil instrument as opposed to a rating of actual performance. Sims (1978), for example, reports the following corrected correlations for Marine Corps training school grades: advanced auto mechanics, .74; electrical equipment repair, .73; field artillery control, .71. For more manual or physical occupations, however, the figures for ratings of performance are: tank crewmen, .22; correction specialists, military police, .37. Valentine (1977) found ASVAB validities of similar magnitude for final grades in forty-three Air Force technical schools.

Swanson (1979) compared ASVAB Form 6 and 7 scores of Navy enlisted men to final grades in 101 technical schools. The median correlation was .43 uncorrected and .73 corrected. For courses in which the recruits continued training until they reached a minimum competency level, the median correlation with time and training was −.21 uncorrected and −.36 corrected. But the various composites of the ASVAB do not differ very much in their predictive validity in the different schools, suggesting that it is mostly the general familiarity with the subject matter or general learning skill that is the main source of the battery's validity.

A limitation of many validity studies, both in the military and civilian sector, is that only success in training is evaluated and not performance on the job. An exception is the study by Larson and Arenson reported by Wilfong (1980), in which two samples of subjects who had voluntarily taken the

ASVAB in high school were followed as they moved into the labor market. The first group consisted of 1,544 11th and 12th grade pupils completing the ASVAB Form 5 (high school version) in the fall of 1976; the second group consisted of 4,657 11th and 12th grade pupils taking the tests during the 1977–78 school year. To obtain criteria of job performance for these individuals, the investigators mailed questionnaires to those pupils who had indicated during testing that their post-graduation plans included work, military service, or undecided. Among the questions was a request for the place of employment and the name and address of the immediate supervisor. These immediate supervisors were then sent questionnaires asking for ratings of on-the-job performance for the individuals they supervised, and based on questionnaires returned, multiple correlations between certain of the high school ASVAB tests and composites were calculated with the performance rating as criterion. The final sample size was not extremely large, and some "shrinkage" of these correlations was expected when the regression weights were applied to the ratings returned for the second group of subjects. Results for this cross-validation sample are shown in Table B.2. These correlations have not been corrected for restriction of range due to selection because it was not possible in this study to know how selection was operating.

Considering the relatively crude criterion measure, the typical reluctance of supervisors to report poor performance and the absence of a correction for restriction of range, the validities of the ASVAB tests for success on the job are reasonably good. They must be viewed only as lower bounds on the actual validities, which probably are substantially higher. It seems safe to conclude that the ASVAB, although somewhat more abbreviated than a standard aptitude battery such as the DAT or GATB, is roughly comparable to those batteries in its power to predict job performance. Without going into more detailed consideration of how the test functions and what behaviors it draws upon in making these predictions, we have some assurance of its practical value for selecting recruits or employees with the best chance of being productive and successful.

The research cited up to this point seems adequate to confirm the important role that differences in scores on the ASVAB will have on the prospects of young people for success in job training or job performance in either military or civilian life. We have not yet marshalled enough evidence to argue that the ASVAB is measuring the specific skills that are responsible for better job success among the higher scorers. All we know is that, directly or indirectly, the test is able to identify those who will so perform. Possibly the tests are just signaling the success of those persons who have a commitment to responsibility and hard work rather than some special abilities required for job success measured by these tests. We have discussed these questions in some detail in Chapters 3, 4, and 5.

TABLE B.2
Single-Sex Validities of ASVAB Composite Scores as Predictors of Combined Performance Criterion For Job Groups Defined During Cross-Validation (From Larson & Arenson, 1979)

Job Group	N	Verbal VE	Analytic/ Quantitative AQ	Clerical CL	Mechanical ME	Trade/ Technical TT	Academic Ability AA
Service Station Attendant [M]	63	.18	.18	.35**	.19	.09	.15
Driver [M]	133	.22**	.28***	.39***	.24**	.36***	.22**
Data Processing Worker [F]	69	.11	.21*	.10	.05	.10	.16
Guard [M]	43	.05	.17	−.18	.09	.28*	.04
Store Manager [M]	53	−.04	.14	.29**	.07	−.08	.16
Custodian [M]	50	.39**	.35*	.23	.37**	.40**	.37**
Child Care [F]	56	.14	.12	.27*	.22	.15	.14
Logger [M]	49	.34**	.35**	.32*	.36**	.30**	.28*
Sewing Machine Operator [F]	59	.11	.07	.02	.12	.17	.14
Auto Mechanic [M]	142	.16*	.27***	.19*	.15*	.16*	.20**
Plant Maintenance [M]	62	.26*	.28*	.31**	.30**	.27*	.23*
Electronic Technician [M]	92	.19*	.26**	.04	.15	.02	.17

*Coefficient significant at .05 level
**Coefficient significant at .01 level
***Coefficient significant at .001 level
[M] Male Respondents Only
[F] Female Respondents Only

B.3. THE PROBLEM OF DIFFERENTIAL PREDICTIVE VALIDITY

If a vocational test is used to select among persons with highly heterogeneous backgrounds and experience, it may happen that the relationship between the test score and a measure of job performance is different among distinguishable groups of such persons. The test is then said to have "differential predictive validity", such that different selection rules must be formulated for each group. An extreme example would be a population consisting of more than one language group, such as that of Belgium or Switzerland, where a test in the applicant's preferred language might have a different relationship to performance than a test in a second language. In such populations it may be necessary to construct and validate tests in more than one language and to allow the applicant to choose the language in which he or she will be tested. This is the policy, for example, in the Belgium armed services.

Another solution that has been attempted in these situations is to develop a non-language test that is valid for the criterion in question. A number of tests purporting to measure general reasoning ability independent of language have been devised. Best known are the Raven Progressive Matrices and the Thorndike-Lorge Non-Language Tests. Regrettably, these tests, when applied to groups with differing linguistic and cultural backgrounds, typically show differential predictive validities similar to those of their language-based counterparts. It appears that the figural relationships in such tests are not equally comprehensible in groups with different exposures to such conventions.

Less extreme but still consequential effects on predictive validity may also arise from experiential variation among persons who are nominally within the same language population. In a population as diverse as that of the United States, heterogeneity affecting predictive validity might exist at many levels. Whether it exists and in what degree is an empirical question that can be investigated at least for the larger subpopulations for which the necessary data can be obtained. In the U.S., studies of this type have been carried out for the major sociocultural groups—Whites, Blacks, and Hispanics—and for the two sexes.

A differential predictive validity study requires a sample of applicants to be tested at time of selection and measured at a later time with respect to some criterion of job performance. On the basis of these data, the regression line showing the mean of the criterion scores for each value of the predicting test score is calculated by the method of least squares. In most applications it is satisfactory to assume a straight-line relationship in the criterion and predictor scores, in which case we may fit the regression lines by estimating the intercept and the slope in each of the groups in question. If the deviations of the criterion scores from the regression line within each group are normally distributed and have the same variance in all of the groups, analysis of variance methods are available for testing the hypothesis that the regression lines are homogeneous from one group to another. The test has two component hypotheses: H1—equality of slopes between groups—and, given that H1 is accepted, H2—equality of intercepts between groups (see Bock, 1975, Chapter 6; Finn, 1978).

In the case of two groups, schematic regression lines shown in Figure B.2 represent the three possible outcomes of these tests of hypotheses—namely, accept H1 and H2, accept H1 and reject H2, and reject H1 and H2. Panel A of Figure B.2 represents two homogeneous regressions (regression lines collinear—the length of each line represents 99% range of the criterion scores; on average, group 1 in this panel has lower scores on the predictor tests than does group 2, but it also has correspondingly lower average scores on the criterion). For predictive purposes, the tests are functioning in the same manner in both groups, the same regression line can be assumed in each group, and group membership of the applicant can be ignored during selection.

In panel B, the extent to which criterion scores depend upon predictor scores is the same for each group, but the level of performance is uniformly higher in group 2 (i.e., the regression lines are parallel but not coincident). The condition represented in panel B would occur when job performance depends upon two factors, one related to the predictor tests and the other not so related.

It is easy to imagine how this might occur. Suppose, for example, that a test of general verbal ability was used to predict some measure of skill in playing basketball among Black and White boys in an urban high school. It is likely that, within these groups, those Blacks with higher general verbal ability use better strategies and tactics and thus score higher in play than those of lower general ability. At the same time, it may be the case that Blacks devote more time to playing basketball both in and out of school. Compared to Whites of the same general ability, they could therefore be expected to score higher in play, other things being equal. If the amount of such extra practice is unrelated to general verbal ability, the upward displacement of the regression line for that group shown in panel B would result. For purposes of selection, a constant amount equal to the difference in intercepts divided by the slope should be added to the test scores of Blacks to obtain the best prediction of the criterion score. The Blacks and Whites thus selected would have different average general ability scores, but their performance in playing basketball would be equal.

We should also be alert to the possibility that deficiency in the design of the validation study can also produce the result shown in panel B. For example, selection may be influenced by some unknown factor that depends on group membership but is unrelated to predictor scores within groups. Suppose that selection is not done "blind" and that the person responsible for selection is permitted to use discretionary judgement in borderline cases. If these judgments were based on other information about the basketball playing

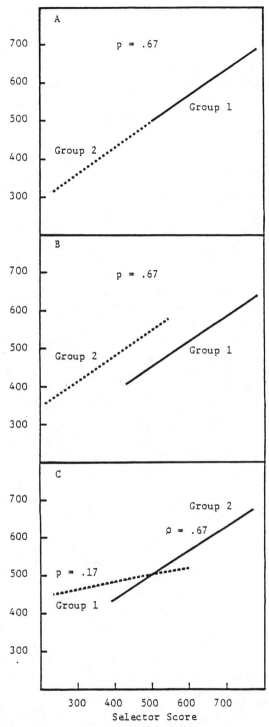

FIG. B.2. Schematic selector-vs.-criterion regression lines for two groups. (A) No differential validity; (B) Selection bias favoring group 1; (C) Differential validity.

183

ability of Blacks, so that in effect the Blacks were being screened more stringently than Whites, the ultimate performance of the Blacks would be higher at given selection scores. This would be especially likely to happen if there were many more Blacks than Whites in the school, and the person doing the selection was attempting to better balance the racial composition of the team. The importance of rigorous controls in carrying out a validation study, especially in the selection of applicants without regard to group membership, cannot be overemphasized.

Finally, panel C depicts a situation in which the selection test is not related to the performance measure to the same extent in both groups. This result, which typically occurs when the groups differ in their average predictor scores, is symptomatic of technical shortcomings of the predictor tests. The tests may not have a uniform distribution of item difficulty, and may be less reliable at lower score ranges than at higher. This is especially a problem in multiple choice tests where the effects of guessing produce less reliable scores in the low range. The resulting non-uniform attenuation of the predictor-criteria correlation can lead to regression lines such as shown in panel C. The greater measurement error in Group 1 has reduced the slope of the regression line relative to that of Group 2 as shown in panel C. The effect of non-uniform reliability of the tests can, of course, be corrected by writing additional items at the required difficulty levels and repeating the validation study.

Another reason for the effect shown in panel C, and one more difficult to correct, is that the dimension measured by the test actually changes as the items increase or decrease in difficulty. It may be that the person constructing the test included additional dimensions to the task when trying to devise more difficult items. If these dimensions are relevant to criterion performance, the validity of the tests will increase as the item difficulty increases. In this case, scores in the lower ranges of the predictor will be less valid than those in the higher ranges, with the result that the regression lines will appear as in panel C. It is even possible that a test may be multidimensional throughout its range, and that some of these dimensions are predictors in one of the groups but not in the other. This would also tend to produce different slopes of the regression lines. These conditions could be corrected only by analysis of the item content, possibly aided by item factor analyses in separate samples from the two groups. New items would have to be written, subjected to item analysis, and a test constructed that is equally valid, and thus having equal regression slopes, in groups at different score levels.

In principle, regression lines with unequal slopes can be used for selection by means of the Johnson-Neyman technique (see Johnson & Neyman, 1936), which assigns different selection rules at different levels of predictive score. The procedure is cumbersome, however, and is less reliable than single or parallel regression line models in comparable data. It has rarely been used in practical personnel selection.

In the interpretation of validity studies, it is of course not just the statistical significance of deviations from homogeneous regression that must be considered, but also the actual sizes of the deviations and the practical effect of possibly ignoring them in favor of a simpler selection rule. When the validation studies are done in very large samples, even minor departures from the assumption of homogeneous regression will be significant. But when the actual effects of the heterogeneity on the types of correct and incorrect classification are calculated by the methods discussed in Section B.2, it might be found that the effects are too small to be of practical importance.

Studies of Differential Validity of the ASVAB and Related Tests in Sociocultural Groups and the Two Sexes

The Armed Services have carried out two major studies of the possible differential validity of their classification tests. The first of these studies was carried out in 1978 by Milton Maier and Edmund Fuchs of the U.S. Army Research Institute for the Behavioral and Social Sciences. Subjects for this study were approximately 14,000 men in various military training programs in 1964 and 1965. From these soldiers, samples of Black and White trainees were selected on the basis of their Army records for purposes of a differential validity study.

The second study was carried out by Lonnie Valentine, Jr., of the Air Force Human Resources Laboratory. Subjects for this study were men and women in the Air Force technical training schools between 1974 and 1977. These subjects were classified as White, Black, other, and as male and female for the purposes of the validity study.

Both these studies used as their main criterion of performance the final course grades in technical training schools operated by the corresponding services. In an earlier report, Maier and Fuchs (1973) discussed the reasons for choosing final training course grades as a measure of job performance in preference to evaluation of actual on-the-job behavior. They argued that because job duties vary so much from one assignment to another it is virtually impossible to obtain a general measure of job performance. A training course and its end-of-course tests sample most of the skill elements required on the job and thus provide a more representative index of how the soldier would perform in a wide variety of situations. In addition, performance in many jobs cannot be measured objectively and must be assessed by means of supervisors' ratings. There is abundant evidence in the literature of applied psychology, however, that supervisors' ratings are extremely unreliable and inconsistent. They are less dependable than the tests used to predict them. End-of-course grades in the military training schools, by contrast, are based on objective tests, usually with reasonably good reliability. Because results on these tests become part of each soldier's record along with his or her classification tests scores, it is relatively easy to gather together the data needed in a validity study.

Army Training Schools. Screening the records of some 25,000 soldiers entering military training programs in 1964 and 1965, Maier and Fuchs (1978) located approximately 14,000 men for whom racial identification and test scores for the Army Classification Battery (ACB) were available. The ACB consists of fifteen tests covering much the same ground as ASVAB but in greater detail. From the scores on these tests, the investigators calculated composite scores using formulas previously developed to predict job performance in the areas shown in Table B.3. This table also shows the number of soldiers classified as White and Black for whom end-of-course grades were available in training programs pertaining to each group of Military Occupational Specialties (MOS). (Data for other racial groups were too limited to be analyzed.)

The scores for both composite predictors and the course grades were standardized to a mean of 100 and standard deviation of 20 in the total sample of 14,127 soldiers. Regressions for each MOS group were obtained in the following way: scores for each predictor were grouped into six successive equal intervals and the mean end-of-course grade was obtained for each. Straight trend lines were then fitted to each set of points with the length of the line indicating the range of scores in the data. Plots of the resulting trend lines, adapted from Maier and Fuchs (1978), are shown in Figure B.3. Data

TABLE B.3
Sample Sizes in Aptitude Area Validation and Racial Studies

MOS group	Sample size			
	Validation	*White*	*Black*	*White & Black*
Combat Arms	1,609	581	131	712
Field Artillery	665	134	41	175
Electronics Repair	3,840	2,036	232	2,268
Operations and Food	1,516	1,166	179	1,345
Surveillance and Communications	2,137	1,243	148	1,391
Mechanical Maintenance	4,395	2,776	266	3,042
General Maintenace	1,139	688	76	764
Clerical	3,502	2,232	446	2,678
Skilled Technical	2,175	1,499	253	1,752
Total	20,978	12,355	1,772	14,127

Source: Milton H. Maier & Edmund F. Fuchs, *Differential Validity of the Army Aptitude Areas for Predicting Army Job Training Performance of Blacks and Whites.* Technical Paper 312. U.S. Army Research Institute for the Behavioral and Social Sciences, Alexandria, VA, 1978, p. 8.

for the field artillery groups were considered too limited to justify plotting. Note that the slopes of the regression lines are in the range 0.5 to 0.75, indicating good validity of the composites for both White and Black soldiers. For two of the specialties, General Maintenance and Clerical, regression lines for Blacks and Whites are practically coincident and clearly indicate that the classification tests are functioning in the same way in both groups. In three of the specialty groups, Electronics Repair, Operators and Food and Motor Maintenance, the regression line for Blacks has slightly lower slope than for Whites, and it crosses the line for Whites near the mean for the Black group. Assuming that these differences in slope are due to reduced reliability or differences in content in the items at lower levels of difficulty, we might expect that if the test were improved in these respects the regression lines for Blacks and Whites would also become essentially coincident for these specialty groups.

Only in the case of Combat Arms, Surveillance and Communications, and the Skilled Technical specialties is there a tendency for the two regression lines to have slightly different slopes and to be sufficiently displaced from one another as not to cross in the region of the score distributions. For Surveillance and Communications, the regression line for Blacks is above that for Whites, and for Skilled Technical below, but in each case the displacement and difference in slope is too small to be of any practical importance. In the Combat Arms specialties, which include Infantry, Armor, and Combat Engineer, the regression line for Blacks has a somewhat smaller slope than that for Whites and is clearly displaced upward. At the highest level of the Combat composite predictor, the mean final combat course grades for the groups are almost equal, while at the lowest level the mean for Blacks exceeds that for Whites by about 0.4 standard deviations.

This result suggests that, at least at lower levels of the predictor score, factors not accounted for by the test are acting to increase the final grades in the combat courses. Without knowing the content of the combat courses or how they were evaluated, it is difficult to know why in this area alone there is evidence of a non-negligible differential validity. Perhaps this is the area where the content of the course is furthest removed from the content of the predictor tests, thus giving more opportunity for other unrelated factors to affect final course grade. Certainly, the predicting composite includes such tests as Arithmetic Reasoning, Trade Information, and Pattern Analysis, which may have limited relationship to combat course performance and on which most low-scoring Blacks may be at a special disadvantage. This is the only specialty area where this study might give some justification for separate selection rules for Blacks and Whites, other policy considerations permitting. In all of the other areas the regression lines for Blacks and Whites are so nearly the same that there would be no justification for distinguishing race during selection.

LEGEND: ———— Validity study regression
— ·— ·— ·— White sample trend line
— — — — Black sample trend line

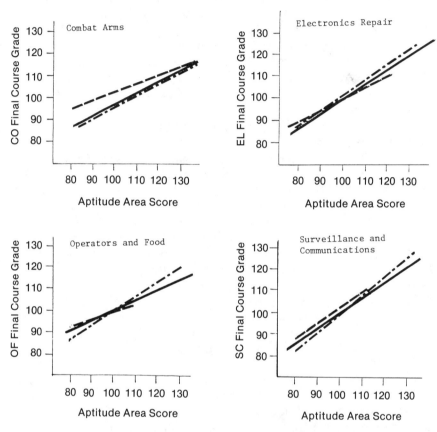

FIG. B.3. Comparative trends of course grades of Whites and Blacks for aptitude scores. Source: Maier and Fuchs, (1978).

Air Force Training Schools. In his differential validity study of the ASVAB, Form 3, Valentine (1977) looked at 43 Air Force technical training schools. For present purposes, we have extracted the results for the eight schools with larger sample sizes. Although Valentine gave results for other minority groups in some cases, we restrict attention to differential validity for Black and White Air Force trainees, and male and female trainees. The names of the schools, numbers of trainees, and the ASVAB composite used

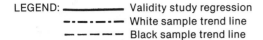

LEGEND: ──────── Validity study regression
        ─·─·─·─· White sample trend line
        ─ ─ ─ ─ Black sample trend line

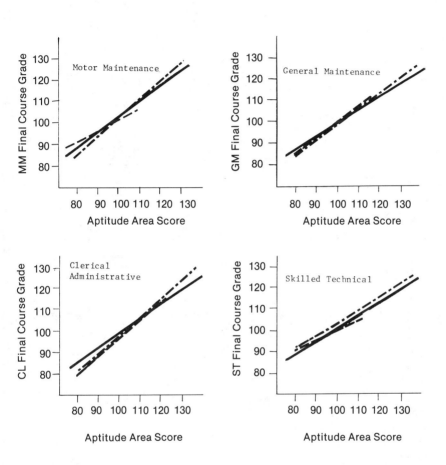

FIG. B.3 (cont'd). Comparative trends of course grades of Whites and Blacks for aptitude scores. Source: Maier and Fuchs, (1978).

for predicting final course grades are shown in Table B.4. The same composites are used in more than one type of training school.

The tests of ASVAB 3 differ somewhat from those of ASVAB 8: Technical Knowledge replaces Science Information, Space Perception replaces Paragraph Comprehension, and Auto and Shop Information are two different tests. The other tests are basically the same in both forms.

Valentine examined the regressions of end-of-training-school grades on four predictor composites of ASVAB 3 test scores. He did not report means

TABLE B.4

Sample Sizes, Corrected and Uncorrected Predictor-Criterion Correlations, Predictor Composite, and Final Grade Raw Score Means and Standard Deviations for Eight Air Force Training Schools: Reported by Sociocultural Group and Sex*

Service School	Sample Size	Correlation		Composite		Final Grades	
		Cor.	Uncor.	Mean	S.D.	Mean	S.D.
Communications-Electronic Systems				(Elect)			
White	1,849	.89	.44	60.0	3.57	85.0	6.01
Black	181	.84	.34	58.2	3.42	81.8	5.34
Male	1,740	.89	.43	59.8	3.55	85.0	6.03
Female	343	.91	.47	58.3	3.56	84.0	5.99
Avionics Systems				(Elect)			
White	2,165	.81	.44	60.2	3.51	84.4	6.38
Black	244	.85	.35	59.0	3.41	81.1	6.44
Male	2,014	.83	.34	60.0	3.49	84.1	6.42
Female	450	.77	.27	58.5	3.39	84.0	6.59
Aircraft Maintenance				(Mech)			
White	4,559	.44	.34	70.4	14.2	84.4	7.78
Black	1,073	.19	.12	63.0	11.81	79.2	7.92
Male	4,468	.57	.38	73.2	11.35	84.0	7.99
Female	1,268	.16	.10	53.7	12.13	81.3	7.98
Aircraft Engineer				(Mech)			
White	1,356	.57	.40	72.0	12.2	85.3	7.41
Black	363	.57	.29	63.2	8.30	80.0	7.00
Male	1,431	.73	.49	71.7	10.02	84.4	7.74
Female	332	.00	.00	61.6	7.03	83.3	7.07

Service School	Sample Size	Correlation		Composite		Final Grades	
		Cor.	Uncor.	Mean	S.D.	Mean	S.D.
Transportation				(Adm)			
White	1,106	.34	.24	68.2	12.40	83.1	6.58
Black	400	.00	.00	66.5	10.50	79.1	5.94
Male	1,346	.28	.18	66.6	11.55	81.9	6.61
Female	200	.36	.21	76.9	10.12	83.3	7.07
Administration				(Adm)			
White	1,503	.38	.22	75.0	10.00	84.6	6.57
Black	1,078	.15	.08	70.8	9.62	81.7	6.34
Male	1,716	.34	.19	72.0	9.88	83.0	6.53
Female	921	.33	.19	75.4	10.05	84.2	6.69
Law Enforcement and Corrections				(Gen)			
White	1,078	.74	.39	53.8	6.42	83.6	5.90
Black	256	.64	.29	51.7	6.10	79.8	6.66
Male	900	.73	.38	53.9	6.55	83.6	6.19
Female	448	.75	.38	52.7	6.03	81.4	6.02
Medical				(Gen)			
White	1,385	.72	.37	58.0	5.47	82.4	6.98
Black	470	.66	.26	55.6	5.11	76.3	6.97
Male	1,283	.81	.42	57.6	5.56	80.9	7.49
Female	620	.70	.29	57.0	5.23	81.0	7.48

* From Valentine, L.D. (1977). Prediction of Air Force Technical Training success from ASVAB** and educational background. Report No. AFHRL-TR-77-18. Brooks Air Force Base, Texas.

** ASVAB, Form 3.

and standard deviations for these composites in the population of applicants, but these statistics can be calculated from the means, standard deviations, and correlations of the ASVAB 3 tests in a large sample of applicants as reported by Seeley, Fischl, and Hicks (1978). The cases in the latter sample were weighted so as to reproduce the AFQT distribution of the World War II mobilization population. The means and standard deviations of the composites computed from Seeley, Fischl, and Hicks's Table 8 appear in Table B.5. The figures in Table B.5 refer to composite scores calculated from the ASVAB 3 raw scores by the formulas shown in the table.

Results from Valentine's study for those schools with larger numbers of trainees are abstracted in Table B.4. Figures for the smaller minority groups have been omitted. The means and standard deviations for composites reported in percentiles by Valentine have been converted to raw score units for comparability with Table B.5. In Table B.4 correlations between each of the four composites—Electronic, Mechanical, Administrative, and General— and the final school grades of trainees selected by these composites are shown both in the uncorrected form given in Valentine's Table 2 and after correction for restriction of range. Comparing the means for the selected groups with the means and standard deviations in Table B.5, we see that selection was quite stringent for all these schools, and especially so for the popular Avionics specialty, where the mean of the selected group is nearly

TABLE B.5
ASVAB–3 Predictor Composites: Unselected Raw Score Population
Means and Standard Deviations**

Composite		Composition*	Mean	S.D.
Electronics	(Elect)	AR + SP + EI	41.3	14.44
Mechanical	(Mech)	TK + MC + SI + AI	58.0	19.31
Administrative	(Adm)	WK + CS	55.1	18.27
General	(Gen)	2 + WK + AR	41.4	16.87

*AR = Arithmetic Reasoning
SP = Space Perception
EI = Electronics Information
TK = Technical Knowledge
MC = Mechanical Comprehension
SI = Shop Information
AI = Auto Information
WK = Word Knowledge
CS = Coding Speed

** From Seeley, L.C., Fischl, M.A., and Hicks, J.M.
(1978). Development of the ASVAB, Forms 2 and 3. Technical
Paper 289, Army Research Institute, Alexandria, Virginia.

one-and-a-half standard deviations above the mean of the general population. It should also be noted that the mean composite score for Blacks is less than that for White males. This indicates that a larger proportion of Blacks are to be found near the cutting point between selection or rejection regions. As we see later in this section, this fact has implications for the regression of final course grades on the predictor composite.

Regression lines for the White and Black, Male and Female groups based on Table B.4 are represented in standardized scores in Figures B.4 and B.5 (mean = 500, standard deviation = 100). Also shown are the results of significance tests for the difference in intercept at the mean and difference in slope calculated by Valentine without correction for restriction in range. One asterisk means that the corresponding F-statistic exceeded the 0.05 point; two asterisks means it exceeded the 0.01 point. Because of the large sample sizes, rather small differences are detected in some cases.

The regression lines in Figure B.4 and B.5 show no evidence whatsoever of biased selection favoring Whites to Blacks or men to women. Indeed, the lines for Avionics Systems, Aircraft Engineering, Law Enforcement and Corrections, and Medical might be construed as evidence of bias in favor of Blacks. A more likely interpretation, however, is that the selection of Blacks near the cutting point (mentioned earlier) tends to include a greater proportion of chance successes than among Whites, whose distribution is shifted toward higher levels on the selection composite (see the distributions in Section 4.2). Because the selection tests are not infallible, some examinees near the cutting point are classified as capable of passing the training course when in fact their chances of doing so are poor. These cases regress to lower values on the final course grade, and bring down the average of their group as seen in the shifting downward of regression lines for Blacks in Figure B.4.

Both Figures B.4 and B.5 show another kind of differential validity affecting the Mechanical and Administrative composites. Unlike the Electronics and General composites, which show excellent and virtually equal validities in all groups, the validities of the Mechanical and Administrative composites are rather poor for Whites and in some cases almost nil for Blacks and females. The slopes of the regression lines indicate that the Mechanical composite has almost no predictive validity for Blacks in the Communications-Electronics Systems course, and none for females in either of the mechanical specialties. The Administrative composite has little or no predictive validity among Blacks for the Transportation or Administration course. Other results reported by Valentine indicate that the General composite would have served much better to predict success in these courses.

These limitations of the ASVAB tests, although not unfair to Blacks or females as groups, are undesirable in individual cases when the composites falsely accept unqualified applicants or falsely reject qualified ones. They are undoubtedly a consequence of the process of development of these tests,

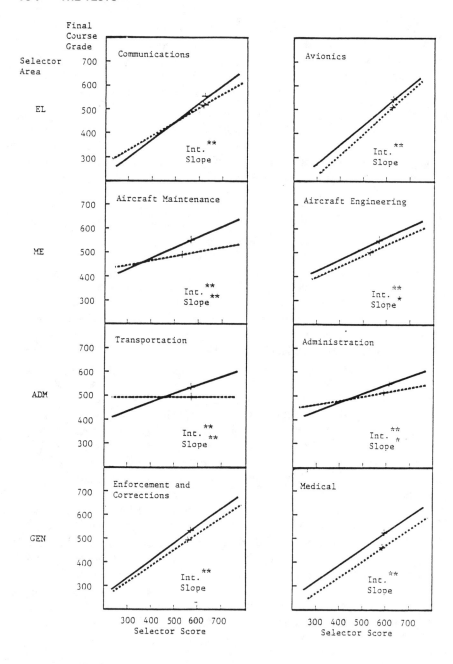

FIG. B.4.   Regressions for White and Black trainees of Final Course Grade on selector composites for Air Force Training Schools. *Slope or intercept significantly different at .05 level; **at .01 level. Solid line = White; broken line = Black.

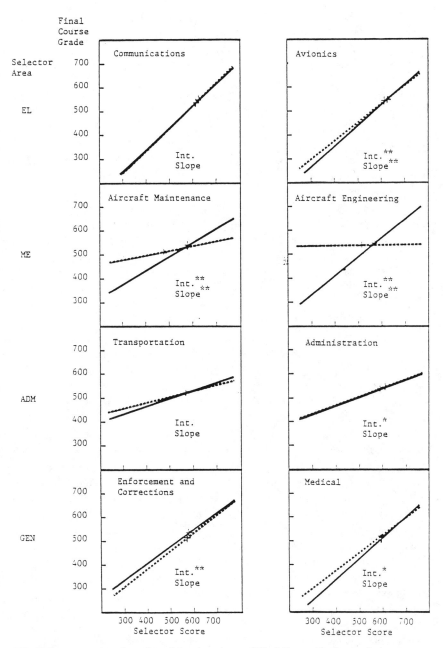

FIG. B.5.   Regressions for male and female trainees of Final Course Grade on selector composites for Air Force Training Schools.   Variance of selector corrected for restriction of range. *Slope or intercept significantly different at .05 level; ** at .01 level. Solid line = Male; broken line = Female.

which was carried out on samples of recruits containing relatively few Blacks or females. The technology of test construction is, regrettably, still so empirical that good psychometric properties cannot be guaranteed without pretesting the items in samples from the relevant subpopulations. It is especially difficult to make a fixed-length test that is equally reliable in groups with widely separated means levels. Bock and Mislevy (1981) estimate the reliability of the Auto and Shop Information tests, which show the largest sex difference in mean scores, to be .83 in males and only .69 in females. Similarly, Mathematics Knowledge, which shows some of the largest sociocultural differences, has reliability .85 in White males aged 19 through 20, whereas the reliabilities in the corresponding Black and Hispanic groups are .71 and .76 respectively.

The results of Valentine's study, reviewed here, seem to indicate that if the problems of differential reliability are solved by improved tests, there will be no differential validity of the ASVAB tests, either for sociocultural group or for sex. His results seem even more favorable in this connection than those of Maier and Fuchs based on earlier tests. There is practically no evidence in either of these studies of bias in favor of Whites or of males.

B.4. PSYCHOMETRIC PROPERTIES OF THE ASVAB TESTS

Reliability. Multiple-choice tests such as those of the ASVAB are by nature fallible measuring instruments and their reliabilities, defined as the ratio of the non-error variance to the total score variance in the population of subjects, are rarely if ever as high as those of physical measuring instruments. In general, the reliability of an objective test is a function of the number of items—longer tests are more reliable than shorter tests. But longer tests require more time to administer, and in a multi-test battery, the test developer must compromise between the number of tests that can be administered in an allotted time and the reliability that can be attained for each separate test. In the case of the ASVAB, the separate tests were kept rather short and the reliability compromised somewhat relative to other vocational aptitude batteries. Table B.6, taken from Bock and Mislevy (1981), compares reliabilities for the ASVAB tests with those of some of the DAT tests. The reliabilities of the ASVAB tests are reasonably high, but not as high as those of the DAT tests. In operational use, however, various composites such as the AFQT composite [WK + PC + AR + (1/2)NO], are employed in selection and classification, and these have reliabilities in excess of .90.

Test Intercorrelations. Although the statistical analysis in the present study is directed toward differences among groups and subgroups defined in the classification of respondents by background factors, some information about variation within the cells of the design results as a byproduct. Table

TABLE B.6
Reliabilities of the ASVAB and the DAT

Test	Number of items	Reliability[1]
ASVAB:		
General Science	25	.86
Arithmetic Reasoning	30	.87
Word Knowledge	35	.86
Paragraph Comprehension	15	.68
Numerical Operations	50	.71
Coding Speed	84	.82
Auto and Shop Knowledge	25	.83
Mathematics Knowledge	25	.84
Mechanical Comprehension	25	.83
Electronics Information	20	.80
DAT:		
Verbal Ability	50	.95
Numerical Ability	40	.93
Mechanical Ability	70	.91
Spatial Ability	60	.95
Spelling	100	.96
Language Usage	60	.91

[1] Complement of the relative average error variance. See Bock & Mislevy (1981).

TABLE B.7
Pooled Within-Cell Correlations (weighted) of ASVAB Subtests

Correl- ations	1 WK	2 PC	3 AR	4 NO	5 CS	6 GS	7 MK	8 MC	9 EI	10 AS
1 WK	1.000									
2 PC	.623	1.000								
3 AR	.557	.539	1.000							
4 NO	.374	.395	.487	1.000						
5 CS	.321	.345	.386	.589	1.000					
6 GS	.681	.532	.557	.320	.227	1.000				
7 MK	.538	.523	.745	.496	.399	.555	1.000			
8 MC	.475	.450	.547	.273	.263	.539	.493	1.000		
9 EI	.573	.468	.477	.267	.233	.615	.443	.553	1.000	
10 AS	.394	.327	.323	.177	.172	.435	.248	.525	.527	1.000
Standard Deviation	71.8	77.7	77.7	81.4	80.6	74.6	78.6	74.8	72.4	67.3

B.7 shows the pooled estimates of within-cell standard deviations and corre-lations of the ASVAB subtests from a weighted multivariate analysis of vari-ance. (The MULTIVARIANCE program was modified especially for this pur-pose.) (In this Table, the tests are ordered according to their content rather than their order of administration. We use this order in the remainder of the text.) On the assumption that the variance and covariance of the scores are homogeneous within cells, the estimates in Table B.7 are obtained by pooling weighted sums of squares and products of deviations from the cell means. The weights used are those of the national probability sample. Thus each respondent contributes to the assessment of variation and covariation in pro-portion to his or her weight in the probability sample.

The figures in Table B.7 exclude all variation due to differences between the cells of the demographic classification. The correlations therefore describe relationships among individual differences within these sub-classes. Covariation due to broader social influences acting on classes as a whole has been eliminated. The latter effects have been discussed as interactions in Chapter 5, 6, and 7.

Because all of the tests have been scaled with standard deviation 100 in the population, it is apparent from the range of the standard deviations between 70 and 80 in Table B.7 that considerable variation remains after the demographic effects have been removed. In terms of variances, about 50- to 65% of the total variance in the national probability sample is due to indivi-dual differences within the cells of the background classification and the remainder is attributable to variation between cells. Background factors con-tribute most to Auto and Shop Information, which is obviously highly experiential knowledge, and least to Numerical Operations, a largely over-learned skill.

To conceptualize sources of individual difference variation, it is helpful to perform an exploratory factor analysis on the correlations in Table B.7. We have done this by the maximum likelihood method using the EFAP II pro-gram of Jöreskog and Sörbom (1978). Assuming simple random sampling, this method provides a statistical test of the number of factors if the degrees of freedom for estimating the correlations are specified. In the present appli-cation to a weighted probability sample, it is difficult to know the actual effective sample size on which these degrees of freedom depend. To be con-servative, we will assume a design effect of 2 and take the effective sample size to be half the number of respondents. That is, we will use 5,453 as the effective sample size. Subtracting 766, which is the number of nonvacant cells in the design, gives 4,687 degrees of freedom for calculating the chi-square statistics for goodness of fit after 1, 2, 3, 4, and 5 factors have been inserted in the factor analysis model. Because the program assumes a correc-tion to the general mean, the effective number of degrees of freedom is 4,688. The results of the tests of fit are shown in Table B.8.

TABLE B.8
Likelihood Ratio Chi-Square for Fit of the Factor Analytic
Model Assuming 1, 2, 3, 4 and 5 Factors (N = 4688)

Number of factors	Chi-square	df
1	4238	35
2	1866	26
3	863	18
4	90	11
5	17	5

Strictly speaking, Table B.8 would indicate that five factors are required. But the fifth factor is a singleton involving only General Science, and its introduction produces a negative correlation in the promax rotated factor pattern. The four-factor solution therefore seems more satisfactory, and it is also suggested by the nearly ten-fold decrease in chi-square when the fourth factor is added. The factor loadings, uniqueness, and intercorrelations of the promax factors rotated from a preliminary varimax solution are shown in Table B.9 (see Hendrickson & White, 1964).

It is apparent from the substantial correlations among the factors that, within the cells of the background classification, variation in overall indivi-

TABLE B.9
Promax Factor Loadings and Intercorrelations for the ASVAB Test

Test	Factor 1	2	3	4	Uniqueness
WK	.904	.018	−.037	.020	.188
PC	.475	.126	.151	.075	.490
AR	.033	.092	.722	.087	.271
NO	.001	.810	.067	−.022	.290
CS	.007	.687	−.008	.045	.508
GS	.491	−.060	.175	.269	.360
MK	.049	.081	.831	−.059	.225
MC	−.080	−.022	.301	.632	.403
EI	.267	−.029	.037	.553	.410
AS	−.033	.044	−.169	.842	.437

Factor Correlations	1	2	3	4
1	1.000			
2	.469	1.000		
3	.678	.562	1.000	
4	.654	.330	.564	1.000

dual levels of performance enters into all of the test scores. In addition, however, the four major dimensions in the oblique factor structure are needed to describe patterns of performance on the ten tests. Factor 1 is clearly the ever-present verbal attainment factor with large loadings for the Word Knowledge and Paragraph Comprehension tests, some loading of the General Science test, and a still smaller loading on Electronics Information.

Factor 2 is the familiar fluent production factor typically seen in such speeded tests as Numerical Operations and Coding Speed. The fact that Numerical Operations requires knowledge of simple arithmetic does not enter as an important source of individual differences because most of the respondents have mastered this level of skill; they differ only in how fast they can perform the mental operation and mark the result on the answer sheet.

Factor 3 is clearly a quantitative attainment factor with dominant loadings on Arithmetic Reasoning and Mathematics Knowledge. Mechanical Comprehension also makes a small contribution to this factor.

Factor 4 represents special technical knowledge covered by the General Science, Mechanical Comprehension, Electronics Information, and Auto and Shop Information.

Thus, of the three basic factors found in most cognitive tests (Bock, 1973), two are well represented in the ASVAB. They are the verbal ability and fluent production factors. The third, the spatial visualizing ability factor, is not directly represented in the ASVAB tests, but may be reflected to some extent in the Mechanical Comprehension and Arithmetic Reasoning tests. Because the ASVAB is a vocational test battery and not just a cognitive test, it also includes the mathematical and technical content represented in factor 4.

It is important to understand that the within-cell factor analysis represented here systematically excludes the between-cell variation. The pattern of relationships seen in Table B.9 does not therefore necessarily hold in the effects of the background factors, which are between-cell effects. For some background effects, tests on the same factor sometimes vary together and sometimes do not. Sex differences, for example, act in the same way on the tests with large loadings on factors 2 and 4, but somewhat differently on Word Knowledge and Paragraph Comprehension in factor 1, and much differently on Arithmetic Reasoning and Mathematics Knowledge in factor B. This is to be expected: differences in the average performance of the two sexes do not necessarily stem from the same root as the differences among persons of the same sex.

Similar differences in background effects occur between tests involved in the special knowledge factor. Auto and Shop Information differentiates social and economic groups in ways somewhat different from Mechanical Comprehension and Electronics Knowledge or General Science.

With these exceptions, the factor pattern in Table B.9 provides a useful grouping of the tests for discussing many of the background factor effects and interactions. Examples appear in Chapters 3, 4, and 5.

Appendix C
The Analysis

Technical matters in the analysis of the Profile data are reviewed in this appendix.

C.1. SAMPLING CONSIDERATIONS

To apply either univariate or multivariate analysis of variance to a complex cross-classification of survey data, the standard assumption is that within each of the ultimate subclasses (cells), the measurements or scores are normally distributed and have homogeneous variances from one subclass to another. If the measurements are multivariate, as they are in the case of the ASVAB scores in this study, the assumption is one of multivariate normality and homogeneity of variances and covariances. It is also assumed that the observations (that is, scores obtained from different respondents) are independent within the subclasses. Given the latter assumption, and assuming simple random sampling within cells, the sampling variance of the cell mean is equal to the within-cell variance of the particular measure divided by the number of observations within the cell. If we take the reciprocal of the sampling variance of the mean as a measure of the information it supplies to the analysis, then the precision of the analysis is greatest when the contribution of each cell mean to the overall group comparisons is proportional to the number of respondents in the cell.

Unbalanced Design. Note that the analysis of variance places no restriction on the number of respondents in each cell. The requirement of equal or proportional numbers in the cells that is introduced in elementary treatments of the subject is primarily a computational convenience. We do not need that assumption here because the MULTIVARIANCE program is capable of performing an exact analysis on unbalanced designs, even including those with no observations in some subclasses. Although it is more efficient to have equal numbers in the subclasses (in the sense that very large numbers of subjects in a few cells does not much improve overall precision and therefore wastes data), the analysis is not vitiated by the wide range of variation in the numbers of respondents in the cells of the present design. In fact, the oversampling of Hispanics, Blacks, and poverty-level Whites is advantageous in improving the precision of comparisons involving those groups.

Weighted or Unweighted Observations. An important consequence of the invariance of the analysis of variance with respect to arbitrary numbers of observations in the cells is that the weights employed in the population descriptions in Chapter 2 are not needed to correct the oversampling, provided that sampling allocations correspond to the classes or subclasses contained in the analysis of variance design. In that case, the design breaks up the sample on the same criteria used in assigning weights for the probability sample, and the weights within the cells of the analysis of variance design are uniform. This is very nearly true of the data. The only variation in weights within cells applies to certain metropolitan and nonmetropolitan census tracts, but even that variation is largely absorbed in the classification by respondent's highest grade completed and mother's highest grade completed. For the purposes of group comparisons, the weights can safely be ignored. If we have any doubt on this matter, we can perform the multivariate analysis of variance with and without the weights and compare the results. If the estimated between-group effects and interactions are essentially the same in both analyses, then any variation in weights within cells is small and can be ignored.

We have in fact performed such an analysis and find there is no appreciable difference in the between-group analysis based on weighted and unweighted data. For example, Table C.1 compares weighted and unweighted estimates of sociocultural by economic status by education effects. Differences between the estimates are inconsequential and show no pattern that would suggest systematic bias in the weighted estimates. The assumption of homogeneous weights within the ultimate subclasses of the six-way analysis of variance design therefore appears quite justifiable.

Since the two results are so similar, one may ask why the unweighted analysis is performed at all. The reason is that only the unweighted analysis makes efficient use of the additional information contained in the oversampling of poor Whites, Blacks, and Hispanics. The means for these groups are determined more accurately than would be indicated by the use of weighted proportions of respondents in these groups. Another reason for not using the weights is that they violate the assumptions of the tests of significance used in the model fitting. In the presence of the weights it would be difficult to judge whether certain interactions should be included or excluded from the model for the estimation of between-group effects.

Methodological research now underway aims to apply the weights within cells while retaining all information between cells. When these developments reach the stage of practical application, the Profile data could be reanalyzed without the assumption of homogeneous weights within cells and without loss of overall efficiency. In view of the near identity of this approach to the unweighted and inefficient weighted analysis referred to above, however, it is unlikely that the reanalyses would noticeably change the unweighted results.

Intraclass Correlation. When there is replication within the cells of the analysis of variance design, as there is in the present study, it is important to know whether or not the observations within cells are independent. If not, a correction may be required when calculating the pooled within-cell estimates of variance and covariance. Lack of independence within cells does not alter the expected mean for the cell, and hence has no bearing on the estimation of between-group effects; but it does alter the estimate of within-cell variance and so affects the statistical tests and confidence intervals. This consideration is important in the present study because the data were obtained by area cluster sampling. The factor by which the cluster sampling reduces error

TABLE C.1
Weighted and Unweighted Estimates of Sociocultural Group by
Economic Status by Education Effects for the Word Knowledge Test

Highest Grade Completed	White		Black		Hispanic	
	Weighted	Unweighted	Weighted	Unweighted	Weighted	Unweighted
			Poor			
0–8	408	404	366	364	388	391
9–11	460	450	389	391	441	443
12	517	509	419	422	486	490
13+	588	581	473	481	540	541
			Nonpoor			
0–8	433	426	370	367	427	422
9–11	501	498	421	423	467	468
12	532	538	451	455	512	514
13+	581	584	500	503	549	549

variation, called the "design effect," can be estimated and is reported for various levels of aggregation of the data by Frankel and McWilliams (1981). In general, the design effect due to this type of cluster sampling is smaller for narrow subdivisions of the sample and increases as subsamples are aggregated. With a few exceptions, the largest design effects observed are about 2; that is, the sampling variance can be reduced by as much as a factor of 2 as a result of the cluster sampling.

In the present analysis, the ultimate subclasses are defined at such a detailed level that there is little apparent effect of cluster sampling on the within-cell variation. The cluster sampling effects have been largely absorbed into the high-order interaction of the background classes. The evidence for this is that the F-statistics for high-order interactions (residual) that we will see in Table C.2 are very close to unity. This means that both the residual variation and the within-cell variation are estimating the same sampling error variation. This suggests that we should assume a design effect somewhere between 1 and 1.5 when interpreting the tests of significance in Table C.3. And there is other evidence for the correctness of this conclusion: interactions that appeared to be only modestly above the level of nominal significance have reasonable interpretations when the corresponding interaction plot is examined. The case in point is the plot of mother's education and sociocultural group shown in Figure 4.3, the interaction of which has a plausible interpretation from what we know of the Hispanic family structure. If the more commonly assumed design effect of 2 were used, this interaction would not be judged significant; yet its reasonable interpretation convinces us of its reality. For these reasons we use a figure of 1.25 times the nominal percentage points of the multivariate and univariate test statistics when judging the statistical significance of between-group effects and interactions.

Because the interpretation of the tests of hypothesis depends upon our assumptions about the design effect, we have chosen not to assign probability levels to the multivariate and univariate F-statistics in Tables C.2 and C.3. Instead, we give the nominal .05 and .01 points of their null distributions. These values can be multiplied by a factor to take into account the design effect when interpreting the statistics in each column of these tables. We believe that a factor of 1.25 is sufficiently conservative for this purpose. In other words, we would consider a statistic in the tables significant if it exceeds the nominal .05 or .01 point by a factor of 1.25. Note, however, that we interpret the univariate F-statistics only under the protection of the multivariate F for that effect; that is, the univariate statistics for a given effect are interpreted only if the multivariate statistic for that effect is significant. Effects that are not multivariate significant are not included in the model for purposes of estimation. (See Bock, 1975, Chapter 6, for a discussion of protected F-tests.)

TABLE C.2
Multivariate and Univariate Test Statistics for Effects of Background Factors: First Analysis

	Respondent's Education (HGC)	Economic Status (EcS)	Sociocultural Group (ScG)	Sex	Mother's Education (MHGC)	Region (Reg)	HGC × ScG	Sex × ScG	Sex × HGC	ScG × EcS	AGC × EcS	Sex × EcS	ScG × Reg	Sex × Reg	EcS × Reg	Sex × MHGC	ScG × MHGC	MHGC × EcS	ScG × HGC × EcS	Sex × ScG × EcS	ScG × EcS × Reg	Residual
Likelihood ratio: F-approximation	208.1	190.8	210.7	896.3	31.4	16.2	5.0	24.3	9.0	3.3	2.9	8.7	3.6	1.9	0.9	2.0	2.1	0.9	1.7	1.8	1.1	1.04
F(.05)	1.5	1.8	1.5	1.8	1.4	1.5	1.3	1.6	1.5	1.5	1.5	1.8	1.3	1.5	1.5	1.4	1.3	1.4	1.3	1.6	1.3	1.00
F(.01)	1.7	2.3	1.7	2.3	1.6	1.7	1.5	1.9	1.7	1.7	1.7	2.3	1.5	1.7	1.7	1.6	1.4	1.6	1.5	1.9	1.5	1.00
Univariate F																						
WK	1679.8	1259.2	1227.2	0.6	226.2	25.2	7.3	2.4	4.1	1.0	11.0	2.2	6.2	2.6	0.6	0.8	1.7	0.5	3.1	3.4	2.5	1.24
PC	1153.2	957.9	800.8	80.8	147.5	7.2	6.2	1.2	4.4	2.3	16.0	1.5	7.5	1.4	0.6	1.3	0.9	0.2	4.1	3.5	2.1	1.17
AR	1018.9	920.0	1042.4	296.4	143.5	14.1	19.5	10.6	15.8	20.4	6.9	0.2	8.0	1.9	1.8	2.4	3.6	0.9	2.7	3.5	1.1	1.10
NO	859.0	685.0	501.4	143.9	87.1	12.6	2.6	0.2	7.1	1.4	8.5	4.3	5.3	1.4	0.5	0.7	2.0	0.8	0.8	5.4	2.0	1.23
CS	953.9	550.2	586.2	590.2	55.1	17.2	3.9	3.3	4.3	0.3	7.1	6.2	3.5	0.9	0.3	1.2	1.2	0.8	1.1	0.2	0.9	1.07
GS	1139.3	1054.5	1236.4	596.6	198.5	4.8	4.5	24.5	15.9	1.3	10.4	1.1	4.9	3.1	0.8	2.2	3.5	1.1	3.6	4.6	1.7	1.12
MK	1013.7	1094.7	595.9	33.3	205.2	17.8	11.3	4.1	19.3	6.7	12.5	0.6	6.2	2.1	2.1	0.3	3.3	1.0	4.8	6.9	0.8	1.23
MC	595.3	974.4	1286.9	20.61	98.9	22.2	10.8	78.0	21.1	9.2	6.9	18.4	7.7	2.6	0.5	3.8	2.9	0.9	3.4	2.3	0.7	1.02
EI	968.0	976.1	1251.6	2153.9	91.4	8.3	11.6	36.9	34.9	2.3	3.5	12.8	4.3	5.3	0.1	4.3	2.9	0.3	1.5	4.2	3.5	1.12
AS	614.2	1094.7	1461.5	4926.3	31.6	52.2	6.6	154.2	38.8	1.8	2.2	40.0	6.6	6.1	0.5	1.4	4.3	0.4	0.9	1.1	2.6	1.09
F(.05)	2.6	3.8	2.6	3.8	2.4	2.6	2.1	3.0	2.6	2.6	2.6	3.8	2.1	2.6	2.6	2.4	1.9	2.4	2.1	3.0	2.1	1.00
F(.01)	3.8	6.6	3.8	6.6	3.3	3.8	2.8	4.6	3.8	3.8	3.8	6.6	2.8	3.8	3.8	3.3	2.5	3.3	2.8	4.6	2.6	1.00

TABLE C.3
Multivariate and Univariate Test Statistics for Effects
of Background Factors: Second Analysis

HGC through *Sex* × *Region*	*Sex* × *MHGC*	*ScG* × *MHGC*	*ScG* × *HGC* × *EcS*	*Sex* × *ScG* × *Ecs*	*Residual*
Likelihood ratio:					
F-approximation	2.0	2.1	1.6	1.8	1.04
F(.05)	1.4	1.3	1.3	1.6	1.00
F(.01)	1.6	1.4	1.5	1.9	1.00
WK	0.8	1.8	3.1	3.3	1.24
PC	1.3	1.0	4.0	3.6	1.17
AR	2.4	3.7	2.6	3.6	1.10
NO	0.7	2.0	0.8	5.4	1.23
CS	1.2	1.2	1.1	0.2	1.07
GS	2.2	3.5	3.6	4.5	1.13
MK	0.3	3.2	4.4	7.0	1.23
MC	3.9	2.9	3.6	2.1	1.02
EI	4.3	2.9	1.6	4.2	1.14
AS	1.4	4.3	0.9	1.1	1.10
F(.05)	2.4	1.9	2.1	3.0	1.0
F(.01)	3.3	2.5	2.8	4.6	1.0

C.2. DATA PROPERTIES

Multivariate analysis of variance makes two demands of the data that are not always easy to satisfy in nonexperimental studies. First, the data for each respondent must be complete. If there are multiple response variables (such as the scores on the ten ASVAB tests), each respondent must have a valid measurement of each variable. In addition, the assignment of the respondents to the classes of the analysis of variance design must be unambiguous. For the Profile study, this means that valid background information must be available for each respondent and that the respondents must be correctly classified.

Second, the distribution of score variation within the ultimate sub-classes of the analysis of variance design is assumed to be multivariate normal and homogeneous in variance and covariance from one subclass to another. No assumption is made about the distribution of scores in the population as a whole. In fact, in application to a comparative study of group effects, the analysis of variance regards the data as arising, not from a single population, but from as many populations as there are cells in the cross-classification of the subjects. It is only the individual-difference variation within these cells that is treated as random and for which distribution assumptions must be made (see Bock, 1975, Chapter 1, for a discussion of the assumptions made in the analysis of variance of experiments, comparative studies, and surveys). In this section, we examine questions of how well the Profile study meets the data-property requirements and what effects any variation might have on the analysis of variance.

Missing Observations. The assumption of complete response measurements on each respondent was met by excluding, from among the 11,914 cases tested, 36 who did not complete the tests under the standard conditions for administration of the ASVAB battery. In addition, some cases had to be excluded because their background information was missing or unclassifiable. As indicated in Chapter 2, the information on Age, Sex, and Sociocultural Group was complete; no cases were excluded for want of this information. But a total of 973 lacked valid information on respondent's Highest Grade Completed, Mother's Education, Region of Residence at Age 14, or Economic Status relative to the official OMB definition of poverty.

Counted among the cases for whom information is missing must also be the 772 among the 12,686 interviewed who declined to be tested or were otherwise lost from the initial NLS sample. If these missing or excluded 1,781 cases have the same ability distribution as the 10,905 cases in the analysis, no bias will result; the effect will be only a small reduction in the power of the statistical tests and about 7% increase in the standard errors of estimate effects.

One way to check on the characteristics of the missing cases is to compare the estimates of the population composition based on the interview sample with those based on the respondents used in the present analysis. For example, Table C.4 shows for these respondents the estimated population percentage for the background factors that are, as we have seen in Chapters 3 through 5, most related to levels of ASVAB test performance. This table may be compared with the similar estimates in Table 2.12. Differences between these tables are attributable to the cases not tested or lacking background information.

As we see, the figures in these two tables are, with one exception, identical to about .1%. The exception is a slight tendency for the analysis sample to contain fewer Hispanics with not more than eight years of education and more with thirteen or more years. In other words, there is some indication that Hispanics in the analysis sample are drawn from slightly higher educational levels than those in the general population. In view of the correlation between educational level and test performance, this might suggest that those found in the Highest Grade Completed classes are of somewhat higher ability than those in these classes in the population. The differences are small, how-

TABLE C.4
Population Composition for the Age Groups 15 through 22 Estimated
from the Weighted Analysis Sample: Highest Grade Completed
by Sociocultural Group by Economic Status (N = 10,905)

Economic Status		White		Black		Hispanic		All	
		Poor	Non-Poor	Poor	Non-Poor	Poor	Non-Poor	Poor	Non-Poor
Highest	0–8	14.3	4.0	13.2	5.7	20.2	8.3	14.6	4.4
Grade	9–11	42.3	44.6	59.3	46.0	53.2	51.5	49.7	45.0
Completed	12	22.7	31.3	18.2	30.4	17.3	24.4	20.4	30.9
	13+	20.8	20.1	9.3	17.9	9.3	15.7	15.3	19.7
TOTAL		100.1	100.0	100.0	100.0	100.0	99.9	100.0	100.0
Percent		7.7	72.9	5.4	8.4	1.7	4.0	14.7	85.3

ever, and are unlikely to have any important effect on the group comparisons. No such differences are found in the White and Black groups.

C.3. TESTS OF THE MODEL

In the analysis of variance of unbalanced designs, all of the estimated effects are in general intercorrelated and the actual numerical values obtained are influenced by the number of terms included in the model. Following the general experience that high-order interactions are rarely seen in nature, we attempt to account for the data by a model that includes only main-class effects and low-order interactions. According to the hierarchical principle, all lower-order effects represented in a higher-order interaction must be included in the model. For this reason, we test the partial effect of adding higher-order interaction terms after the variation between subclass means due to lower-order effects and interactions has been accounted for. Our objective is to exclude from the model those interactions that contribute nothing to between-subgroup effects.

The results of the multivariate analysis of variance for choosing terms in the model are shown in Tables C.2 and C.3. In each case we show the multivariate test statistic for the hypothesis that the corresponding effect or interaction is null. They are presented in the form of Rao's F-approximation for the likelihood ratio statistic. These F-statistics may be compared with the .05 and .01 points of the F-distribution, for the approximate number of degrees of freedom, shown in the following two lines. In addition, we show for each of the ASVAB tests the univariate F-statistic on the same null hypothesis, and at the bottom of the table we give the .05 and .01 points with which they may be compared.

As is apparent in Table C.2, these statistics are extremely large for the main effects and for such two-factor interactions as sociocultural group by highest grade completed, sex by sociocultural groups, sex by highest grade completed, sociocultural group by economic status, highest grade completed by economic status, sex by economic status, and sociocultural group by region. At this point in the model building, significance levels drop off sharply. There is some evidence of sex by region effects, especially for the male-specialized subjects of Auto and Shop Information and Electronics Information; and there is no evidence of interaction of region by socioeconomic status. There appear to be very marginal interactions between sex and mother's education, and between sociocultural group and mother's education. As mentioned earlier, the latter have a clear interpretation and probably are real. We are less certain about sex by mother's education. There is no evidence whatsoever of interaction between mother's education and economic status, so this term can be dropped from the model.

Among the triple interactions we consider only sociocultural group by highest grade completed by economic status, and sex by sociocultural group by economic status. The latter is of borderline multivariate significance and possibly could have been omitted. However, it has a fair-sized effect for the Mathematics Knowledge test, which is of special interest in the discussion of sex differences (Chapter 5). For this reason, sex by sociocultural group by economic status was retained in the model. Both of these interactions are highly specific to certain of the groups and certain of the variables. In the case of sociocultural group by highest grade completed by economic status, the interaction, as we saw in Chapter 3, is entirely due to the lack of any economic status effect in Whites with one or more years of college. In the case of sex by sociocultural group by economic status, the effect is confined to female Blacks, primarily in the Mathematics Knowledge test.

The final interaction that is considered separately—sociocultural group by economic status by region—is clearly nonsignificant and can be dropped from the model. All remaining interactions and the remaining triple interactions that have little plausibility are pooled and tested jointly against the within-cell error. Although, because of the enormous number of degrees of freedom in this test, the multivariate test statistic for the residual is significant and some of the univariate test statistics are significant, the F-ratios for the individual measures cluster so closely around their theoretical value of 1.0 that there seems little reason to attempt to include any additional terms in the model for estimation. All subsequent analysis of the data is therefore based on the model with 69 degrees of freedom, including all of the terms in Table C.2 except the sociocultural group by economic status by region interaction, the mother's education by economic status interaction, and the region by economic status interaction. Statistics for the analysis under the abbreviated model are shown in Table C.3.

References

Allen, W. R. (1980). Preludes to attainment: Race, sex, and student achievement orientations. *The Sociological Quarterly, 21,* 65-79.

Alvarez, R. (1976). The psycho-historical and socioeconomic development of the Chicano community in the United States. In C. A. Hernandez, M. J. Haug, & N. Wagner (Eds.), *Chicanos: Social and psychological perspectives.* St. Louis, MO: C. V. Mosby Co.

Anastasi, A. (1964). *Differential psychology: Individual and group differences in behavior.* New York: The MacMillan Company, Inc.

Anastasi, A. (1982). *Psychological testing.* New York: MacMillan Publishing Co., Inc.

Anastasi, A., & Cordova, F. A. (1953). Some effects of bilingualism upon intelligence test performance of Puerto Rican children in New York City. *Journal of Educational Psychology, 44,* 1-19.

Armstrong, J. M. (1980, March). *Achievement and participation of women in mathematics: An overview.* Report of a two-year study funded by the National Institute of Education.

Armstrong, J. M. (1981). Achievement and participation of women in mathematics: Results of two national surveys. *Journal for Research in Mathematics Education, 12*(5), 356-372.

Asbury, C. A. (1973). Cognitive correlates of discrepant achievement in reading. *Journal of Negro Education, 42,* 123-33.

Ashton, G. C., Polovina, J. J., & Vandenburg, S. C. (1979). Segregation analysis of family data for 15 tests of cognitive ability. *Behavior Genetics, 9,* 329-347.

Astin, A. W. (1982). *Minorities in American higher education.* San Francisco: Jossey-Bass.

ASVAB Working Group. (1980, March). *History of the Armed Services Vocational Aptitude Battery: 1974-1980.* Washington, D.C.: Office of the Assistant Secretary of Defense (Manpower, Reserve Affairs and Logistics).

Atwater, D. C., & Abrahams, N. M. (1980). *Evaluation of Alternative ASVAB Composites for Selected Navy Technical Schools.* (NPRDC-TR 80-15). San Diego, CA: Navy Personnel Research and Development Center.

Barral, D. P. (1977). *Achievement levels among foreign born and native born Mexican American students.* San Francisco: R & E Research Associates.

Bem, S., & Lenney, E. (1976). Sex-typing and the avoidance of cross-sex behavior. *Journal of Personality and Social Psychology, 33*(1), 48-54.

Benbow, C. P., & Stanley, J. C. (1980). Sex differences in mathematical ability: fact or artifact? *Science, 210*, 1262–1264.

Bennett, G. K., Seashore, H. G., & Wesman, A. G. (1974). *Differential Aptitude Tests.* New York: The Psychological Corporation.

Bennett, G. K., Seashore, H. G., & Wesman, A. G. (1974). *Fifth Edition Manual for the Differential Aptitude Tests Forms S and T.* New York: The Psychological Corporation.

Bernstein, B. (1961). Social class and linguistic development. In A. J. Halsey, J. Floud, & C. A. Anderson (Eds.), *Education, economy, and society.* New York: Free Press.

Blau, P. M., & Duncan, O. D. (1967). *The American occupational structure.* New York: Wiley.

Blau, Z. S. (1981). *Black children-White children: Competence, socialization, and social structure.* New York: Free Press.

Bloom, B. S. (1964). *Stability and change in human characteristics.* New York: Wiley.

Bloom B. S., Davis, A., & Hess, R. (1963). *Compensatory education for cultural deprivation.* New York: Holt.

Bock, R. D. (1973). Word and image: Sources of the verbal and spatial factors in mental test scores. *Psychometrika, 38*, 437–457.

Bock, R. D. (1974). Book review of *Educability and group differences*, by A. R. Jensen. *Perspectives in Biology and Medicine, 17*, 594–597.

Bock, R. D. (1975). *Multivariate Statistical Methods in Behavioral Research.* New York: McGraw-Hill.

Bock, R. D. (1976). Basic issues in the measurement of change. In D. N. M. de Gruijter & L. J. T. van der Kamp (Eds.), *Advances in psychological and educational measurement.* London: Wiley.

Bock, R. D. (1985). Unusual growth patterns in the Fels data. Paper presented at the proceedings of the Fourth International Conference on Auxology, in Montreal. May, 1985.

Bock, R. D., & Kolakowski, D. (1973). Further evidence of sex-linked major-gene influence on human spatial visualizing ability. *American Journal of Human Genetics, 25*, 1–14.

Bock, R. D., & Mislevy, R. J. (1981). *The profile of American youth: Data quality and analysis of the Armed Services Vocational Aptitude Battery.* Chicago: National Opinion Research Center.

Bock, R. D., & Perline, R. (1979). A Lod score method for detecting linkage on the X-chromosome between a market locus and a major-gene locus for a qualitative character. *Behavior Genetics, 9*, 139–149.

Bock, R. D., Zimowski, M. F., & Laciny, C. (1986). *Sex differences in cognitive profiles: A developmental theory.* Submitted for publication.

Bodmer, W. F., & Cavalli-Sforza, L. L. (1971). *The genetics of human population.* San Francisco: Freeman.

Bouchard, T. J., Jr., & McGee, M. G. (1977). Sex differences in human spatial ability: Not an X-linked recessive gene effect. *Social Biology, 24*, 332–335.

Bouchard, T. J., Jr., & McGue, J. L. (1981). Familial studies in intelligence: A review. *Science, 212*, 1055–1059.

Bray, D. W., & Moses, J. L. (1972). Personnel selection. In P. H. Mussen and M. R. Rosenzweig (Eds.), *Annual Review of Psychology, 23*, 545–576.

Brim, O. G., & Kagan, J. (Eds.) (1980). *Constancy and change in human development.* Cambridge, MA: Harvard University Press.

Bronowski, J. (1947). Mathematics. In D. Thompson and J. Reeves (Eds.), *The Quality of Education.* London: Muller.

Brookover, W. B., Beady, C., Flood, P., Schwietzer, J., & Wisenbaker, J. (1979). *School, social systems, and student achievement: Schools can make a difference.* New York: Praeger.

Broverman, D. M., & Klaiber, E. L. (1969). Negative relationships between abilities. *Psychometrika, 34*, 5–20.

Brown, F., Carter, D. G. & Harris, J. J. (1978). Minority students, ability grouping, and career development. *Journal of Black Studies, 8,* 477–488.

Brown, G. H., Rosen, N. L., Hill, S. T., & Olivas, M. A. (1980). *The condition of education for Hispanic Americans.* Washington, D.C.: National Center for Education Statistics.

Brush, L. R. (1980). *Encouraging girls in mathematics: The problem and the solutions.* Cambridge, Mass.: Abt Associates.

Burnett, S. A., Lane, D. M., & Dratt, L. M. (1979). Spatial visualization and sex differences in quantitative ability. *Intelligence, 3,* 345–354.

Burton, N. W., & Jones, C. V. (1982). Recent trends in achievement levels of Black and White youth. *Educational Researcher, 12,* 10–14, 17.

Carter, T. P. (1970). *Mexican-Americans in school: A history of educational neglect.* New York: College Entrance Examination Board.

Casserly, P. L. (1980). Factors affecting females' participation in advanced placement in mathematics, chemistry, and science. In L. H. Fox, L. Brody, and D. Tobin (Eds.), *Women and the mathematical mystique.* Baltimore: The Johns Hopkins University Press.

Cattell, R. B. (1967). The theory of fluid and crystallized intelligence. *British Journal of Educational Psychology, 37,* 209–224.

Centra, J. A. (1974). *Women, men, and the doctorate.* Princeton, NJ: Educational Testing Service.

Chan, K. S., & Rueda, R. (1979). Poverty and culture in education: Separate but equal. *Exceptional Children, 45,* 422–428.

Clarke, A. M., & Clarke, A. D. B. (1976). *Early experience: Myth and Evidence.* New York: Free Press.

Cleary, T., Humphreys, L., Kendrick, S., & Wesman, A. (1975). Educational uses of tests with disadvantaged students. *American Psychologist, 30,* 15–41.

Cole, M., & Bruner, J. (1971). Cultural differences and inferences about psychological processes. *American Psychologist, 26,* 867–876.

Coleman, J. S., Campbell, E. Q., Hobson, C. J., McPartland, J., Mood, A. M., Weinfeld, F. D., & York, R. L. (1966). *Equality of educational opportunity.* Washington, DC: U.S. Government Printing Office.

College Board, Admission Testing Program. (1981). *National report, 1981.* New York: College Entrance Examination Board.

Cook, M. A. & Alexander, K. L. (1981). *Tracking and training in the academic switchboard: Curricula, course-work and the equity of school organization.* Unpublished paper. Cleveland: Case Western Reserve University.

Crandall, V., Preston, A., & Rabson, A. (1969). Maternal reactions and the development of independence and achievement behavior. *Child Development, 31,* 243–251.

Crim, A. (1981). A community of believers. *Daedalus, 110*(4), 145–162.

Cuevas, G. J. (1984). Mathematics learning in English as a second language. *Journal for Research in Mathematics education, 15* (2), 134–144.

Crim, A. (1983). Community of believers. In *Educating our citizens: The search for excellence.* Washington, D.C.: Center for National Policy, 15–24.

Crim, A. (Personal communication, 1983.)

Cuevas, G. J. (1984). Mathematics learning in English a second language. *Journal for Research in Mathematics Education, 15* (2), 134–144

Cummins, J. (1979). Linguistic interdependence and educational development of bilingual children. *Review of Educational Research, 49,* 222–251.

Dave, R. H. (1963). *The identification and measurement of environmental variables that are related to educational achievement.* Unpublished Ph.D. dissertation, Department of Education, University of Chicago, 1963.

DeFries, J. C., Ashton, G. C., Johnson, R. D., Kuse, A. R., McClearn, G. E., Mi, M. P., Rashad, M. N., Vandenberg, S. G., & Wilson, J. R. (1976). Parent-offspring resemblance for specific cognitive abilities in two ethnic groups. *Nature, 261,* 131–133.

Douglas, J. W. B. (1964). *The home and the school.* London: McGibbon and Kee.

Duncan, O. D., Featherman, D. L., & Duncan, B. (1972). *Socioeconomic background and achievement.* New York: Seminar Press.

Edwards, O. (1979). Cohort and sex changes in Black educational attainment. *Sociology and Social Issues, 59*, 110–120.

Eitelberg, M. & Doering, Z. D. (1982, August 24). *Profile in perspective: The policy and research implications of the "Profile of American Youth."* Paper presented at the Annual Meeting of the American Psychological Association, Washington, D.C.

Erikson, E. H. (1968). *Childhood and society* (3rd edition). New York: W. W. Norton.

Erlenmeyer-Kimling, L., & Jarvik, L. (1963). Genetics and intelligence. *Science, 142*, 1477–1479.

Erlick, A. C. & Lebold, W. K. (1977). *Factors influencing the science Career Plans of Women and Minorities.* West Lafayette, Indiana: Purdue Opinion Panel, Measurement and Research Center, Purdue University.

Farran, D. C., Haskins, R., & Gallagher, J. J. (1980). Poverty and mental retardation: A search for explanations. In J. J. Gallagher (Ed.), *New directions for exceptional children* (Vol. 1). San Francisco: Jossey-Bass.

Featherman, D. L. (1980). Schooling and occupational careers: Constancy and change in wordly success. In O. Brim and J. Kagan (Eds.), *Constancy and change in human development.* Cambridge, MA: Harvard University Press.

Felmlee, D. & Eber, D. (1983). Contextual effects in the classroom: The impact of ability groups on student attention. *Sociology of Education, 56*, 77–87.

Fennema, E. (1974). Mathematics learning and the sexes: A review. *Journal of Research in Mathematics, 5*, 126–139.

Fennema, E. (1982, February). *Women and mathematics: State of the art review.* Paper presented at the Equity in Mathematics Core Conference, Reston, Virginia.

Fennema, E. (1981, August). The sex factor: Real or not in mathematics education. In E. Fennema (Ed.), *Mathematics education research: Implications for the 80s.* Alexandria, VA: Association for Supervision and Curriculum Development.

Fennema, E. (1980). Teachers and sex bias in mathematics. *Mathematics Teacher, 3*, 169–173.

Fennema, E. & Sherman, J. (1977). Sex-related differences in mathematics achievement, spatial visualization, and affective factors. *American Educational Research Journal, 14*(1), 51–71.

Fernandez, C., Espinosa, R. W., & Dornbusch, S. M. (1975). *Factors perpetuating the low academic status of Chicano high school students.* (Research and development memorandum No. 138). Stanford, CA: Stanford Center for Research and Development in Teaching, Stanford University.

Finn, J. D. (1978). *MULTIVARIANCE: Univariate and multivariance analysis of variance, covariance, regression, and repeated measures.* Mooresville, IN: Scientific Software, Inc.

Foster, D. (Personal communication, 1981.)

Fox, L. H. (1977). The effects of sex role socialization on mathematics participation an achievement. In *Women and mathematics research: Perspectives for change.* Washington, DC: National Institute of Education.

Fox, L. H., & Cohn, S. (1980). Sex differences in the development of precocious mathematics talent. In L. H. Fox, L. Brody, & D. Tobin (Eds.), *Women and the mathematical mystique.* Baltimore: The Johns Hopkins University Press.

Fox, L. H., Tobin, D., & Brody, L. (1979). Sex-role socialization and achievement in mathematics. In M. A. Wittig, A. C. Petersen & M. Andrisin (Eds.), *Sex-related differences in cognitive functioning.* New York: Academic Press.

Frankel, M. R., & McWilliams, H. (1981). *The profile of American youth: Technical sampling report.* Chicago: National Opinion Research Center.

Garcia, E. E. (1980). Bilingualism in early childhood. *Young Children, 35*(4), 52–66.

Garfinkle, S. H. (1975). Occupations of women and Black workers, 1962-74. *Monthly Labor Review, 98*(11), 25–35.

Garron, D. (1970). Sex-linked recessive inheritance of spatial and numerical abilities and Turner's syndrome. *Psychological Review, 77,* 147–152.

Gastrin, J. (1940). Det intelligenta larandets problem. *Acta Academiae Aboensis, Humaniora 13*(9).

Gazzaniga, M. S. (1970). *The bisected brain.* New York: Appleton-Century-Croft.

Gemmill, L. M., Bustoz, J., & Montiel, M. (1982, August). *Factors influencing mathematics participation of highly able Mexican-American adolescents.* Final Report to the National Science Foundation (Grant No. SED 80–17768).

Geschwind, N. (1970). Organization of language and the brain. *Science, 179,* 940–44.

Geschwind, N. (1974). The anatomical basis of hemispheric differentiation. In S. J. Diamond & J. G. Beaurmont (Eds.), *Hemispheric function in the human brain.* New York: Wiley.

Geschwind, N. & Galaburda, A. M. (1985). Cerebral lateralization biological mechanisms, associations, and pathology: II A hypothesis and a program for research. *Archives of Neurology, 42.*

Gibbons, R. O., Baker, R. J., & Skinner, D. B. (1985). Field articulation testing: A predictor of technical skills in surgical residents. *Journal of Surgical Research,* (in press).

Glick, P. C. (1979). Children of divorced parents in demographic perspective. *Journal of Social Issues, 35,* 170–82.

Golden, M., Birns, B., Bridger, W., & Moss, A. (1971). Social class differentiation among Black children. *Child Development, 42,* 37–45.

Goodenough, D. R., Gandini, E., Olkin, I., Pizzamiglio, L., Thayer, D., & Witkin, H. A. (1977). A study of X chromosome linkage with field dependence and spatial visualization. *Behavior Genetics, 7,* 373–388.

Gregory, M. K. (1977). Sex bias in school referrals. *Journal of School Psychology, 5,* 5–8.

Guilford, J. P., & Hoepfner, R. (1971). *The analysis of intelligence.* New York: McGraw-Hill.

Guilford, J. P., & Zimmerman, W. S. (1953). *Guilford-Zimmerman aptitude survey.* Orange, CA: Sheridan Psychological Services.

Guilford, J. P., & Zimmerman, W. S. (1947). Some A.A.F. findings concerning aptitude factors. *Occupations, 26,* 154–159.

Hale, J. (1980, October). The socialization of black children. *Dimensions,* 43–48.

Hall, V. C., & Kaye, D. B. (1980). Early patterns of cognitive development. *Monographs of the Society for Research in Child Development, 45*(2).

Hartlage, L. C. (1970). Sex-linked inheritance of spatial ability. *Perceptual and Motor Skills, 31,* 610.

Haskins, R., Walden, T., & Ramey, C. T. (1983). Teacher and student behavior in high and low ability groups. *Journal of Educational Psychology, 75,* 865–876.

Haven, E. W. (1971). *Factors associated with selection of advanced academic mathematics by girls in high school.* Ph.D. dissertation, University of Pennsylvania.

Hendrickson, E. A., & White, P. O. (1964). Promax: A quick method for rotation to oblique simple structure. *British Journal of Mathematical and Statistical Psychology, 17,* 65–70.

Hertzig, M. E., Birch, M. G., Thomas, A., & Mendez, O. A. (1968). Class and ethnic differences in responses of preschool children to cognitive demands. *Monographs of the Society for Research in Child Development, 33,* 117.

Hess, R. (1970). Social class and ethnic influences upon socialization. In P. Mussen (Ed.), *Carmichael's manual of child psychology* (third edition), (Vol. 2). New York: Wiley.

Hess, R., & Shipman, V. (1965). Early experience and the socialization of cognitive modes in children. *Child Development, 34,* 869–886.

Hess, R., Shipman, V., Brophy, J., & Bear, R. (1969). *The cognitive environments of urban preschool children: Follow-up phase.* Chicago: Graduate School of Education, University of Chicago.

Hier, D. B. & Crowley, W. F. (1980). Impaired spatial ability in men with hypogonadotropic hypogonadism. *Transactions of the American Neurological Association, 105,* 1–2.

Hier, D. B., & Crowley, W. F. (1982). *Spatial ability in androgen deficient men.* Manuscript submitted for publication.

Hilton, T. C. (1979). ETS study of academic prediction and growth. *New Directions for Testing and Measurement, 2,* 27–44.

Holliday, F. (1940). An investigation into selection of apprentices for the engineering industry. *Occupational Psychology, 14,* 69–81.

Holliday, F. (1943). The relations between psychological test scores and subsequent proficiency of apprentices in the engineering industry. *Occupational Psychology, 17,* 168–185.

Horner, M. S. (1972). Toward an understanding of achievement related conflicts in women. *Journal of Social Issues, 28,* 157–175.

Horowitz, F. D., & Paden, L. (1973). The effectiveness of environmental intervention programs. In B. Caldwell and H. Riccuiti (Eds.), *Review of Child Development Research,* (Vol. 3). Chicago: University of Chicago Press.

Hunt, E. B. (1976). Varieties of cognitive power. In L. B. Resnick (Ed.), *The Nature of Intelligence.* Hillsdale, NJ: Lawrence Erlbaum Associates.

Hyde, J. S., Geiringer, E. R., & Yen, W. M. (1975). On the empirical relations between spatial ability and sex differences in other aspects of cognitive performance. *Multivariate Behavioral Research, 10,* 289–310.

Hyman, H. H., Wright, C. R., & Reed, J. S. (1975). *The enduring effects of education.* Chicago: University of Chicago Press.

Jacklin, C. N. (1979). Epilogue. In M. A. Wittig, A. C. Petersen, & M. Andrisin (Eds.), *Sex-related differences.in cognitive functioning.* New York: Academic Press.

Jackson, J. J. (1973). Black women in a racist society. In C. V. Willie, B. Kramer, & B. Brown (Eds.), *Racism and mental health.* Pittsburgh, PA: University of Pittsburgh Press.

Jencks, C., Bartlett, S., Corcoran, M., Crouse, J., Eaglesfield, D., Jackson, G., McClelland, K., Mueser, P., Olneck, M., Schwartz, J., Ward, S., & McWilliams, J. (1979). *Who gets ahead?* New York: Basic Books.

Jencks, C., Smith, M., Acland, H., Bane, M., Cohen, D., Gintis, H., Heyns, B., & Michelson, S. (1972). *Inequality.* New York: Basic Books.

Jensen, A. R. (1980). *Bias in testing.* New York: Free Press.

Jensen, A. R. (1973). *Educability and Group Differences.* New York: Harper and Row.

Jensen, A. R. (1969). How much can we boost I.Q. and scholastic achievement? *Harvard Educational Review, 39,* 1–123.

Johnson, M. L. (1984). Blacks in Mathematics: A status report. *Journal for Research in Mathematics Education, 15,* 145–153.

Johnson, P. O., & Neyman, J. (1936). Tests of certain linear hypotheses and their applications to some educational problems. *Statistical Research Memoirs, 1,* 57–93.

Jones, H. (1954). The environment and mental development. In L. Carmichael (Ed.), *Manual of child psychology,* (second edition). New York: Wiley.

Jordan, T. E. (1978). Influences on vocabulary attainment: A five-year prospective study. *Child Development, 49,* 1096–1106.

Jöreskog, K. G., & Sörbom, D. (1978). *EFAP II: Exploratory Factor Analysis Program,* Mooresville, IN: Scientific Software, Inc.

Kagin, S., & Buriel, K. (1978). Field-dependence-independence and Mexican-American culture and education. In J. Martinez, *Chicano psychology.* New York: Academic Press.

Kelley, T. L. (1928). *Crossroads in the mind of man.* Stanford, CA: Stanford University Press.

Kerckhoff, A. C., & Campbell, R. T. (1977). Black-White differences in the educational attainment process. *Sociology of Education, 50,* 15–27.

Kimura, D. (1967). Functional asymmetry of the brain in dichotic listening. *Cortex, 3,* 163–178.

Kohn, M. L. (1977). *Class and conformity* (second edition). Chicago: University of Chicago Press.

Kolakowski, D., & Bock, R. D. (1981). A multivariate generalization of probit analysis.

Biometrics, 37, 541–551.

Kulvesky, W. W. (1981, March 25-28). *Gender differences among Mexician American youth.* Paper presented at the Annual Meeting of the Southwest Sociological Association, Dallas, Texas.

Laosa, L. M. (1982). School, occupation, culture and family: The impact of parental schooling on the parent-child relationship. *Journal of Educational Psychology, 2,* 791–827.

Larson, N. C., & Arenson, D. L. (1979). *Validity of ASVAB 5 against civilian job criteria.* Unpublished research report. Associated Consultants International, Chicago, IL.

Lesser, G., Fifer, G., & Clark, D. (1965). Mental abilities of children from different social-class and cultural groups. *Monographs of the Society for Research in Child Development. 30*(4), 1–115.

LeVine, M. (1976). *Identification of reasons why qualified women do not pursue mathematical careers.* Report to National Science Foundation.

Levine, S. & Huttenlocher, J. (1985). *Sex differences in spatial ability of preschool children.* Unpublished manuscript.

Levine, R. A. (1973). Culture, personality, and socialization. In D. A. Goslin (Ed.), *Handbook of socialization theory and research.* Chicago: Rand McNally.

Levy, J. (1984). Interhemispheric collaboration: Single mindedness in the asymmetric brain. In C.T. Best (Ed.), *Developmental neuropsychology and education: Hemispheric specialization and integration.* New York: Academic Press.

Linn, M. C., & Petersen, A. C. (1985). Emergence and characterization of sex differences in spatial ability: a meta-analysis. *Child Development* (in press).

Loehlin, J. C., Sharan, S., & Jacoby, R. (1978). In pursuit of the "spatial gene": A family study. *Behavior Genetics, 8,* 27–41.

Luchins, E. H. (1976). *Women in mathematics: Problems of orientation and reorientation.* Final report, National Science Foundation Grant #GY11316, Rensselaer Polytechnic Institute, Troy, NY. January.

Maccoby, E. E., & Jacklin, C. N. (1974). *The psychology of sex differences.* Stanford, CA: Stanford University Press.

Mackler, B. (1977). *Black superstars: Getting ahead in today's America.* New York: Conch Magazine Limited.

Maier, M. H. & Fuchs, E. F. (1973). *Effectiveness of selection and classification testing.* (Research report 1179), U. S. Army Research Institute for the Behavioral and Social Sciences.

Maier, M. H. & Fuchs, E. F. (1978). *Differential validity of the army aptitude areas for predicting army job training performance of blacks and whites.* (Technical Paper 312), U. S. Army Research Institute for the Behavioral and Social Sciences, Alexandria, VA, p.8.

Marrett, C. B. (1981). *Minority females in high school mathematics and science.* Final Report to the National Institute of Education (on Grant No. 6–79–0110).

Marrett, C. B. (1982). *Minority females in high school mathematics and science.* Madison, WI: Wisconsin Research and Development Center, University of Wisconsin.

Martin, G. C. (1951). Test batteries for auto mechanics and apparel design. *Journal of Applied Psychology, 35,* 20–22.

Matthews, W. (1980, December). *Adding up race and sex: A study of enrollment in high school mathematics classes.* Paper presented for the Program on Women, Northwestern University, Evanston, IL.

Matthews, W. (1983). *Influences on the learning and participation of minorities in mathematics.* (Program Report No. 83–5.) Madison, WI: Wisconsin Center for Education Research, University of Wisconsin.

McClendon, M. J. (1976). The occupational status attainment process of males and fema *American Sociological Review, 41,* 52–64.

McCorquodale, P. (1980, November 20–22). *Interests in science courses and careers: A comparison of Mexican-American and Anglo students.* Paper presented at the Society for the Advancement of Chicanos and Native Americans in Science Conference, Albuquerque, NM.

McCorquodale, P. (Personal communication, 1983.)

McFarlane, M. (1925). A study of practical ability. *British Journal of Psychology,* (Monograph Supplement No. 8).

McGee, M. G. (1979). Human spatial abilities: Psychometric studies and environmental, genetic, hormonal, and neurological influences. *Psychological Bulletin, 86,* 889–918.

McGlone, J. (1980). Sex differences in human brain asymmetry: A critical survey. *Behavioral and Brain Sciences, 3,* 215–263.

Meece, J. L. (1980, April). *A theoretical framework for studying students' course selection in mathematics.* Paper presented at the Annual Meeting of the American Educational Research Association, Boston, MA.

Meece, J. L., Parsons, J. E., Kaczala, C. M., Goff, S. B., & Futterman, R. (1982). Sex differences in math achievement: Toward a model of academic choice. *Psychological Bulletin, 91*(2), 324–48.

Minton, C., Kagan, J., & Levine, J. A. (1971). Maternal control and obedience in two-year-old children. *Child Development, 42,* 1873–1894.

Moore, E. (1980). *The effects of cultural style on black children's intelligence test achievement.* Ph.D. dissertation, University of Chicago.

Moore, E. (1982). Language behavior in the test situation and the IQ test performance of, traditionally and transracially adopted Black children. In L. Feagans and D. Farran (Eds.) *Language of children reared in poverty.* New York: Academic Press.

Moore, E. (1986). Family socialization and the IQ test performace of traditionally and transracially adopted black children. *Developmental Psycology. 22* (3), 317–326.

Mullins, L. (1980). On women, work, and society. *Freedomways,* (First Quarter), 15–24.

Murillo, N. (1976). The Mexican-American family. In C. Hernandez, M. Haug, & N. Wagner (Eds.), *Chicanos: Social and psychological perspectives.* St. Louis: C. V. Mosby Company.

Nash, S. C. (1979). Sex role as a mediator of intellectual functioning. In M. A. Wittig, A. C. Petersen, & M. Andrisin, (Eds.), *Sex-related differences in cognitive functioning.* New York: Academic Press.

National Assessment of Educational Progress. (1979). Mathematical applications, 1977–1978. Denver: Education Commission of the States.

National Bureau of Standards. (1959). *Bureau of Standards Tables of Bivariate Normal Distribution Function and Related Functions. Applied Mathematics Series 50.* Washington: U.S. Government Printing Office.

National Science Foundation. (1982). *Women and Minorities in Science and Engineering.* (NSF 82–302.) Washington.

Nebes, R. D., & Sperry, R. W. (1971). Cerebral dominance in perception. *Neuropsychologia, 9,* 247.

Nichols, P. L., & Anderson, V. (1973). Intellectual performance, race, and socioeconomic status. *Social Biology, 30,* 367–374.

O'Connor, J. (1943). Structural Visualization. Boston: Human Engineering Lab.

Ogbu, J. (1978). *Minority education and caste.* New York: Academic Press.

Ornstein, R. E. (1973). *The psychology of consciousness.* San Francisco: Freeman.

Pallas, A. M., & Alexander, K. L. (1983). Sex differences in quantitative SAT performance: New evidence on the differential coursework hypothesis. *American Educational Research Journal, 20,* 165–182.

Park, J., Johnson, R. C., et al. (1978). Parent-offspring resemblances for specific cognitive abilities in Korea. *Behavior Genetics, 8,* 43–52.

Parsons, J. E., Kaczala, C. M., & Meece, J. L. (1982). Socialization of achievement attitudes and beliefs: Classroom experiences. *Child Development, 53,* 322–339.

Pedersen, E., Faucher, T. A., & Eaton, W. W. (1978). A new perspective on the effects of first-grade teachers on children's subsequent adult status. *Harvard Educational Review, 43*(1), 1–31.

Pedraza-Bailey, A. (1982). Cubans and Mexicans in the United States: The functions of political and economic migration. *Cuban Studies/Estudios Cubanos, 11*:2/12:1, 79–97.

Petersen, A. C. (1979). Hormones and cognitive functioning in normal development. In M. A. Wittig, A. C. Petersen, & M. Andrisin, (Eds.), *Sex related differences in cognitive functioning.* New York: Academic Press.

Petersen, A. C. (1976). Physical androgyny and cognitive functioning in adolescence. *Developmental Psychology, 12,* 524–533.

Porter, J. N. (1974). Race, socialization, and mobility in educational and early occupational attainment. *American Sociological Review, 39,* 303–316.

Portes, A., McLeod, S. A., & Parker, R. N. (1978). Immigrant aspirations. *Sociology of Education, 51,* 241–260.

Portes, A., & Wilson, K. L. (1976). Black-White differences in educational attainment. *American Sociological Review, 41,* 414–431.

Ramey, C. T., & Haskins, R. (1981). Early education, intellectual development, and school performance: A reply to Arthur Jensen and J. McVicker Hunt. *Intelligence, 5,* 41–48.

Ramirez, M. (1973). Cognitive styles and cultural democracy in education. *Social Science Quarterly, 53,* 895–904.

Rist, R. C. (1973). *The urban school as a factory for failure.* Cambridge, MA: M.I.T. Press.

Rosenberg, M., & Rosenberg, F. (1978, September 28-October 1). *The occupational self: A developmental study.* Paper presented at the Self-Concept Symposium, Boston, MA.

Rubovits, P. (1975). Early experience and the achieving orientations of American middle class girls. In M. Maehr & W. Stallings (Eds.), *Culture, child, and school.* Monterey, CA: Brooks/Cole.

Scarr, S. (1980). Commentary on V.C. Hall and D.B. Kaye, Early patterns of cognitive development. *Monographs of the Society for Research in Child Development, 45,* No. 2.

Scarr, S. (1975). Genetics and the development of intelligence. In F.D. Horowitz (Ed.) *Review of child development research* (Vol. 4). Chicago: University of Chicago Press.

Scarr, S. (1971). Race, social class, and I.Q. *Science, 174,* 1285–1292.

Scarr, S., Pakstis, A., Katz., & Barker, W. (1977). The absence of a relationship between degree of White ancestry and intellectual skills within the Black population. *Human Genetics, 39,* 69–86.

Scarr, S. & Weinberg, R. (1976). I.Q. test performance of Black children adopted by White families. *American Psychologist, 31,* 726–739.

Schiff, M., Duyme, M., Dumaret, A. & Tomkiewicz, S. (1982). How much would we boost scholastic achievement and I.Q. scores?: A direct answer from a French adoption study. *Cognition, 12,* 165–96.

Seeley, L. C., Fischel, M. A., & Hicks, J. M. (1978). *Development of the ASVAB, Forms 2 and 3.* (Technical Paper 289). Alexandria, VA: Army Research Institute.

Segal, N. L. (1982). *Cooperation, competition, and altruism within twin-sets: A reappraisal* Ph.D. dissertation, University of Chicago.

Sells, L. W. The mathematics filter and the education of women and minorities. In L. H. Fox, L. Brody, & D. Tobin (Eds.), *Women and the mathematical mystique.* Baltimore: The Johns Hopkins University Press, 1980.

Serbin, L., O'Leary, K., Kent, R., & Tonick, I. (1973). A comparison of teacher response to the pre-academic and problem behavior of boys and girls. *Child Development, 44,* 796–804.

Sewell, T., Farley, F. H., Manni, J., & Hunt, P. (1982). Motivation, social reinforcement, and intelligence as predictors of academic achievement in Black adolescents. *Adolescence, 18,* 647–56.

Sewell, T. E. & Martin, R. P. (1976). Racial patterns of occupational choice in adolescents. *Psychology in the School, 13*, 326–333.

Sewell, W. H., & Hauser, R. M. (1975). *Education, occupation, and earnings.* New York: Academic Press.

Shenkel, K. F., Leedy, H. B., Rosenberg, N., & Mundy, J. P. (1957). Evaluation of the Puerto Rican screening test (ECFA) against success in training. (Technical Research Report PRB1097). Washington, D.C.: Personnel Research Branch, The adjutant General's Office.

Shepard, R. N., & Metzler, J. (1971). Mental rotation of three-dimensional objects. *Science, 171*, 701–703.

Sherman, J. (1980). Mathematics, spatial visualization, and related factors: Changes in girls and boys, grades 8–11. *Journal of Educational Psychology, 72*, 476–482.

Sherman, J. (1981). Girls' and boys' enrollments in theoretical math courses: A longitudinal study. *Psychology of Women Quarterly, 5*(Supplement), 681–89.

Sherman, J. (1982). Mathematics, the critical filter: A look at some residues. *Psychology of Women Quarterly, 6*(4), 428–45.

Sherman, J. A. (1967). Problem of sex differences in space perception and aspects of intellectual functioning. *Psychological Review, 74*, 290–229.

Sherman, J. M., & Fennema, E. (1977). The study of mathematics among high school girls and boys: Related factors. *American Educational Research Journal, 14*, 159–168.

Shute, V. J., Pellegrino, J. W., Hubert, L., & Reynolds, R. W. (1983). The relationship between androgen levels and human spatial abilities. *Bulletin of the Psychonomic Society, 21*, 465–468.

Sims, W. H. (1978). *Interim results of an examination of the Armed Services Vocational Aptitude Battery (ASVAB) Forms 6 and 7 for the classification of Marine Corps recruits.* (CNA Report 78–3081). Alexandria, VA: Center for Naval Analysis.

Sitkei, E., & Meyers, C. (1969). Comparative structure of intellect in middle and lower class four-year-olds of two ethnic groups. *Developmental Psychology, 1*, 592–604.

Slater, P. (1941). Tests for selecting secondary and technical school children. *Occupational Psychology, 15*, 10.

Slaughter, D. T. (1983). Education and the family. Evanston, IL: Northwestern University, School of Education, (unpublished manuscript).

Slaughter, D. T. (1972). On becoming an Afro-American woman. *School Review, 80*, 299–318.

Slaughter, D. T. 6 Epps, E. (forthcoming). Home enviromnent and the academic achievement of American minority children and Youth. *Journal of Negro Education.*

Smith, I. M. (1964). *Spatial ability.* San Diego: Robert R. Knapp.

Solomon, L. C., & Taubman, P. (Eds.) (1973). *Does college matter?* New York: Academic Press.

Sperry, R. W. (1970). Perception in the absence of neocortical commisures. In *Perception and its disorders,* Res. Publ. A.R.N.M.D., vol. 48, The Association for Research in Nervous and Mental Disease.

Stafford, R. E. (1965). Mental arithmetic problems (Form AA). Revised edition multilithed, Vocational and Educational Guidance Associates.

Stafford, R. E. (1961). Sex differences in spatial visualization as evidence of sex-linked inheritance. *Perceptual and Motor Skills, 13*, 428.

Streissguth, A. P., & Bee, H. L. (1972). Mother-child interactions and cognitive development in children. In W. W. Hartup (Ed.), *The young child: Reviews of research* (Vol. 2). Washington, D.C.: Association for the Education of Young Children.

Super, D. E., & Crites, J. O. (1962). *Appraising vocational fitness by means of psychological tests.* New York: Harper and Row.

Swanson, L. (1979). Armed Services Vocational Aptitude Battery, Forms 6 and 7: Validation Against School Performance in Navy Enlisted Schools (July 1976-February 1978). *NPRDC Technical Report 80–1.* San Diego, CA: Navy Personnel and Training Research Laboratory.

Sympson, J. B., & Weiss, D. J. (1981). *Predictive validity of conventional and adaptive tests in an Air Force training environment*. (Final report on Contract No. F33615-77-C-0061). Brooks Air Force Base, TX: Air Force Human Resources Laboratory.

Tanner, J. M. (1978). *Fetus into man: Physical growth from conception to maturity*. Cambridge, MA: Harvard University Press.

Taylor, H. C. & Russell, J. T. (1939). The relationship of validity coefficients to the practical effectiveness of tests in selection: Discussion and tables. *Journal of Applied Psychology, 28*, 565-578.

Thoday, J. M. (1969). Limitations of genetic comparisons of populations. *Journal of Biosocial Science* (Supplement), 3-14.

Thomas, G. E. (1980). Race and sex differences and similarities in the process of college entry. *Higher Education, 9*, 179-202.

Thomas, G. E., Alexander, K. L., & Eckland, B. K. (1979). Access to higher education: The importance of race, sex, social class, and academic credentials. *School Review, 87*, 133-56.

Thurstone, L. L. & Thurstone, T. G. (1941). Factorial studies of intelligence. *Psychometric Monographs* (no. 2). Chicago: University of Chicago Press.

Thurstone, L. L. & Thurstone, T. G. (1947). *The primary mental abilities*. Chicago: Science Research Associates.

Treiman, D. J., & Terrell, K. (1975). Sex and the process of status attainment: A comparison of working women and men. *American Sociological Review, 40*, 174-200.

Trotman, F. (1977). Race, (1977). I.Q. and the middle class. *Journal of Educational Psychology, 69*, 266-273.

Tulkin, S., & Covitz, F. (1975). *Mother-infant interaction and intellectual functioning at age 6*. Paper presented at the Biennial Meetings of the Society for Research in Child Development, Denver, CO.

Tulkin, S., & Kagan, J. (1972). Mother-infant interaction in the first year of life. *Child Development, 43*, 31-41.

Turner, H. (Personal communication, 1983.)

Vaidya, S., & Chansky, N. (1980). Cognitive development and cognitive style in mathematics achievement. *Journal of Educational Psychology, 72*, 326-330.

Valentine, L. D. (1977). Prediction of Air Force technical training success from ASVAB and educational background. (AFHRL-TR-77-18). Brooks Air Force Base, Texas, Air Force Human Resources Laboratory.

Vandenberg, S. G. (1975). Sources of variance in performance on spatial tests. In J. Eliot & N. J. Salkind (Eds.), *Children's spatial development*. Springfield, IL: Charles C. Thomas.

Vandenberg, S. G. (1972). Assortive mating, or who marries whom? *Behavior Genetics, 2*, 127-157.

Vandenberg, S. G. (1967). Hereditary factors in psychological variables in man, with special emphasis on cognition. In J. N. Spuhler (Ed.), *Genetic diversity and behavior*. Chicago: Aldine.

Vitola, B. M., Mullins, C. J., & Croll, P. R. (1973). *Validity of Armed Services Vocational Aptitude Battery Form 1, to predict technical school success*. (AFHRL-TR Report 73-7.) Brooks Air Force Base, TX: Air Force Human Resources Laboratory.

Walker, J. T., Krasnoff, A. G., & Peoco, D. (1981). Visual spatial perception in adolescents and their parents: The X-linked recessive hypothesis. *Behavior Genetics, 11*, 403-413.

Werdelin, I. (1961). *Geometrical ability and space factors in boys and girls*. Lund, Sweden: University of Lund.

Wilfong, H. D. (1980). *ASVAB: Technical supplement to the high school counselor's guide*. Fort Sheridan, IL: Directorate of Testing, United States Military Enlistment Processing Command.

Willerman, L., & Stafford, R. E. (1972). Maternal effects on intellectual functioning. *Behavior Genetics, 2*(4), 321-325.

Williams, J. H., & Whitney, D. (1978). Vocational interests of minority disadvantaged students: Are they different? *The Negro Educational Review, 29,* 97–103.

Williams, T. (1976). Abilities and environments. In W. H. Sewell, R. M. Hauser, & D. L. Featherman (Eds.), *Schooling and achievement in American society.* New York: Academic Press.

Wilson, K. L., & Portes, A. (1980). Immigrant enclaves: An analysis of labor market experiences of Cubans in Miami. *American Journal of Sociology, 86,* 295–319.

Wilson, R. S. (1975). Twins: Patterns of cognitive development as measured on the Wechsler Preschool and Primary Scale of Intelligence. *Developmental Psychology II,* 126–134.

Winer, B. J. (1971). *Statistical principles in experimental design.* New York: McGraw-Hill.

Witelson, S. F. (1976). Sex and the single hemisphere: Specialization of the right hemisphere for spatial processing. *Science, 193,* 425—427.

Witkin, H., Dyk, R., Paterson, H., Goodenough, D., & Karp, S. (1962). *Psychological differentiation.* New York: Wiley.

Wittig, M. Petersen, A & Andrisin, M. (Eds.) (1979). *Sex-related differences in cognitive functioning.* New York: Academic Press.

Witty, P., Garfield, S., & Brink, W. (1941). A comparison of vocational interests of Negro and White high school students. *Journal of Educational Psychology, 32,* 124–132.

Wolf, R. (1964). The measurement of environments. In A. Anastasi (Ed.), *Testing problems in perspective.* New York: American Council on Education.

Wolleat, P. L., Pedro, J. D., Becker, A., & Fennema, E. (1980). Sex differences in high school students' attribution of performance in mathematics. *Journal for Research in Mathematics Education,* 357–366.

Yen, W. M. (1975). Sex-linked major-gene influences on selected types of spatial performance. *Behavior Genetics, 5,* 281–298.

Zimowski, M. F. (1985). *Attributes of spatial test items that influence cognitive processing.* Unpublished doctoral dissertation, University of Chicago, Chicago, IL.

Author Index

Subject Index

A000013514198